LORI COPELAND

Simple Gifts

ZONDERVAN®

ZONDERVAN.com/
AUTHORTRACKER
follow your favorite authors

ZONDERVAN®

Simple Gifts

Requests for information should be addressed to:

Zondervan, *Grand Rapids, Michigan 49530*

Library of Congress Cataloging-in-Publication Data

Copeland, Lori.
Simple gifts / Lori Copeland.
p. cm.
ISBN-10: 0-310-26350-6
ISBN-13: 978-0-310-26350-0
I. Title.
PS3553.O6336S56 2007
813'.54—dc22

2007000442

Published in association with the literary agency of Alive Communications, Inc., 5375 Roundup Dr., Colorado Springs, CO 80910

Interior design by Michelle Espinoza

Printed in the United States of America

07 08 09 10 11 12 • 20 19 18 17 16 15 14 13 12 11 10 9 8 7 6 5 4 3 2 1

Simple Gifts

One

"*My momma always said 'Life was like a box of chocolates. You never know what you're gonna get.'*"

Forrest Gump's mother was right. About *my* life, anyway. It *was* a box of chocolates—and someone had eaten the creams and left me the nuts.

Nothing was clearer to me that April day when I stepped onto the plane to go home to Parnass Springs, Missouri. Pleasant memories and warm fires didn't await me. My childhood had been tumultuous, to put it kindly; not the kind you wanted to revisit.

But headed back I was, to settle the estate of Aunt Beth, the woman who had helped raise me, and to further fuel a lie I'd lived practically from the moment I'd left Parnass. I was still cowardly Marlene Queens, in too deep to ever confess the pointless lie (that didn't even make sense to me now) even to those I loved most. Even to Joe Brewster.

And especially to Joe's son, Vic.

I had nine days to endure, and I knew it wouldn't be easy, but most of life wasn't.

My immediate problem was Sara, my only child. I'd spoiled her rotten. My daughter was like the lilies of the field—she toiled not, neither did she spin. You could add housekeeping and laundry to that list. Sara was the love of my life, but my daughter had an unhealthy dependence on me, even though she was a mother now.

On top of that, I had been battling diabetes and a host of other stress-related problems, including migraines and just plain exhaustion. And Sara was coming down with something—she'd moped for days, complaining that she didn't feel well. I needed a break, even though this trip didn't have peace and quiet stamped all over it.

But Aunt Ingrid had finally given consent to liquidate her and Beth's jointly owned property, and since I was considered the closest thing Beth had to a daughter, her estate liquidation fell to me. The battle had been going on for over two years, and I for one was thrilled it was coming to an end. The upcoming skirmish would throw me into Vic Brewster's path, and I wasn't looking forward to that. Over the years we had remained the best of friends—or so it appeared on the surface, but only I knew the secret behind my lying facade.

I sighed. How many mistakes did God allow one woman? But I, like a tiger, was in too deep to change my stripes now. And granted, I'd drifted about as far away from God as one could get without drowning. Funny. I knew that, but I continued to ignore my condition—the way I ignored most things I didn't want to face.

I'd never let Vic know that Noel Queens, my husband and a gifted thoracic surgeon, had walked out on me when Sara was two. When Vic married, I knew he was lost to me forever. So what if my pride wouldn't let me admit my own marriage had failed? After all, the esteemed Dr. Queens and I weren't together long—just long enough to bear a child and discover that the Devil, not the Lord, had spawned our relationship. I hadn't lied about failure. *Maybe* I'd deceived Vic and my family about my marriage. A little. But deceit was certainly more acceptable than flat-out lying.

No, Marlene. You lied. You continue to lie. Face it.

Now that I'd be seeing Vic again, could I keep up the subterfuge? Did I want to? He was a widower. The guilt that I carried seemed so needless.

"Have you found Jesus yet, Gump?"

"I didn't know I was supposed to be looking for him, sir."

Oh, I'd found Jesus years ago during one of Joe Brewster's spring revivals. Vic's dad brought in one of those fancy Kansas City preachers who wore a white suit and pinkie ring and scared the living fire right out of backslidden church members. Even Beth and Ingrid became agreeable for a few weeks, but then the fire died to trailing smoke, and my aunts returned to more comfortable ways—church Sunday and Wednesday nights, and the rest of the time you just had to put up with them.

I'd found God during my youth, but then misplaced him when I married Noel. My actions of the past years were anything but Christlike.

Forrest said, *"Momma said 'stupid is as stupid does.'"*

Forrest's mom was a smart woman.

It was doubtful I'd avoid Vic. He lived in the guest cottage behind his dad's house across the street from Beth's and Ingrid's houses, and I'd be sure to bump into him at the annual Parnass Springs cemetery cleanup. So no use pretending I wouldn't see him. I simply needed to make sure we didn't collide head-on.

A dark cloud hung in the west when I disembarked in Columbia, Missouri. I got my luggage, rented a car, and was on the road in twenty minutes. A gust of wind rocked the Grand Am, shaking the small compact the way a dog shakes a dead squirrel. A first-class Missouri spring line squall hit as I headed out of town. Rain and hail inundated my travel.

Why couldn't the storm have held off until I had made the thirty-minute drive? More to the point, why couldn't the guy behind the rental desk have filled the gas tank? My eyes locked on the needle hovering between a fourth of a tank and empty—maybe I had a malfunctioning gauge?

I couldn't hear squat above the storm's fury and hail pinging the roof. The rental company had better have good insurance, because the smooth candy-apple red surface on their shiny car looked like bubble wrap.

A mile from Parnass Springs, a tire blew. I veered the car onto the shoulder and stared at the driving rain. Malfunctioning gas gauges, blowouts. *Great start, Marlene. And you chose not to take the rental insurance.*

All right, Lord. This was supposed to be a freeing trip. Guilt flooded me. Who was I to talk to God like we were best buddies? I always seemed to find him when *I* needed something. Sara needed me, and here I had run from responsibility like a scared rabbit.

Les Swank's image popped in my mind. I'd raced to the senior doctor at the Chicago Shriner's Hospital when I almost blacked out last week. He knew me from my job there, in the cardiac care unit.

He'd eyed me over his bifocals. "What seems to be the problem?"

"My sugar's 376."

He shook his head. "Marlene. And you're a nurse."

"I know. I'll watch my diet. I'll ignore carbs—live on salads and protein."

"And you'll add a second Glyburide at night, you'll exercise more, and you'll stop by my office in the morning for a full checkup."

"Barbarian."

"Hardhead." He took the prescription pad I offered and began to write.

I spoke his mind before he could. "I need my rest. I'm not a spring chicken anymore."

"You're what? Forty-three? That's young, and you've still got what it takes to generate any man's interest. It's your health that's starting to turn ugly. When are you going to slow down?"

"Slow what?" The foreign term threw me.

He tore off the prescription and handed it over. "You promised to slow down years ago, get more exercise, and eat right."

"I will. Starting now. I'm going to Parnass Springs for a week—nine days, if you count the weekend."

"Good choice. It should be lovely this time of year."

Yeah, lovely. I'm sure I'd agree if it weren't for the haunting memories of matters that had never been settled.

Why, oh why, didn't I just stay home?

Thunder cracked. The wind whipped and howled while I dragged the doughnut-sized spare tire out of the trunk, breaking a nail in the process. The tire hit the pavement. Wringing my smarting finger, I watched rubber bounce wiggly niggly across the asphalt. Motorists slammed on brakes. Tires screeched on wet pavement. The tire bounced mid-treetop level and landed in a ditch on the opposite side of the highway.

Great.

I should have waited in the car until the rain slacked, but by now, there wasn't a dry thread on me. A half hour later, I'd fixed the flat.

I was drenched to the bone, and rain had plastered my hair against my head. I caught a glimpse of myself in the rearview mirror and saw one soggy, darkened strand stuck to my forehead. Water rolled down the bridge of my nose in a nasty drip. I had brown eyes—liquid brown eyes, I'd been told. They were very liquid at the moment.

Waiting to pull back onto the highway, I noticed a line of motorcyclists. I counted twenty-one ahead of me. The riders and passengers were all decked out in leather jackets and rain gear. "Hell's Angels" blazoned across the backs of their jackets. I backed off the gas and followed, wanting to pass but leery in the driving rain. The big bikes hummed like a swarm of hornets as rubber met wet pavement. Ah, the good old days. Vic and a neighbor had taught me to ride many years ago.

I hit the brake when a cloudburst consumed the car.

The trip was starting off great. Very relaxing. My stress level had peaked somewhere between high and you gotta be kidding.

I reached to flip the wipers to high and my hand hit the horn. *Beep!* Then *beeeeeep!* I smacked the center of the leather-covered steering wheel trying to make it stop. The thing was stuck! I cranked down the window and stuck my head out, waving my arms to communicate that the horn was stuck. A female driver turned and motioned me past. I couldn't pass. I couldn't see!

I followed the twenty-one, none-too-happy Hell's Angels, horn blaring at decibel levels that even the dead would have found objectionable. Lucky me. I got some lethal looks as

I rolled into town on a wing and a prayer, just before dusk, soaked and chilled to the bone.

The day couldn't get any worse—

How silly of me. Of *course* it could. The town's one gas station could be closed.

The station came into sight, and I sat up straight, hoping against hope—then almost swallowed my tongue.

Oh, it could get much *worse.*

The gas station was open. But who was standing at the gas pump, filling an older-model pickup and looking better than any man his age should look? None other than Vic Brewster, Mr. Clark Kent and Indiana Jones rolled into one, wearing a pair of brown cords and a blue shirt.

This was too coincidental. Too romance novelish. Too *stupid* to bear.

My first instinct was to hide, to slump down behind the wheel and ease through the pump section with only my hands visible on the steering wheel. It'd look weird, true, but it would save me from a heap of embarrassment.

Ducking it was.

I hunched, watching for pump clearance from the corner of my left eye, the one with twenty-forty vision. I'd shoot right on through, zip onto the highway, and then pull over to the shoulder a safe distance away. When good ole Vic finished fueling and left, I'd go back.

Vic Brewster. The last man I wanted to bump into looking like flotsam dredged up from the bottom of the lake. A glance in my rearview mirror showed it was worse than I thought. Not only was I was drenched to the skin, hair hanging in wet coils, but mascara ran in black streaks down my cheeks, and every trace of makeup had vanished.

I eased up on the gas pedal, my rented car creeping past the tall, familiar figure, praying he wouldn't notice me. The convenience store clerk gawked from the window at the seemingly driverless car, but desperate times called for desperate measures. The car cleared the last pump, and I sighed. I'd made it. Now all I had to do was sit up enough to spot any oncoming traffic before I pulled—

Bam!

My thoughts shattered at the sound.

Bolting upright, I focused down the hood of the car at a sight I didn't care to see again if I lived to be a hundred. I'd hit a Coke display—maybe fifty 12-can cases suddenly spewed a sticky, sweet soda geyser. My foot slipped and hit the gas. The display emitted an ear-piercing screech, scraping across the cement. My hands gripped the steering wheel so hard, my knuckles turned white. I couldn't see anything for the soda washing my wipers. Stop and I'd die of humiliation; continue and I'd push the entire foaming display out onto the highway, possibly cause a wreck, hurt someone, or kill myself.

Or I could slam on the brakes, revealing myself to Vic and the curious convenience store clerk. Hmm. Die of humiliation or cause an accident?

Accident didn't sound too bad.

The driver's side door flew open, my options evaporating when I met a pair of startled, but oh-so-familiar dark eyes. Recognition dawned on those rugged features.

Dear Father, open this floor and let this car swallow me. Now!

"Marlene?"

I did the only self-respecting thing a woman could do in such circumstances. I pretended to faint.

"Marlene!" A male's piercing whistle split the air. "Hey! She's fainted!"

Drama had never been my strong suit, but a merciful God allowed me an Emmy-winning performance. When Vic and the store clerk eased me out of the car onto the cold concrete, I moaned. Then I slumped in my make-believe semi-conscious state, pulling the light blanket someone had donated over my head. Vic promptly yanked it back. Questioning voices, curious bystanders, innocent victims of my ploy who had stopped for gas or for a loaf of bread on their way home, witnessed my sterling performance.

Vic's rich timbre floated above the others. "She must have fainted when she pulled into the drive. I'll take her to the clinic."

The clinic? *His* clinic? He was the town vet! Groan. Through slatted eyes I saw a young man, maybe the clerk, tower above me. "Lucky for her she hit soda pop instead of a gas pump."

Well, yeah. I was just oozing luck today.

So, fine. What I'd done was incredibly dumb. I could have seriously injured someone. Hitting a pump could have blown us all to kingdom come. Why hadn't I just driven past the pumps when I recognized Vic, and returned later? Now, here I was, headed to a *vet* clinic, when there was nothing wrong with me but a colossal case of sheer stupidity.

Two men loaded me into the front seat of a pickup, Vic behind the wheel. Why did men age so much more gracefully than women? If anything, Vic looked better than ever. Though never handsome, he was striking; a man's man, tall, a ruddy complexion, dancing dark eyes, and a hint of silver at his temples.

He started the pickup, and I blurted out the principal thought on my mind. "*Where* are you taking me?"

He grinned. "The medical clinic. Did you think I was planning to take you to the veterinary clinic?"

"Well, I wondered."

"I could check you out, but I'd have the law breathing down my neck. Besides, I'd like to know why you fainted. We'll let Doc Johnson decide the cause."

He was worried about me. Guilt hit like a steamroller. *Marlene, you can get yourself into the worst messes. When are you planning to grow up?*

Doc Johnson was older, barrel-chested, and brusque, with white hair and penetrating blue eyes, and a failing memory. He barely remembered my name. "Fainted, huh? You make a habit of doing that?"

I shook my head. "No . . . this is a first."

"Well, come on to the back and we'll see what's ailing you."

He ran a preliminary exam, asking questions and checking my vitals. I faked grogginess. The ruse had gone on too long to confess now, even with my conscience taking bites out of my pebbling gooseflesh.

I had misled so long that lies were coming almost naturally.

About the time *CSI* came on, Dr. Johnson gave up on the tests when he (duh) failed to find a physical reason for my fainting spell. By now my hair and clothing had dried and I had finger combed my curly locks into a semblance of order.

Someone had stuck my purse near my jacket. I fumbled around to find a tube of lip gloss and ran it over my dry lips. When Vic walked back into the brightly lit room, my appearance had improved to merely semi-pathetic. I wanted to cry. He looked so together—I'm talking confident and focused. The years had been kind to him.

I, on the other hand, must have looked like a dried fig.

"Hi," he said, studying me carefully.

"Hi," I murmured. "You waited."

"I wanted to make sure you got home all right."

I tried to glance away, but the years fell back, and suddenly it was Vic, my best friend Vic, looking at me, his features grave with concern.

"So. Long time no see."

"Way too long." His eyes crinkled at the corners. "You gave me a scare."

"Sorry."

"I didn't know you were expected back. You didn't say anything when we talked at Christmas."

"Aunt Ingrid finally decided to be sensible. She's agreed to let me settle Beth's estate. Guess she got tired of fighting me." Aunt Ingrid was technically my father's stepmother, but she had always seemed like another aunt to me.

He pulled up a chair and sat down beside the table. "I'll bet you didn't know I was mayor of Parnass Springs, did you?"

"No kidding?" Vic? Town mayor? He'd broken out enough city-hall windows to own the place, so I guess that was only fair.

"Well, acting mayor while Eric Wells is on a fact-finding mission."

I shook my head, trying to look lethargic. "Mayor? I never expected you to go into politics."

"Next stop, the White House." He reached for my hands and his eyes turned grave. "Doc says you have diabetes. Why didn't you tell me?"

For the same reason I hadn't told him a lot of things. Health issues meant I was weak. Noel walking out meant I was a failure. I didn't *want* to be weak or a failure in Vic's eyes.

I tried to focus. "My blood sugar's been a little high lately, but I'm on medication—is it high now?" I'd barely eaten anything today—I'd think it would be dangerously low.

"A little. Have you been taking care of yourself?"

"Oh? Well. On occasion."

Tell him the truth, Marlene. Tell him you "fainted" from embarrassment.

Not in a million years. I brushed a languid hand across my forehead. Oscar-winning stuff. When, exactly, had lying come so easily? "So, what ... what happened?"

"Not sure, but you pulled into the station and hit a pop display. We were able to get the car stopped before you shot back onto the highway."

I kept silent. Cowards are like that.

"How are you feeling?"

"Like a complete and utter fool, but health-wise, good." I opened an eye and met his gaze. "How are you?"

He grinned, a lopsided, cocky, totally Vic smile that never failed to send my heart into spasms.

"Great. It's good to see you. You look wonderful."

Heat blanketed my cheeks. He was being kind, of course. I wasn't the fresh-faced girl of my youth. I felt old and tired—and who wouldn't be, carrying a load of guilt as big as a Clydesdale? Here I was, occupying a clinic bed, taking up a doctor's time, and lying—to my best friend. Because of one split moment's insane decision.

God, forgive me. When will I ever learn? How long are you willing to put up with me? "Do I need to stay overnight?"

"Doc says you're free to go, but he wants to see you in the morning. You need a good night's sleep. Why don't you come by the vet clinic tomorrow, and I'll bring you back here so Doc can check your blood sugar and see if you're following instructions. You can't mess around with diabetes, Marlene."

"You work on Saturdays?"

"I work every day."

Well, I supposed a vet would be on call most of the time.

The nurse unhooked me from the various paraphernalia and left the room, saying I could take my time about sitting up and putting on my shoes.

Vic rose from the chair and pulled me into a sitting position. "Here. Let me help."

He slipped my shoes on, tying them one by one and then helped me stand. My jacket was still damp and wrinkled, but I didn't protest when he pulled it around my shoulders. Maybe I didn't mind because his hands were warm and comforting, or maybe just because it was Vic standing beside me.

"Wait a minute." He left and then returned with a wheelchair.

"I can walk."

"Forget it. You go out in a wheelchair or you spend the night here. Take your choice."

I sighed and climbed on board, letting him push me out through the lobby to his truck.

"Wait! Don't I have to sign insurance papers?"

"We'll take care of that tomorrow." He opened the passenger door, and warm air rushed over me. "Tonight you're going home, soaking in a hot bath, and tomorrow morning you're sleeping in."

"Okay, fine. You're the doctor. I'm staying at Beth's house."

He helped me inside, and I leaned back against the headrest, closed my eyes, and prayed again for that hole to open up and swallow me. Granted, I loved seeing Vic, but not this way. When I thought about the things I hadn't told him over the years, vital bits of my life I had deliberately left out . . . He knew all about me, yet he knew nothing. And part of what he thought he knew was wrong. The times we'd talked, I'd not been . . . forthcoming.

He drove into Aunt Beth's driveway and helped me up the porch steps and into the house. I waited in the doorway as he hit the switch, flooding the room with light.

A chill raced through me. This house was my past whether I liked it or not. Standing here right now, I didn't like it.

"You're sure you'll be all right?" His strong arm reinforced me.

"I'll be fine. I phoned ahead to have the utilities turned on, the water heater lit. All the comforts of home, if a pipe doesn't leak or the ceiling doesn't cave in."

His gaze roamed the cracked plaster. "It's a mess."

It was. Nearly as bad as my life. I wanted to see the house through his eyes, without the chill of childhood memories. Realistically it was falling down. A large brown spot on the dining room ceiling meant a new roof was in order. I sniffed. Mice. Place was probably overrun with the furry little creatures.

Vic's brows lifted.

"I'll be all right. Nothing will bother me here." Not an easy job, sounding convincing with cobwebs hanging from the light fixtures and dangling in obscure places. Mice I could handle. Spiders? The thought of coming across a furry, eight-legged creature strung my nerves tighter than banjo strings.

And then there were the rocks. Aunt Beth had been an avid collector of many things. Of course she didn't collect anything valuable, just other people's junk, throwaways, and rocks. Lots of rocks. Which she kept in the house.

I'd always expected the living room floor to fall into the basement some day, taking half a ton of boulders with it.

I took a deep, sustaining breath. "Don't worry, I'm feeling much stronger. I'll have a cup of tea and go to bed."

"There's an extra bedroom at Pop's house. You're welcome to stay there."

I still had enough common sense to know *that* was a bad idea. I was here to get rid of the past, not to promote it. "A good night's sleep will do wonders. Thanks for all you've done."

And may he never know how unnecessary it'd been. I couldn't believe I'd perpetrated something so foolish.

Believe it Marlene. You made an impression on the entire community. I'd envisioned returning home with a tad more dignity.

But dignity never was yours. Not ever.

"All right then. I'll see you tomorrow. Come by when you're up and around." He reached as if to brush a lock of hair off my forehead, then withdrew his hand. I thought he might kiss me—a bird peck on the cheek, nothing unusual for friends—but he stepped back and turned an eye to the night sky. "Looks like the storm is over."

"Yeah." Standing beside him, aware of his special scent—male, and some killer cologne—I had the unsettled feeling the storm was just about to break.

He descended the steps and strode to the driveway. I stood in the shadows of the porch, watching him back the truck across the street to his dad's house.

Finally I went inside and switched on every light in the place as I walked through the rooms, remembering the hours I'd spent here. Aunt Beth had always been strange—bizarre, actually—but if not for her kindness, I would have gone to an orphanage. Clean sheets bearing a faint scent of lavender awaited me in the linen chest. The lid fit tight so the mice hadn't been able to get to them. I made the bed in the front bedroom, the one with the large window, and went back downstairs.

I ran a sink full of sudsy water and washed enough dishes for breakfast. Someone—Joe most likely—had left a box of tea and a fresh loaf of bread on the table. Ingrid would have told him I was coming . . .

I frowned. Odd that he didn't tell Vic—

Eww! Well, I was right. The kitchen was overrun with mice. No, they weren't in sight, but their droppings were scattered all around the room.

I filled the teakettle, and when it whistled, I poured hot water over the tea bag and added a shot of honey. On a whim I carried my cup out to the side porch. The porch swing seemed sturdy enough, so I sat, swaying to and fro. I'd forgotten how peaceful it was. The people here were part of my past, and the older I got, the more I longed for solid roots.

I focused on the small parsonage across the street. Joe Brewster, Vic's father, Parnass's spiritual leader, lived there. Had the years been kind to him? Joe had shepherded four generations in this small rural community. His endless compassion, combined with a few amusing quirks and a passion for inventing useless gadgets, endeared him to the town. His revivals were notorious for both fun and sobriety. Joe knew how to make a Christian laugh, to enjoy the richness of life, yet honor their Maker. He'd been my surrogate father in my younger years.

A light came on in the small cottage out back of the parsonage. Vic's place, though according to him, Joe had been after him to move back into the house. Had our unexpected encounter today stirred memories for Vic too? Did he ever think about his earlier years and the way I'd destroyed what we'd once thought was an irrevocable bond between us?

My increasingly morose thoughts ended when the "William Tell Overture" sprang to life. My cell phone. I flipped it open and Sara's panicked voice brought me the rest of the way back to reality. With a thud.

"Mom!"

"What, darling?" I knew I shouldn't have left. What had happened now? Why was she calling so late?

"It's Petey."

"Something's wrong with Petey?"

He had a cold when I left. It must have turned into pneumonia! I knew I should've stayed in Glen Ellyn instead of running off to Parnass Springs. What had I been thinking? My little grandson was dying, and I wasn't even there—

"I can't find Mr. Bear, and he refuses to go to bed without it."

My heart, which had been doing a fairly decent imitation of a jackhammer, slowed. A bear? She called me at this time of night about a stuffed bear? I closed my eyes and took a deep breath, struggling for control. "Where did he last have it?"

"He can't remember."

"Did you look in the hall closet?" He used the space for a "club house."

"I never thought of that. I'll look now."

I waited, gripping the phone. *Be strong, Marlene. This is her first test. Let her handle this crisis alone.*

"Mom? It's not there."

"Did you check Emma's room?"

I waited five minutes. Sara returned. "It's not there either. I don't know what I'll do if we don't find it!"

Life, as we knew it, would go on, but I didn't miss the unspoken reproach in her tone of voice—I had no right to go off and leave her alone.

"It's there somewhere. You'll have to look until you find it, sweetie. Give me a call tomorrow and let me know where it was."

Before I lost my nerve, I did something I'd never done before. I hung up. Sara was young—much too young to have two children under the age of four. She'd been too young to marry, but Pete was older and I thought he would stabilize her. Instead, he worked so many long hours in residency that he'd made Sara even more dependent on me.

For a few minutes I sat staring at the phone as if Sara might reach through the wire and throttle me. When it seemed safe that she wouldn't, I cleared my throat, smiled, and released a pent-up breath.

There. That wasn't so hard.

I fixed a fresh cup of tea and returned to the swing, rocking, letting the quiet seep through my soul. Spring frogs croaked; the mild air saturated my frayed nerves.

Peace and quiet. At this point of my life, that wasn't unreasonable, was it?

Two

I tried to sleep in Saturday morning, but noisy birds and sunshine woke me. I knew I was back in Aunt Beth's house before I opened my eyes. Her unique fragrance drifted above the musk and mouse piddles. Eccentric, she was, but she always smelled of lavender soap. I bet I'd find at least thirty bars of Yardley Lavender in the linen closet.

I stretched and pulled the sheet around my chin. Peaceful. No traffic, no need to leap out of bed and rush through my usual ritual: shower, blow-dry my hair, brush my teeth, slap on makeup, down a cup of coffee, a handful of medication, and a piece of wheat toast. I had nothing pressing to do and not one soul to make demands on my time. No stress, no hurry. Sheer bliss.

I lay there for over thirty minutes, savoring the absence of repercussions for my laziness. Then it hit me.

Coffee. I needed coffee.

I'd planned to buy supplies at the local convenience store, the Scat and Git, but my filling station detour through cuckoo-land had shot that down. I'd grab a cup on the way to Vic's office.

Lukewarm water blasted my face, reminding me that the house needed a new water heater. After drying off from my shower, I pulled on jeans and a red sweatshirt. In a hurry now, I combed my medium-length bob and pulled on a ball cap, collected my purse, and got into the rental car some kind soul had thoughtfully delivered. Aunt Ingrid, Aunt Beth's fraternal twin, stuck her head out of her open kitchen window as I was backing out of the drive.

Ingrid was another quirky sort—always had been off in her own world. She'd married Eugene Moss later in life. Uncle Eugene became the town mayor, but then he'd gone nuts thirteen years ago and ran off with the local café waitress, Prue Levitt. Once again, a Moss scandal had rocked the town and caused a widening rift between Ingrid and Beth—one that remained until the day Beth died. The cause of the rift? That Beth refused to take sides.

Beth had never been overly fond of her sister, and Eugene used that weakness to forge a bond with Beth, who remained steadfastly neutral.

Ever incensed at Beth's impartiality, Ingrid refused to speak to her sister or have anything to do with her personal estate, though the two Parnass sisters jointly owned three-fourths of the town and multiple real estate holdings in Columbia—a legal nightmare to be sure. I had no idea of the two women's collective worth, only that it was big. Since Aunt Beth raised me, and the mere mention of Ingrid set her teeth ajar, the task of liquidating Beth's house and personal belongings had fallen to me.

"You home, Marlene?"

I slammed on the brakes. "I'm in a bit of a hurry, Aunt Ingrid. Do you need something?" I should have stopped to see her the night before, but by the time I left the clinic, it had been past Ingrid's usual bedtime.

"I'd like a minute of your time when you're not too busy." Ingrid stepped over to the hedge. I took in her housecoat and ragged slippers, her flame-red—I looked again—*flame-red* hair wound in red Velcro curlers. She'd changed her hair color. The flamboyant red made her round, deep-set eyes disappear. She carried the ever familiar plastic rain bonnet in case of a sudden wind or rain shower. The woman was purely paranoid about wet hair.

I glanced at the wavering gas gauge. Did I need fuel or not? Any reputable rental service would have filled the tank, yet dare I chance it?

"I'll catch you later Aunt Ingrid. I'm supposed to be somewhere in a few minutes."

She blocked the drive. "I have a right to know when you're in town. I'm family, you know."

"I know. Talk to you when I get back." Good old Ingrid, she never changed. Through death, storms, and taxes, Ingrid held on to her "rights."

I arrived at the vet clinic a little before nine. Vic glanced up, eyes widening, probably at seeing me up and around so early. "Hey. I thought you were supposed to sleep in?"

"I did. I usually get up at four-thirty."

"You've got to be kidding. There really is a 4:30 a.m.?"

"It should be outlawed, but there is. I work the seven-to-three shift."

He shook his head. "Better move back here. It's a slower pace."

"Animals don't get sick at inconvenient times of the day here?"

He winked. "City ordinance. Nine to four-thirty, and then we cut it off." He got up and poured me a cup of strong black coffee. I hated black coffee but drank it anyway.

"Let's drive over to the clinic and see how the blood sugar is this morning."

"I know how it is—I have my Glucometer—"

"Doc says he wants to test you personally."

I got into his pickup, and in a few minutes I was inside the clinic. I couldn't get sick while I was here. Sara would never forgive me if I stayed longer than my allotted time.

The reading was down, an acceptable ninety-two. I wanted to burst into song.

"No lasting effect from your Coke fight?" Vic grinned.

I was far too old for a girlish blush, but my cheeks didn't seem to know that. "None, and it was sugar-free Coke, not real Coke. I'm not that tough."

A brow shot up. "Tough enough to eat my meat loaf tonight?"

Most women would recognize an invitation to dinner, but I wasn't most women. I was rusty at this man-woman business, and besides, this was Vic, and admittedly I do silly things. "Not *that* tough. Why don't I make lasagna?"

"Okay by me. What time?"

"Provided the stove will light? Six. That too early?"

"I'll be there. What can I bring?"

"An appetite."

He drove me back to the vet clinic, and I left a few minutes later, humming. I liked lasagna. Hadn't had it in a month, and dinner—an innocent dinner with an old friend—had nothing to do with my sudden burst of well-being.

I doubled back to a convenience store some five miles away, not wanting to bump into anyone until last night's debacle had faded from memory.

On second thought, I couldn't stay hidden that long.

I reached for the cell phone and punched in the number for a plumber that I'd gotten from an old telephone directory at Beth's house. Here's hoping the place was still in business. The line rang ten times before someone finally picked up.

"Yup?"

"Kelo Plumbing?"

"Yup."

"I need a hot water heater replaced, and a drippy kitchen faucet repaired. Can you help?"

"Yup."

I rattled off the address. "Know where that is?"

"Yup. You Herman's kid?"

And so it begins. "Can you come today?"

"Nope."

"Monday?"

"Yup. Afternoon. Late."

"Okay. Thanks."

"Yup."

I clicked off, humming a tune at my progress. Now all I had to do was find a ceiling man and a roofer who could talk in complete sentences.

Mayer's Quick Shop was like any home-owned stop-and-shop. I pulled up to the pump and filled my gas tank, enjoying morning sunshine and the lack of traffic. Parnass Springs's slower pace suited me just fine. Ingrid and Beth's great-great grandfather had founded the town and built the covered bridge. The town drew a fair amount of tourists with the historical landmark and trendy gift shops.

I browsed the shelves, picking up basic food items: milk, bread, eggs, canned goods, D-Con, and mouse traps, plus stuff for lasagna. I was looking forward to the impromptu dinner date. Vic was still the only man who made me giddy.

Yeah, giddy.

The thirtysomething lady behind the counter had long, straight brown hair, and braces on her teeth accentuating a friendly smile. She totaled my purchases and raised her eyebrows. "Will that be all?"

"Yes. No ... wait." My nose detected fresh doughnuts. Not Krispy Kreme, but close. "I'll take a dozen glazed."

Not on my diet, but one wouldn't hurt. The sugary fragrance tormented me on the drive home.

Back at Aunt Beth's house I washed the cabinet shelves and put away the groceries. The plumber had recognized my address. That didn't surprise me, but I'd hoped the memory of Herman had faded. I'd loved Herman, of course I had, but a part of me resented him. And yes, a bigger part of me was ashamed of him. One didn't easily overcome the stigma of a father accused of molesting a young woman.

"Herman isn't all there." Ingrid's words from so long ago rang in my ears. "You have to be kind to your father—he has the mind of a seven-year-old."

Unfortunately, he also had a youth's hormones. So it was that Herman Moss, Aunt Ingrid's stepson, impregnated a girl living in the same assisted-living home. The result? Me. Marlene Moss—innocent victim of a mentally challenged couple. Some insisted Herman had molested the girl, but Ingrid vehemently denied the charge. Herman was simple, not a pervert.

Ingrid and Eugene allowed the pregnancy and refused to discuss adoption. Why Ingrid and Beth wanted to raise

Herman's child was beyond me, but maybe that was the answer: they both wanted *their* way and their way was me. Both women were strong pro-lifers. The girl's family favored adoption, but Ingrid and Beth fought for Herman's "parental" rights. Though Herman certainly couldn't raise me, neither could the young woman involved. After custody was awarded to my aunts, my mother was immediately moved to another facility.

I was left to face collateral damage. Namely me, Aunt Ingrid, and Aunt Beth.

Parnass Springs was a close-knit town, and the incident created a real scandal. Cruel accusations flew back and forth about Herman, the funny man that stood head and shoulders above others, whose front teeth hung over his bottom lip. Who was loud. So loud. People excused his unacceptable behavior because of his innocence, and Aunt Beth and Ingrid upheld their decision. For unfeeling women, they showed unusual compassion to an infant who had no say in the matter.

I shook the uninvited memories away, surprised they were still so strong. I wasn't going to think about Herman. That part of my life was over.

On impulse I picked up the box of doughnuts and walked across the street. The parsonage hadn't changed much, and neither had the small white clapboard church with the narrow steeple. I pictured the polished solid-oak pews, the round white globe light fixtures, and the oak cross at the back of the baptistery. The church was as familiar to me as Aunt Beth's house.

I stepped up to the porch and knocked. Joe Brewster answered. We studied each other for a moment. He was older;

his hair as white as the clouds skipping overhead, but his sturdy frame was unbowed. Warm brown eyes still saw through my facade right to the heart. His smile was as genuine and full of mischief as the day I'd left all those many years ago. I walked into his arms. He hugged me close and I hugged him back.

"Marlene. Let me look at you."

I smiled, knowing what he would see. The passing years hadn't been kind to the young woman he'd known. A wayward husband, raising a daughter alone, keeping the wolf from the door—it all took a toll. But neither Joe nor Vic knew my secret. Nor, for that matter, did anyone else in Parnass Springs.

I assumed when Vic married Julie that I'd lost him forever. By then I'd dug myself in so deep with my made-up stories that I didn't know how to find my way back to the truth.

Joe kissed my forehead. "Still pretty as a picture. Come on in here, little one. You've stayed away too long."

The warmth of his greeting wrapped around me like a favorite blanket. I floated over the threshold and into the kitchen on a wave of goodwill.

"Are those doughnuts I smell?" Joe bustled about the small kitchen, clearing a place at the cluttered table.

I stared at the contraption that looked like a modern moonshine still sitting on the kitchen counter. Coffee bubbled through coiled glass tubing before rushing into the waiting cup.

"What is that?"

"My latest invention." He grinned. "State-of-the-art coffeemaker. Does everything but put it in a saucer and blow on it. It double filters the coffee so it's extra pure, even adds cream and sugar."

"Extra pure. How about that." I sipped from the cup he handed me and made appropriate lip-smacking noises, rolling my eyes. "Heavenly. So, you're still inventing?"

"Vic swears the machine is nuts, but with a little more tinkering, I can get the bugs worked out. The widow Hanks wasn't too pleased with my new back scratcher, but that woman doesn't appreciate what it takes to come up with high-tech quality."

I choked on my coffee. "What happened?"

"Well shoot, the thing almost took the hide off her back. I had a bolt set a little too loose and it slipped into high gear. Got to scratching a bit too furious and Verna got all vexed. Said it clawed like a riled cat."

I burst out laughing. If Verna Hanks was anything like I remembered, I'd bet Joe got a tongue-lashing he hadn't forgotten. "Was she upset?"

"You could say that, but there wasn't any reason for her to call me a menace to society. I offered to give her money back."

He filtered another cup of coffee. There were similarities in father and son's features, but Vic favored his mother. Odd. Vic and I had talked every New Year's Eve—hadn't missed a year since the day I left Parnass Springs. I'd kept up on everything going on in town, and what Vic hadn't told me, Aunt Beth and Ingrid had. Yet I hadn't seen him in what? Twelve years? Not since he'd been in Chicago for a veterinary convention and I met him for dinner downtown. We'd talked for hours. Noel had left me, but my pride wouldn't allow me to tell Vic that I'd made a terrible mistake by leaving Parnass and him. Besides, by then he was happily settled with Julie.

That night was crystal clear in my mind, the night I'd first deceived this man. I was crazy, confused, so happy to see him, but sick at heart that I had made the biggest mistake of my life by walking away and marrying Noel. Of course the subject came up over dinner.

Stirring his coffee, Vic had faced me, solemn faced. "You loved Noel enough to run away and marry him? Without talking to me? That hurt, Marlene."

Looking anywhere but at him, I'd said softly, "I thought I loved him. When you're eighteen, you're not thinking clearly—at least I wasn't."

"But you're happy?" His eyes searched mine, looking for—what? Confession that I had been the biggest of fools and wished I'd never heard the name Noel Queens? If I spoke the damning words, what difference would it make to him now? Julie was waiting at home—a lovely woman whom Vic loved with all his heart and soul.

And so the lies began.

"Very happy!" I pasted on my brightest smile and asked for the dessert menu, as if Key lime pie would absolve sin. Only briefly had I thought I loved Noel Queens. I was an idealist at eighteen. I thought I wanted to spare Vic a life without children. At the time I was so sure I had his interests at heart, but within a couple of years my sacrificial instincts had turned to rot, and I knew I'd married Noel to get away from Parnass and Herman's memories.

What sort of person admits she's so shallow that she has to run—and continue to lie—to avoid her past?

Me. Marlene Queens.

So shallow that I would rather live a lie than let Ingrid, Beth, Vic, or Joe know I was that sort of wretch. And once the lie was spoken, it was relatively easy to keep alive.

Joe brought me back to the present when he offered the doughnuts. I shook my head. "Diabetes. I thought I might have one when I bought them, but I think I'll pass." The lower blood sugar reading this morning had encouraged me. "So, what's going on in Parnass Springs?"

"I'm retiring and the church is throwing a big bash next Sunday night." Joe stirred his coffee.

"Retiring?" I couldn't believe it. Of course, he had to be sixty-five at least. "How many years have you been the pastor at Mount Pleasant?"

"Forty years this spring. Sure seems longer than that."

Forty years preaching the gospel. How many souls would be in heaven because of his ministry? How many familiar faces would be there to greet him when he entered the gates? I was humbled just thinking about it. "When did you say the celebration is?"

"Next Sunday night. You'll come, won't you?" He reached for a second doughnut.

"I wouldn't miss it." Sara didn't expect me home until Monday evening. "Do you remember the time Vic and I emptied four quarts of red food coloring into the baptistery?"

"And I had a baptism that morning?" His eyes lit with humor. "The water turned Mrs. Bradley's silver hair a serious shade of pink. She joined the Methodists shortly after that. Claimed they took sacred rituals more seriously."

"I can't believe we did that." I shook my head. Kids. My daughter had embarrassed me more times than I cared to remember. I guess she was her mother's daughter.

Joe chuckled. "You know the time that sticks in my mind? When you two troublemakers turned a couple of gerbils loose in the middle of Sunday morning worship service. I don't believe anyone got much out of the sermon that day."

"When the pets scattered under the pews, everyone on that row swung their legs up. And one got in Ed Rankin's pant leg." I laughed so hard I spilled my coffee. "I never saw a man move so fast."

We visited for the better part of an hour before I realized the time and left. If I'd let myself, I'd have stayed forever.

My cell phone rang late afternoon. I fumbled for it, knowing who it must be. "Hello, Sara." I was surprised she waited this long to call after her panic on Friday evening.

My daughter's breathless voice came over the line. "Mom!"

"Hi. Where did you find the bear?"

"Under the sofa, but Mom! I forgot to tell you that I went to the doctor on Friday, and he just called. I have the most exciting news!" Before I could ask what, she barreled on. "Can't you guess?"

I sat down on one of the kitchen chairs, my heart suddenly hammering in my throat. I'd welcome a diagnosis on why my daughter had been under the weather for the past month and a half, but the mother in me always feared the worst. What if she had some horrible, incurable disease?

"You'll never guess what he said!"

"Flu?"

There'd been a particularly nasty strain going around, and I feared Sara would get it. She hadn't fully regained her strength from the last bout.

"Not the flu."

"Mono. It's flared again."

"No, silly. I'm expecting!"

I nearly dropped the phone. *Oh, please, tell me you're joking.*

"Did you hear me, Mom? Isn't it exciting? Petey and Emma Grace will have a brother or sister in December!"

Thrilling. From the silence, I realized I was expected to rejoice, but three kids in less than five years? "Oh ... my."

"Pete's walking on air. Oh, wait a minute, Mom. Petey just took a neon tetra out of the aquarium. Petey! Put that fish back in the water!" My daughter's voice came back on the line. "Isn't this wonderful, Mom? I am just too, too excited."

Another baby. Sara, have you lost your mind? I closed my eyes, taking a moment to stem my concerns. She couldn't handle the children she had.

"Another baby. Well, imagine that." Twenty-three and a third child on the way.

Enthusiasm didn't exactly pour from my mouth. All I could think of was a mountain of diapers and getting up at night to feed a crying baby while Sara slept, content to let someone else do the grunt work. I was too old to raise another baby, and I had no illusions as to who would take over when Sara collapsed from fatigue. I had to talk to my son-in-law, Pete. When God said to go forth and replenish the earth, I'm sure he didn't intend for Pete and Sara to take it on as a one-couple commission. At any rate, it seemed we had another baby on the way, and I would be expected to stay with the family until Sara recuperated.

I tossed and turned most of the night, then finally got up before dawn and made a pot of coffee. Mornings had always been my favorite time of the day, but today I could barely relish the peace. The house was so quiet.

The sun barely topped the trees now, bright green growth, glistening with dew as I drove the familiar route to the country cemetery, past Eddie's Café and Parnass Park where families picnicked and children caught fireflies on the summer nights and stuck them in mayonnaise jars. I'd heard the café had a fire recently, but repairs had been made and it was open, once again the hub of the coffee-drinking set.

The cemetery appeared ahead. I took a deep breath and braked. Almost anyone who'd ever lived in Parnass Springs was buried here. Even those who moved away sometimes came back to be planted in the town burial ground, much like pigeons returning to the roost.

Our plot sat ... where? You'd think I could remember the exact location, but it had been a long time since I was last here. I hadn't made it back for Herman's services ...

No. I wasn't going to give in to regret this morning. That was five years ago. Past history.

The annual cemetery cleanup was scheduled for a week from today, a hoopla that included the whole town. I'd participate then, but I wanted to get a head start on our plots. If I knew Ingrid, and I knew Ingrid, years of dead branches and winter's remaining debris buried the granite and marble headstones.

Loaded with tools I'd brought from the car trunk, I clanged toward the gravesites. Juggling a 32-ounce Styrofoam cup of coffee, a rake, shovel, and plastic pail containing a trowel, my gloves, and a cushion to kneel on, I was amazed the noise hadn't caused the dead to waken and gripe at my intrusion.

I paused at the headstone where Uncle Eugene's foot was buried. Poor Uncle Eugene. He loved the women. His first wife caught him in a compromising situation with the town strumpet; she divorced him and left him with their handicapped child, Herman. Ingrid married him a few years later, and then Prue Levitt claimed him. This gravesite was surely one for the record books. When he died a few years back, his parents planned to bury him in his hometown, Olathe, because Prue, the third wife, didn't have the funds to transport him to Hawaii where she planned to relocate, to be near her son by a previous marriage. Aunt Ingrid had a conniption when Hawaii was mentioned and coerced Eugene's parents into burying him in their family plot in Kansas. Well … *most* of him. Years before the divorce, Eugene had lost a foot in a hunting accident. Since he'd been married to Ingrid at the time, the foot rested here in Parnass Cemetery.

To some families that might seem a weird story. For my family? Par for the course.

It took a few minutes to locate the family plot. It had been what? More years than I cared to admit since I'd last stood here in front of the simple granite markers that lay flat to the ground. Aunt Beth died two years ago, Herman a few years earlier. My eyes skipped over the markers. I hadn't come back for either Aunt Beth or Herman. In fact, Sara was a toddler the last time I'd visited here.

The "William Tell Overture" shattered the serenity. *Guess who? Sara, what am I going to do with you?*

I set the pail down, dropped the shovel and rake, and fumbled in my jacket pocket for my cell phone, the true curse of the modern generation. Oh, for the days I only had to deal with an occasional interruption when someone could track me down to say that I had a phone call. Now, twenty-four hours a day the thing could ring, jolting me from sleep, interrupting work.

I hit the answer button. "Yes?"

"Mom! Did I tell you that I've been up since five this morning? This pregnancy is worse than the others. I'm going to be sick twenty-four/seven. I've got to have some rest, Mom. I'm so tired I can hardly keep my eyes open. The mono will come back if I don't get my rest. It's barely eleven o'clock and I'm exhausted!"

This had to be the fastest developing case of morning sickness on record.

"Calm down, honey." My daughter had the power to make herself sick just by thinking about it.

"I am so glad God made you my mother." Pause. "You're still coming home Monday, right?"

Yes, but not a moment sooner. I was staying for Joe's retirement party. Joe had tirelessly served his community and God for over forty years. Morning sickness wasn't fatal, only uncomfortable. Sara would survive.

"Honey, calm down. The house needs a new water heater and roof. I've talked to a plumber—well, sort of—and he's coming soon. I have a call in to the roofer. The repairs need to be done before I can put Beth's house on the market."

Why didn't I mention Joe's retirement party? Sara knew my deep affection for the minister, and she would understand my need to be here. Wouldn't she? Then again, understanding wasn't exactly her long suit.

Coward. You're afraid of your daughter.

I wasn't afraid, just cautious about choosing my battles. This wasn't the time or place to upset her. I knew my lack of gusto for her exciting news hurt her, but her quest for a big family was impractical and foolish. She had no concern for what could happen when both sides of the family were impaired. I'd gotten along without a large family just fine.

"Mom! Can't you come home *before* Monday?"

My jaw firmed. "Monday, Sara." Maybe longer but I didn't say it. Not yet. She would have to get by for a few more days. I was staying until after the retirement party.

I glanced around and spotted Joe getting out of his car and reaching for the pail he kept in the back floorboard. He must be here to visit Melba.

Sara sighed. "I wish you were here. I'd feel better."

"You'd feel the same."

What mother didn't need to hear she was needed? Wanted. I glanced at Joe, who by now had transported his tools and was busy raking debris from his wife's grave. Melba's gravesite was three plots over from Aunt Beth's. I knew the breeze carried our phone conversation. "Honey, I have to go. Try to get some rest."

"Mom, call me later?"

"Sure, hon."

I clicked off, giving Joe an apologetic smile. He smiled back.

"Sara all right?"

"She's pregnant."

Joe paused, leaning on the rake handle. "Have mercy."

My exact sentiments.

I picked up my rake and started to work. Birds soared overhead; the sky was a bright turquoise blue. Suddenly it was good to be alive, to breathe in the fragrant spring air. I didn't have an ache anywhere, my feet didn't hurt, and for once I was complaint free.

Lilac and spirea bushes lined the cemetery. I caught an occasional whiff of the fragrant early iris growing near Herman's stone. My dad's stone.

My dad.

The words stuck in my throat as relentlessly as they had so many years ago. The man who showed up at every PTA meeting and sat in the front row at every one of my programs, occasionally standing to wave at me before someone made him sit. The man who when he ate and talked, sprayed spit in your face. He came to every Christmas pageant, wedged between Aunt Beth and Aunt Ingrid. He even came to my prom and danced with all my friends.

Pride had stood out all over him as he watched me from the sidelines, all the while shelling peanuts and throwing the hulls on the gym floor. The memory still made my skin itch.

"Iris sure smells good."

I glanced to see Joe standing beside me, admiring the deep lavender blooms. He knelt beside my work pails, breathing deeply of the heady fragrance.

"The scent reminds me of Aunt Beth." I dropped to my knees to pull weeds away from the granite, stopping to brush my hand over the fading inscription. "I'm not pleased with the stonework. The dates are almost impossible to read."

"You should talk to Carl Summers. He's got a place off Highway 86. Does some fine stonework."

"Thanks, I'll call him."

I got up, brushing off the seat of my jeans. Joe removed his ball cap, squinting at the sun. Deep in thought, I had failed to notice the late morning hour.

"Say—" Joe turned to face me—"how about sharing my peanut butter and jelly sandwich?"

"Is it lunchtime already?"

I'd been so engrossed, I'd forgotten the hour. In Parnass Springs time seemed to matter little, if at all. No frenetic pace, no demanding schedules. My stress shriveled like a marshmallow over a hot fire. I eyed Joe with a serious look. "Peanut butter and jelly, huh?"

"Made it myself."

"What kind of jelly?"

"Peach preserves."

I reached out to shake his hand. "Deal."

We found a shady spot and Joe opened his lunch pail, a Wal-Mart sack. He tore the sandwich in two, put half on a napkin and handed it to me. After uncapping the thermos, he poured the cup full of hot coffee and passed it over.

"What about you?"

"I'll sip out of the thermos."

I bit into the bread, and creamy peanut butter and peach preserves exploded my taste buds. How nice to share a meal with a good friend under a spreading oak on a mild spring afternoon.

Joe's presence was a balm to my spirit. It was so good to see him, this man I loved almost as much as I had his son …

I swallowed the bite of a sandwich. Did Joe still carry a silent hurt because I'd married Noel? He'd been so sure Vic and I belonged together, but if I'd stayed in Parnass Springs and married Vic, I would have caved in eventually and given him children.

No, marrying Noel may have been a frantic effort to break all ties with Parnass, but it had been necessary. I loved Vic; I wanted more for him than I could give. That much was the truth.

And, if one considered my aunts, I'd done Vic a favor. I liked to think I was different from Aunt Ingrid and Aunt Beth, but no one knew better than I, that blood was thick. Sometimes too much so.

Aunt Ingrid and Aunt Beth were cold. I sometimes wondered if they knew the meaning of love. I still wasn't sure they even noticed when I left all those years ago. To this day, Ingrid never asked me to come home for holidays, and though I had carefully calculated lies to cover Noel's constant absence, they were never needed. Neither aunt ever asked or seemed overly curious about the man I'd run away with, nor about the daughter I'd raised. Oh, the folly of youth.

When I left Parnass on a cold, stormy day, my decision seemed courageous and self-sacrificing for the man I truly loved, Vic Brewster. Now I recognized the flaws in that belief. My impetuosity had reaped a life of regret.

I'd met Noel my first week in nurse's training. I was a green trainee, and he was a handsome, suave man well into his second year of med school. I was attracted by the nurse/doctor scenario, and I so desperately wanted to break free of Parnass. We dated two months, and one night we decided to get married. How nuts. Married at eighteen, and Noel much older.

Then, when I became pregnant, a season of utter terror.

I worried myself sick the entire nine months I carried Sara, fearing my parents' genes would affect my baby. Noel, of course, was convinced I was paranoid about Herman. He wanted children, and my fears were foolish in his sight. When Sara was born, though, God blessed us. We beat the odds. My daughter was bright and talented and showed not a hint of Herman or Lexy's imperfections.

"Penny for your thoughts."

I took another bite of sandwich, silently chuckling. I hadn't heard the old colloquial phrase in years.

"Oh, I was thinking maybe I'd ask you to marry me, Joe. This is the best peanut butter and jelly sandwich I've ever eaten."

He nodded, as if marriage proposals, even in jest, were an everyday occurrence.

"You'll have to get in line. The mere mention of my name is nectar to some of these widow women."

He looked up and grinned, and I knew without a doubt where Vic's orneriness originated.

"Ah. You're a hunted animal, huh?"

"You don't know the half of it."

He winked and took a bite of his sandwich. It was hard to believe that he was sixty-five, vibrant, healthy, and single. I'd bet the women swarmed him like flies at a picnic. I doubted that he would marry again; Melba had been his life. When a stroke and then paralysis struck Vic's mom, everyone thought that Joe would die along with her. Aunt Beth had written that he hung in there for five years nursing Melba, lovingly caring for her every need until one morning she failed to wake. Then he'd insisted on preaching her funeral service.

I wasn't there, but when I got his letter telling me the preaching hour had been the hardest of his life, I sat down and wept for Joe and Melba and a love so few couples ever find.

"So. Little Marlene."

The familiar nickname almost brought me to tears. Every day when I came home from school with Vic and we raided the Brewster cookie jar, Joe called me that. Melba's big old kitchen always smelled of flour and sugar. She was a small woman, but she cooked and ate like a lumberjack. I could never understand how she wasn't as big as a Mack truck, but she retained her slim, youthful body through plates of creamy walnut fudge, five-layer lemon cakes, and the best cherry cobbler this side of heaven.

"How come you decided to come home? You haven't been back in what . . . a very long time?"

"Way too long."

"You don't like us anymore?"

"Can't stand you. You're wretched."

He feigned hurt. "And I gave you half of my sandwich."

I polished off the last crumb and wiped my hands on the grass, then answered his question. "I'm home to put Aunt Beth's house on the market. It's about time, don't you think? It's been two years."

"Ah, yes. She and Ingrid still weren't speaking when she passed away. I sure hate to see the place change hands, but I know a house will deteriorate if it's not lived in. I'm glad Ingrid's finally consented to let you settle the estate. By the way, does Ingrid look in your window instead of ringing the doorbell when she comes to visit?"

I laughed. Aunt Ingrid did peek in windows to see if anyone was home. In most towns the police would have hauled her off to jail, but the reason she gave for the bizarre habit? She didn't want to bother anyone if they were busy.

"Odd lady, but good deep down," Joe admitted.

"I'm glad you think so." I grinned.

"Here to put Beth's house on the market—that's what you said?" He lay back, crossing his hands over his stomach.

Unlike Melba, he couldn't eat anything he wanted and keep a thin waistline. Apparently no one had told him. "That's good. Beth's house needs occupants, and the estate should be settled. It's good to have you back, little one. How's life treated you?"

"It sucker punches me every once in a while."

I leaned back against the tree trunk and filled him in on the years, things I'd told him in letters and Christmas cards—minus Noel, of course. He always asked about Noel, so I got the chance to use my well-devised explanations for his absence: overseas medical conferences, training, fact-finding trips. I had all the answers, and bless Joe, he never dwelled on the subject. I did get the sense, though, that he knew I had loved Vic with all my heart and had settled for less ...

"It appears, Little Marlene, you've done a good job making lemonade from life's little lemons."

I was *not* going to cry. "Ha. Fooled you, haven't I?"

"Oh, now—" He sat up, facing me. "You've raised a child, have two grandchildren and another on the way, a successful husband. God's been good."

"Yes, he has." God had been good, but the deceit stuck in my throat like sawdust. I leaned over and put my hand on his arm. "How about you? You doing okay?"

For the briefest of moments, tears sprang to his eyes, and I realized Melba was uppermost in his mind. The mist cleared. "I'm making it—can't say I don't miss what I've lost, but life goes on."

Life goes on. How many times had I thrown myself that line?

"I suppose my biggest worry these days is Vic."

"Vic?" I sat up straighter, all ears. "What about my buddy? He looks fine." And then some.

"He's working himself to death. Putting in long hours at the clinic, and now he's taken on this mayor's job. It's only temporary, but people are hounding him to death. Every time a barking dog wakes a neighbor, someone thinks they need to call the mayor and get him to do something about it."

I laughed. "Well, if I know Vic, he'll do his best."

"I wonder ..."

He stared into the distance. We were the only visitors in the cemetery, just me and Joe in the quiet serenity.

"What?"

He sighed. "I can't help but wonder what would have happened if you had stayed, Marlene, married Vic, and raised a family."

"I've thought of that." Every day of my life.

"Vic would have a wife. I thought he'd remarry after Julie died, but he didn't. That was just such a shock ..."

I could imagine. To lose your wife in a train-crossing accident ... that had to be terrible. The track ran the length of Parnass Springs. Every day a dozen or more trains blew through. Aunt Beth said one afternoon Julie must not have heard the train whistle. Vic had turned reclusive for a while after her death, and who could blame him?

Joe went on. "In a few more years he'll be too old to want to raise young' uns. He'd be an old man by the time they'd graduate high school."

I tried to allay a father's fears. "He can still marry a young woman who could give him lots of children."

"No, Vic wouldn't marry just to have children. He doesn't give his love that easily." He looked over and winked. "When you left, you took his heart with you."

As much as I loved the thought, I knew it wasn't true. Vic had made it fine without me. And the good Lord knew that at my age, no matter how crazy I was about the man, I wouldn't want a baby. Not now. Not ever.

Three

Sunday afternoon I took a long nap.

Monday, I took another nap to recover.

Shortly after I woke, Vic brought Joe over for a lunch of sandwiches and we caught up on old times. Sara called twice while I was cleaning up. I'd start to do one thing, and the "William Tell" would ring out. I caught Joe and Vic exchanging numerous glances.

Vic reached for another handful of chips. "Did the roofer ever call back?"

"He'll be here end of the week." Again, I saw the dubious look between the two men, but the roofer had been honest. "He'd said he was very busy but he'd work me in."

Vic reached out and took a cookie out of my hand.

"Vic!"

"You're not supposed to be eating cookies." He popped the sweet in his mouth.

"Thanks a lot."

Reaching for a pear, he tossed it to me. "Knock yourself out."

"Who appointed you my guardian?"

Shrugging, he bit another cookie. "Me, I guess. Any problems with that?"

"A few come to mind."

Quite a few.

Late that afternoon I bumped into Joe as he was exiting the church. "What are you up to so late in the day?"

He grinned like an unrepentant four-year-old kid. "I've just installed an automatic page-turner for Mattie. It'll make her work easier."

"Mattie's still playing the organ?" Mercy! How old was she? Near ninety? "What if she's not ready to turn the page?"

He sobered. "It's fully automated. All she has to do is press the button before she starts playing, and after a certain time lapse, the device automatically turns the page."

"Really." His newest invention sounded like a disaster waiting to happen. Well, at least this one shouldn't attack anyone. "I'm surprised Miss Mattie's still in good health."

"Hasn't missed a Sunday in forty years."

I noticed he didn't sound exactly cheerful about the milestone.

"How old is she now?"

"Ninety-four and deaf as a stump. Should have retired years ago, but no one's had nerve enough to suggest it."

Miss Mattie Hensley. Ah, the memories I had of her. The banker's wife had been meaner than a snake when I was growing up. She'd terrorized generations of young girls who grew into her Sunday school province—what we called her class. It didn't sound as if her disposition had mellowed with age.

Joe brightened. "The new minister's wife plays the piano and the organ. Very proficient—and on key! Mattie can't carry on forever."

I laughed.

His expression deflated. "Yeah, you're right. She'll outlive us all. You been over to the house to see Vic?"

"No, I'm on my way to run errands." I scanned the near empty street. "Looks like a lot has changed. New shops, great café."

"We're getting real modern. There's a new animal shelter too. Have you seen it?"

"No, I haven't."

"You will. Coming to the service Wednesday night?"

Would I miss a chance to see Mattie give Joe's automatic page-turner a trial run? Not on your life. "I'll be there. What time?"

"Meeting starts at seven." He leaned closer. "Better get a seat in the front row. You won't want to miss the look on Mattie's face when she sees what I've done."

I'd be there early.

He flashed me a wicked grin, gave a little wave, and walked on only to turn around again. "Noticed you had quite of bit of bread and pastrami left over at lunch. Would it be all right if I stop by around suppertime? Just hate to cook for one—you know how that is."

"I'd be honored."

I watched him leave, loving the odd little inventor, but in reality, my heart ached for him.

Wednesday evening I slipped inside the church and proceeded to the front row, eyes searching for Vic. He said he'd be there barring an emergency. I was still seething from the long day I'd put in waiting on the plumber and roofer. Mr.

"Yup" called late last night to say he hadn't got around to me (no kidding), but he'd be there first thing this morning. I'd waited. And waited. Neither the plumber nor the roofer had shown. The roofer hadn't phoned, so I didn't know his plans, but "Yup" called to say he'd run into a little trouble on the previous job and couldn't get around to me that day. Tomorrow morning. For certain.

Yup. I'd believe it when I saw it.

Linda Bates, who used to be Linda Andrews, my best friend in high school, greeted me with open arms.

"Marlene! You rascal! Why didn't you let me know you were coming?" She shook her head. "You look fantastic! Slim, you've let your hair grow out, and *what* eye shadow are you wearing? It makes your eyes positively sparkle! How long are you here for?"

"Until Monday—"

"Oh, you're not! Now that we've got you, we're going to make you stay for a decent visit."

The congregation settled down and reached for hymnbooks. We sank onto the scarred pew, giggling. Joe peered at us from the dais.

Frank Qullian, song leader for the last twenty-five years, announced the first hymn and threw out his arms, motioning us to rise (Moses with a lead-pencil baton). Miss Mattie hit the opening chords, and our voices lifted in harmony. I guess she must have pushed the button on the page, because right in the middle of "Amazing Grace" she abruptly switched to "Showers of Blessing." The congregation exchanged bewildered glances and struggled to catch up.

The page-turner swung into action again, and Mattie, looking a trifle confused, swung with it, right into the ringing notes of "Revive Us Again."

This was one of my favorites, and I put my heart into the chorus. "Hallelujah! Thine the Glory!"

The page turned and Miss Mattie switched octaves. Frank shot her a look as the congregation gamely belted out "When the Saints Go Marching In!"

Linda broke up beside me. I wasn't going to look because if I started laughing I'd never stop. I shot Joe a helpless glance. He sat on the dais, transfixed with an angelic expression on his face, as if he hadn't a clue what was going on.

Smart. Miss Mattie was going to throttle him.

The elderly organist ended her rather spirited—and different—medley with "The Battle Hymn of the Republic." The congregation struggled mightily and roared out the closing words: "Our God is marching on!"

Mattie rose from the bench looking regal, if slightly dazed. I was proud of her. I would have mopped the floor with Joe Brewster.

Joe immediately charged to the podium and opened with prayer, which gave us a chance to pull ourselves together. The prayer was long and involved and included everyone from the president to the church janitor. Finally we heard "amen" and gratefully opened our Bibles. I kept an eye out for Vic, but he didn't show. I was used to men not showing up. There had been long days and nights when I'd waited for Noel to come home, never knowing if he was detained by business or pleasure. In Vic's case, I guessed it wasn't my concern.

Tears stung my eyes, blurring the printed page. God had been good to me, and I was too quick to feel that I was the only one with problems. I'd failed him numerous times, but other than Herman, he'd never failed me. He'd given me a beautiful, healthy, loving daughter, and I was hiding from her like a hunted animal.

Shame on you, Marlene. He gave you the responsibility of raising a child. If Sara's a clinging vine, you have no one to blame but yourself.

Sad, but true. I couldn't blame Noel; he'd never been around to help. He sent presents and showered our daughter with attention the few times he decided to make an appearance, but he left the parenting to me. I didn't do all that badly, but I'd made mistakes. Didn't I always?

After services, Linda pushed a young man toward me. "Marlene, I want you to meet Johnny Weeks, our new pastor. He's taking Joe's place."

I gripped the fair-skinned-man's hand, captivated by his shy smile, his warm blue eyes, and the golden curls tumbling over his forehead.

He introduced me to his wife, Rachel—petite, blonde, blue-eyed, and bubbly. According to her, the congregation had been supportive and immensely helpful during their move, and Joe was a saint.

With Joe hovering benevolently in the background, the transition would be smooth.

In small groups and in pairs, the congregation dwindled and headed home for the evening. I said good-bye to Linda, promising to visit before I left, and then wandered down the road toward the convenience store. I wanted something cold to drink before I walked home. Overhead, the stars stretched in an awesome celestial awning. I paused in front of the gas station, transfixed by the glory of God's handiwork.

Out of the blue, I heard Herman's voice in my mind. *"C'mon, Marly. I got a nickel. We can buy ice cream!"*

I'd been a small girl—no more than five, but I knew Herman was just plain stupid. A nickel wouldn't buy ice cream—

maybe bubble gum, but not ice cream. Aunt Beth and Aunt Ingrid relented and decided to spend the money. They had taken us for a walk and an ice-cream cone on a hot summer night. Herman laughed all the way, that horsey sound, showing a row of buckteeth. I shied away, like always, taking Aunt Beth's hand and walking on the opposite side of Ingrid and Herman. Later, he came up to me, wanting a lick of my chocolate cone. He offered his strawberry in exchange, and I shook my head.

"Good," he'd coaxed. He pushed the cone closer and closer until the ice cream touched my nose and I squealed.

Ingrid jerked Herman back to her side, knocking his cone to the ground. She pulled him along, scowling at him. His mystified eyes locked with mine, and I wanted to turn and run. But I didn't. I hated him and I pitied him. I hated Aunt Ingrid and Aunt Beth for allowing him to be my father. Other kids' fathers were strong and handsome. They didn't have big teeth and a loud laugh and stick ice-cream cones in their daughter's faces.

Other kids were proud of their daddies.

Why couldn't he go away and never come back? But he was always there, at the breakfast table or in the door, waving good-bye as I left for school. At school carnivals, basketball and baseball games, working in the concession stand, blowing up balloons, pinning banners to the gym wall. I could never escape him, and my resentment had grown into an ugly, festering sore …

"You'll get a crick in your neck staring up like that."

My heart double-timed when I heard Vic's tease. "Probably so." I turned to face him. "I was looking at the stars. I'd forgotten how breathtaking they could be. I can't see them as clearly in Glen Ellyn."

"One of the reasons I've stayed in Parnass Springs." He joined my admiration of cosmos glory. "You still like ice cream?"

"Love it."

"Wait here." He entered the station while I wandered over to sit down at the outside picnic table. He returned a few minutes later carrying two ice-cream bars. One was sugar free. I could have kissed him. Noel would have bought regular and expected me to eat it since he'd gone to the trouble to buy it.

We enjoyed the ice cream in silence, concentrating on eating the cold treat before it melted. Vic still wore work clothes: denims and a plaid shirt that smelled like a horse.

"Missed you at the service tonight."

He glanced at me, eyes going gentle. "I intended to come, but I had a mare down."

Before he could explain further, we heard approaching footsteps.

"Well imagine this, two of my favorite people. What are you little hoodlums cooking up now?"

I hadn't heard Joe approach, but there he stood, eyes twinkling with mischief.

"Ice cream, Pop?"

"I better not, just out for my evening stroll." He focused on me. "Quite a lively service tonight."

I bit my lip to keep from giggling and concentrated on my ice cream. "Quite."

Vic frowned. "Lively? At Mount Pleasant?"

"Well—different," Joe admitted.

"How was Miss Mattie after services?" I nibbled chocolate coating off my bar.

Joe visibly cringed. "A tad upset with me, I fear."

"Miss Mattie?" Vic turned to look at me. "Why would Mattie be upset with Pop?"

"Ask him about his automatic page turner."

Deep crimson flooded Joe's face, evident in the glow of the overhead streetlight. "Guess there's still a few bugs in the invention. I'll have to work on it a bit more before she uses it again."

I filled Vic in on the musical fiasco. He chuckled.

"And I missed the excitement," he said.

"You'd have loved it."

Joe grinned. "Well, it did liven up the meeting." He lifted a hand. "I'll see you two later. The evening air is bad for old folks." He gave me an exaggerated wink and left, hailing a tall, dark-haired man leaving the convenience store. They continued down the road together, deep in conversation.

Silence closed around us. Not a siren to be heard. A chorus of frogs sang a nocturnal concert.

Vic laughed. "A little different from Glen Ellyn, I guess."

"Very different."

"Bored?"

"Not in the least." Truth be told, I was in heaven; I hated the thought of going home almost as much as I missed Sara and my grandbabies.

A carload of teenagers passed, radio cranked to the max. "Reminds me of the way we used to hang out."

I smiled. "Yeah. Those were the days, huh?"

"How's Noel?"

I licked the stick clean and disposed of it in the nearby trash receptacle. "Now I'm cold."

"I can remedy that." He hooked an arm around my neck like he had so many years ago, a brotherly gesture, and we set off for home. I hadn't answered his question. I didn't intend to.

"Ever feel like we're getting old, Marlene?"

"All the time." I pressed closer. How could I get any older than I felt right now? Where had the years gone? Why had I thought my plan for my life was wiser than God's?

"You know, when we were kids we didn't think much about life. We had it all ahead of us. We thought it would all be good. Coming up roses."

"Turned out to have a little crabgrass mixed in."

He leaned closer and grinned. "We're not old. We're in our prime; the best is yet to come."

I laughed. "Nice try, but I know baloney when I hear it."

"I mean it. There's something to be said for experience. Kids think they know everything, but they only know enough to mislead and confuse them. They don't start to live until life throws them a few curveballs."

"Hummm." I'd had my share of curveballs and sliders. I missed my naiveté.

"Your life hasn't been all laughs?"

Ha! "I can't complain. Sara's been a blessing."

"If she's anything like you, she must be great."

I studied the way one corner of his mouth lifted higher than the other when he smiled, the familiar planes in his face—how I'd missed him. So much that it hurt. With some effort I pulled my attention back to the conversation. "She's a little dependent on me."

Like a leech, a barnacle on a ship's hull, a piece of lichen on a rock. Why had I never insisted she stand on her own feet? I stopped, stunned that I could think such thoughts about my darling daughter. But her dependence on me was a reality I couldn't deny.

Vic didn't appear to notice my lapse. He pointed to the white church, steeple pricking the dark velvet sky. "I took God for granted when I was young. After Julie died, I saw him differently."

I was a little surprised by the admission. I'd sensed a change in him for years, but we'd never talked about his spiritual awakening. Our conversations had always centered on the immediate. The Vic I remembered had been a little defiant where religion was concerned, determined to be one of the boys instead of the preacher's kid.

"I'm sorry about your wife. That wasn't fair."

"Yeah. Thanks. Life is seldom fair. They say whatever doesn't kill you makes you stronger—or something to that effect. Losing Julie nearly killed me, but it also made me stop and examine my life. Priorities. You know—the prodigal son returneth." He grinned. "I always knew Dad was right about God. I was even proud of him and the solid beliefs he held, but I was a kid. Faith didn't mean a lot to me then, but it does now."

I'd done a fair share of scrutinizing my own situation when Noel left, and I had lived with a bitter heart. Now I couldn't help wondering ... How could I have let one person spoil a large part of my life? Well, two, if you counted Herman.

Either way, I was about to decide bitterness wasn't worth it. It was like living on bacon cheeseburgers and hoping the other guy had the heart attack.

While Vic had grown spiritually stronger, I'd moved away from the church. Oh, I still believed in God. I sure had called on him in hard times, but when I married Noel, we'd both worked, and we never had time for church. Free Sundays were spent in worldly pursuits. I gradually slipped away.

Then there was always this animosity in me. If only I hadn't wanted to leave my father and past behind; if only I had made smarter choices in a mate; if only I had stayed in Parnass; if *only.*

I told myself that this *was* God's plan for my life. Then I'd get mad at God.

I glanced at my watch. "Look at the time. I need to be getting home. The plumber and roofer will be here early."

"You're not serious."

My heart sank when I heard the humor in his voice. "You think they won't come?"

"Folks around here don't get in any hurry. They mean well, but they have their own agendas. They may come and they may not."

"Never?"

"No, they'll come—just when they get around to it."

"I only have a few days to line up the work."

"Well, miracles happen."

Croak. What was that supposed to mean?

I slid the key in Beth's front lock. In the time I'd been here I'd managed to get the floors cleaned, the curtains washed and ironed, and even hauled out a couple of smaller rocks. My back was killing me. How was I to accomplish all I needed to do in what time I had left? No one would buy the house with a leaking roof. And the dripping faucets would leave rust stains on the sink, making it impossible to clean.

"That you, Marlene?"

The question penetrated the darkness, reminding me of the raven in the Edgar Allen Poe poem, the one that kept croaking "Nevermore." I jumped, resisting the urge to demand "Who goes there?"

"It's me, Ingrid." She'd basically left me alone since I'd been back—but then, she was like that, unless she wanted something. I couldn't imagine what she'd want, but I knew something was on her mind if she was out after dark.

Her imposing figure stepped from the shadows—tall, fairly wide, red hair pulled back in a long braid and tightly secured by her plastic rain bonnet. Gold-rimmed glasses perched on her nose. Matriarch of Parnass Springs, ruling with a firm, if not always tactful, hand.

The last person I wanted to see tonight.

She strode across the wet grass, garbed in a pink flannel gown with a rose print and a ratty green terry-cloth robe. She hadn't changed much. She was older, of course—ninety-two now. Maybe a tad plumper, but I'd be willing to bet those blue eyes never missed a thing.

I sat down on the porch swing and waited.

She marched across the lawn, and I gave thanks she hadn't heard about my entrance to town—or if she had, she hadn't demanded to know why I'd disgraced her. She'd have seen through my phony act in a second. I'd never been able to fool her.

She climbed the steps and settled on the swing beside me. The seat sagged beneath her bulk. "Don't know where you disappear to for such long periods."

I resisted the urge to say she didn't need to know. She always said her age gave her the right to pry, but I knew from experience, give her an inch, and she'd take the whole yardstick.

"I went to services."

"I wasn't there," Ingrid stated.

"I noticed."

"Don't be smart with me. I go occasionally."

We sat in the silence. What did she want?

She peered at me over her glasses. "Joe long-winded tonight?"

"Not at all. His sermon was very inspiring."

"Vic, there?"

"He wasn't at the service. I saw him later."

"You're a married woman."

Was she worried about Noel? Why? She'd never been concerned about him before.

"Vic's an old friend, nothing more."

"That's what they all say."

Why the interrogation? I knew Aunt Ingrid was suspicious of every man, but this was ridiculous.

"Well, he's a good man," she said. "He didn't turn his back on the place where he grew up, like some I could name."

Yeah, yeah, bad ole Marlene. "I didn't have a choice." I was desperate to get away from Herman, but I couldn't tell her that. "Vic did."

"Oh, choice." She waved her hand in a dismissive gesture. "We usually do what we want."

Yeah, right. I'd wanted Herman for a father. I'd wanted to be a single mother raising a child by myself. When I married Noel Queens, he promised me the moon. I'd thought we'd have a good marriage, though like most thoracic surgeons, he worked long hours. One night, when Sara was two, he left to make his hospital rounds and ended up in Vegas with a pretty psychiatrist. He'd made the rounds all right. Evidently he'd been making them for some time while carefully cleaning out our joint bank accounts and putting everything in his name.

I'd divorced him and he'd married his psychiatrist. That marriage lasted seven years. The third wife managed to corral him for two years. Or maybe I had that wrong. It was possible she'd wised up quicker than wives number one and two.

Aunt Ingrid shoved to her feet. "Well, I'll be getting along and let the cat in. Saw the light on and wanted to make sure you were all right. Town's not as safe as it once was. Some strange man stopped Mildred Folsom a month ago and wanted directions to Kansas City. Never know *what* crazies are running loose."

"I'll be fine. Thanks for your concern." She hadn't mentioned Beth. Even in death, bitterness ruled.

"I'm glad you've come home, Marlene. I've been praying that you'd come to your senses and move back to Parnass Springs. The town needs a firm hand, and I'm not going to be around forever."

"I'm only here a few days."

"Better stay longer. Vic needs a wife. Half the time his socks don't match."

She wandered off into the darkness, and I stared after her, mouth hanging open. Was she going senile? *Vic needs a wife?* She knew I was married—at least she thought I was. As for the firm hand, not even in my wildest thoughts would I consider replacing Ingrid when she passed. I didn't have that sort of Rottweiler mentality.

I let myself in the front door, flipped on the lights, and tripped a circuit breaker.

I yelped. The house was as dark as a witch's heart. *Please God, let it be a simple fix and nothing that requires an*—I could barely bring myself to even think the word "electrician."

I groped my way upstairs, trying to find the circuit breakers in the dark. I reset the tripped one, then fumbled for a wall switch, and light flooded the room. Score one for Little Marlene.

A yawn stretched my mouth. Fine. Trouble could just go away. My mission was simple: Rest. Get Beth's house on the market. Break Sara's dependency. Put the past behind me.

I had four whole days left to complete those tasks.

No problem.

I'd no more than rolled out of bed Thursday morning before I heard someone pounding on the front door. Not even in my wildest expectations did I hope to find the plumber or roofer. Good thing, because I didn't.

I found Aunt Ingrid, wide-eyed and bushy-tailed, as my Grandpa Parnass used to say.

I stared at her disheveled appearance—crimson cheeks, eyes bright as a possum caught in a headlight. Was she having a heart attack? Her flushed face glowed tomato red, her eyes dilated. Prone as she was to dramatics, I'd never seen her so distressed. "What's wrong?"

"I've heard from the hussy."

"The who?"

"The hussy!"

"Oh." That hussy. Prue—the waitress who'd run off with Uncle Eugene... how long ago? Too many years to remember. Prue Levitt. No, make that Prue Levitt Moss. I didn't think the two rivals spoke.

"And?"

"And you'll never guess what that homewrecker wants."

I couldn't. Not in a million years. To be truthful, I didn't even want to try. All I wanted was to see a plumber's or roofer's truck pull up in front of the house.

"She wants Eugene's foot."

Okay. That got my attention. "Uncle Eugene's foot?"

"His *foot.*"

"The one buried in the cemetery?"

She looked at me like I'd left my common sense in Illinois. "He only had two. He took one to the grave with him. The other he left here, and if that woman thinks for one minute she's going to get it, she's sadly mistaken."

I shook my head. With any luck, I was dreaming. The cell phone sang out, and I ignored it. Sara could wait.

"Why—" I paused, trying to clear my head—"Why would Prue want Uncle Eugene's foot after all these years?" He'd been dead ten years—his whole body, I mean. The foot had been in the grave years longer.

"To spite me."

"Aunt Ingrid. Surely the woman didn't call—"

"She didn't call. Sent me a wire." She waved a paper in my face. "Coward!"

And I thought *I* had problems. "Why does she want the bone?"

"Foot!" my aunt snapped. "She claims she can't afford to have the whole body shipped to Maui. She can only pay to have the foot shipped, said she was tired of not having something of Eugene to pay her respects to."

Good grief. I wanted to slap my forehead in a V8 moment. Uncle Eugene. They were still haggling over him.

"Well, Prue Levitt can jump off a cliff. That foot isn't going anywhere. I'll turn the whole mess over to the mayor. It's *his* job to deal with nutcases."

I took a deep breath. I was pretty sure a mayor wouldn't concern himself in a catfight over a severed limb. Especially not this mayor. "Aunt Ingrid, I think the two of you should work this out and not involve Vic."

She narrowed her eyes. "I don't talk to the shameless broad. You'll be my go-between. I'll tell you what to say, and you can tell her where to get off."

Tell her where to get off, my brain mouthed. I didn't tell people where to get on, let alone off. This wasn't my fight. I had enough problems of my own, and I was not getting involved in this spat. Ingrid was on her own.

Aunt Ingrid wasn't through. "That lunatic. If it hadn't been for her, Eugene would be here, in Parnass Springs instead of Kansas. Said she didn't have enough money to bury him—*I* would have buried him! I'd have someone to carry flowers to on Memorial Day. How do you think I feel hauling a bouquet to a foot? Everyone in town has someone under a gravestone. I have a *foot.*" Ingrid drew a fortifying breath and crossed her arms. "I'm keeping it."

I stepped back, closing my eyes and watching my last few days in Parnass going straight down the tube.

"Oh, by the way, you have to head a committee."

My eyes flew open. "Committee? *What* committee?"

"The animal shelter wants to pay homage to Herman."

"Herman?"

"Your father. Herman."

My heart sank. Why would anyone want to pay tribute to him?

"If you're wondering why, I'll tell you young lady. When Eugene died, he left his son a large trust. Your father's grandparents had old money. They never used a cent that wasn't necessary, so it accumulated to a large estate. Since you'd never accept anything from Herman, he had an animal shelter built in your name, gave money to the public library, and then put the rest in a trust for you. Didn't know that, did you? You thought he was so ignorant he couldn't feel love. Well, he did, young lady, and that shelter is a monument to you. He didn't want you to know, but I think it's about time you accepted your responsibility. The shelter's requested a statue of Herman be erected on the front lawn. As his daughter, you will head the committee."

My mouth flapped like a battered flag. Being Herman's daughter wasn't enough? I now had to face the shame of erecting a lawn statue on a public site in his honor? I groped the doorway for support.

No way ... Absolutely *no way*, would I subject myself to this disgrace.

And there was no way she could make me.

Four

"*Who* owns the foot?" R J Rexall, senior partner of Rexall, Rexall, and Bextal, Attorneys-at-Law, reared back in his chair on Friday and rolled his eyes to the ceiling as if the answer to the perplexing problem flashed in red neon up there. I suppressed a sympathetic smile. Ingrid had little use for Rexall's son or his nephew, Bextal, but she agreed with R J's counsel some of, if not all, the time. I prayed this would be one of the rare moments when a client took the paid lawyer's advice, though I didn't count on it.

"No need to waste time. All I want is a legal paper to get that woman off my back." My aunt was a pitiful sight this morning. I'd pleaded with her to at least comb her hair, but she said—her exact words—"Let others see what the Husband Stealer's done to me." The Husband Stealer being Prue Levitt, of course, who wouldn't be there to see her. I'd tried to talk reason to the woman and where did it get me? Sitting there listening to her argue with her attorney, that was where.

I'd even gone to Joe for advice, and he was no help. He said he didn't think I had much choice; Ingrid was old and couldn't fight this battle. She'd need help, and much as he hated to say it, it was a Christian's duty to help kin.

"Now Ingrid." R J, an austere-looking man with salt-and-pepper hair and dressed in a dark, designer-label suit and bright red tie, peered down the bridge of his nose. "I'll have to research this matter since I've rarely, if ever, dealt with anything quite like it."

Well, no kidding. I uncrossed my legs and tried to squeeze feeling back into my foot. I'd be willing to bet there were few, if any, lawyers who'd faced this kind of quandary. But when I remembered how much he charged for his services, my sympathy evaporated for the controversy he'd have to confront.

Ingrid's lip puckered. "Do whatever you want, but I'm telling you, the foot belongs to me."

I gave her a warning look. We'd had a long conversation on the drive over about cooperation, tact, and manners—all things Ingrid not only lacked but apparently wasn't interested in acquiring. She'd promised to be nice, but it seemed we each had a different concept of the word.

"Granted, one could argue that Prue was married to Eugene at the time of his death— "

"On paper only. They were in the process of divorce." Ingrid's expression was as belligerent as a disgruntled pug with a grudge.

"I understand, nevertheless, one could argue that the present wife would have certain rights. On the other hand, there's a valid argument that the whole matter would be determined by Eugene's estate, which I understand was in a bit of a muddle when he passed."

"Eugene didn't worry much about technicalities." Ingrid twitched at the light sweater around her shoulders. "His folks had to bury him. I wanted to, but *Ms.* Levitt refused my offer."

R J delivered a patient expression. "Understood. Lacking a will or trust, by intestate law—"

"Eugene's foot is not an asset of the will. It's a completed gift." Ingrid's tone didn't brook dissent.

The attorney nodded, and I saw at least four more gray hairs pop out on his temple. If we stayed here much longer the man would look downright distinguished, elderly statesman and all that. What was I doing here in Rexall, Rexall, and Bextal's office when I vowed I would stay out of the catfight? I didn't know to whom the foot belonged, but I figured it didn't really matter except to two women intent on taking their grudge to the grave.

Literally.

"I'd like to counter sue."

I choked, Aunt Ingrid's unexpected declaration catching me off guard.

R J's carefully molded brow furrowed like uneven corn rows. "Pardon?"

"I *want* to counter sue."

"For what intent?"

"I want Eugene moved back to Parnass Springs." She leaned forward, her eyes fixed on the attorney. "Do you have any idea what it's like to take flowers to a foot?"

He shook his head, looking slightly dazed, and sent another glance toward the ceiling. I could almost hear him asking, "Why me, Lord?" I identified with the sentiment.

Ingrid persisted. "Not pleasant, I can assure you. I want Eugene moved here, buried in his rightful plot, the one he purchased when he was alive. He knew where he wanted to be buried or he wouldn't have bought the space."

"Aunt Ingrid." I found my voice, keeping my tone gentle but firm. "You can't sue Prue for Eugene's body. She had nothing to do with his resting place. His parents buried him in Olathe because his divorce to Prue wasn't final when he died, and well—you know she didn't have the funds at the time to see to the matter." I thought over what I'd just said. *Sue Prue?* Sounded like the schoolmarm in an old-time B western, which I was sorry to admit, I was old enough to remember. But she really couldn't bring a lawsuit in a case like this, could she? One look at her tight lips and high color, and I figured she could do anything she pleased, and nothing I could say would make any difference. But I had to try.

She squinted at me. "So?"

"So. Who are you suing?"

"Prue. I'll sue her twice. She shouldn't have buried him in Olathe—I told her not to—told her he had a perfectly good grave here in Parnass Springs, but would she listen to me?" She snorted.

R J offered me a look that asked, "Is she senile or what?"

I couldn't say; she wasn't thinking clearly and she'd always hinged on the unconventional, but this was disgraceful. I leaned close to her, keeping my voice to a whisper. "Mr. Rexall's fee is one hundred twenty-five dollars an hour."

That should grab her attention. It had certainly grabbed mine.

She paled, shifted in her seat, and swallowed hard. "I'll spend every cent if I have to."

Exhuming a body that wasn't yours and a foot that had been buried for over a decade, would take time and a good deal of money. Of that I was certain. I was even more certain it was time I didn't have to spare. Sara needed me.

But, according to Joe Brewster, so did Aunt Ingrid.

Exactly *where* did my responsibilities lie? Here in Parnass Springs with Aunt Ingrid, whose health was clearly failing, or with a healthy, helpless daughter who depended on me to make the world revolve.

Either scenario gave me the willies.

R J dismissed the meeting with the promise to research the subject and get back to Ingrid.

Ingrid, who had reached the door, now paused. "Why are you researching?"

"To ascertain your rights."

"Doesn't matter. I'm keeping the foot." She turned and hobbled out of the office.

Rexall looked as helpless as I. I understood only too well the air of relief I glimpsed in his expression as I closed the door behind us. Lucky me, I was the designated driver.

I got in the car and waited until she was belted in before starting up the motor. One glance at the set of her jaw and I knew we hadn't accomplished one thing. Might as well have stayed at home and missed the whole humiliating episode.

On the way home, Ingrid requested that we stop at the covered bridge. The scenic spot had been Eugene's favorite. Ronald Parnass, Ingrid's grandfather, had single-handedly built the passage using a horse and wagon to haul the heavy limestone gleaned from the hillsides.

Ingrid's melancholy, albeit belligerent, disposition conquered her mood. I drove to the bridge hoping to sweeten her attitude, but not really expecting much from the effort.

I'd forgotten how pretty it was there. We sat in the car, admiring the spring morning. Birds chirped. Bright new green ivy covered the historical attraction. Tourists often stopped to admire the piece of history. Vic and I had sat beneath this monument so many summer nights, watching the carnival lights.

Every spring, large semitrucks would pull into town and set up shop on the open grounds adjacent to the bridge. Ferris wheels, the tilt-a-whirl, bumper cars, and the whip occupied our minds for a full week. Vic and I had gone every night just to ride the Ferris wheel and spit off the top.

As sweet as my memories were, I knew Ingrid also had her poignant recollections. "Did you and Eugene come here often?"

She sat staring at splattered raindrops rolling down the windshield, her watery eyes mirroring … what? Hurt? Did tough-as-a-thirty-cent-steak Ingrid, *my* Aunt Ingrid, hurt? Could anyone who vowed to hold on to a mere bone have a conscience? She'd never shown any sign of having one.

"I loved him, you know."

I reached over and rested a hand on her arm. For all her tough veneer, she was brittle; her life was crumbling to an end. You couldn't have picked two more unlikely people to fall in love: staid librarian and flashy, but homely, traveling tire salesman.

Eugene hadn't been much for looks, but he knew how to dress, and personality oozed from his pores. He must have dazzled a younger Ingrid. Eugene had loved Ingrid; trouble was, he loved all women; the more the better. With one failed marriage behind him, and a mentally challenged child in the wings, he'd swept Parnass Springs and Ingrid off her feet. The marriage had been a good one for years, before Devil Restlessness had again attacked Eugene.

He'd gotten involved with a pretty young café waitress, and that was that. The tire salesman quit his job and family, and left Ingrid alone with bookshelves full of romance novels. Bitterness set in, and Ingrid persisted in a vegetative state. Parnass Springs, in spite of its sterling community, held hurtful memories not only for its young but for the aged.

"Tammy Wynette had it right."

"About what, Aunt Ingrid?"

"Sometimes it's hard to be a woman." She drew a deep, gut-wrenching breath. "Givin' all your love to just one man." Another profound breath. "He'll have the good times. You'll have the bad times."

She got that right. No one knew better than I the joys and pitfalls of womanhood. Eve should have thought before she leaped. The craziest notion came over me then.

I wanted to confess my lie of all these years, to tell Ingrid about Noel and my hurt.

Why not? Certainly she'd understand, maybe better than I did. But cowardly Marlene pushed back the thought, afraid that in one of my aunt's less defenseless moments, she would blurt out the truth—and the truth would find Vic.

Oh, I didn't kid myself. My day of reckoning was imminent, I just wasn't ready to face it. I didn't try to kid myself that I'd take my secret to the grave. I would be found out, I just wasn't sure how and when. If lucky—really lucky—I would leave Parnass Springs with Vic none the wiser about my failure. Only God knew my secret, and that was bad enough.

If I wasn't lucky . . .

I didn't want to think about that. About the disappointment in Vic's eyes when he discovered I was a fraud.

I'd returned again and again to Scripture. One verse especially—John 14:14: "You may ask me for anything in my name, and I will do it."

All right, so what I wanted to ask wasn't exactly righteous. My faith knew its limits, and I wasn't proud of it. My mistakes were many—some insurmountable. No do-overs for me. And as far as I'd let myself go with this deception, I hadn't crossed the line where I'd actually ask God to help me out with it.

Even I could only go so far.

Ingrid and I sat quietly, dealing with past hurts. Why hadn't I realized we had so much in common? Compassion stirred past my resentment, especially when I sensed, rather than saw, her shiver. The morning's events, combined with painful memories, had caught up with her. For the moment she was quiet. Beaten.

"Do you want to go home, Aunt Ingrid?"

She turned, blinking back tears. "I want to go home."

I decided I was ahead of the game, so I started the car. On impulse, I reached over and tried to smooth her hair. Cowlicks stuck straight up. The jagged pillow crease across the back of her head looked awful. She needed a barrette. When had she started letting herself go?

Her eyes met mine. "Butchie was a good dog."

I went along with her wanderings. "Butchie was a great dog—a loyal friend." Her long-term memory was good; short-term didn't seem to be so hot. There wasn't just one Butchie. There must have been nine during Herman's life. When a Butchie died, Ingrid bought a new pup and Herman named him. Herman never ran out of Butchies. If only I had recycled the good things in my life.

"Herman loved him."

"Yeah, Herman loved him." He had indeed. I remembered Butchie being gone for two days and the way Herman had grieved, refusing to eat. Yeah, Herman had loved Butchie.

And Herman loved you.

A sharp jab of guilt hit my heart. Herman loved me. He couldn't help what he was, any more than I could help that he wasn't what I'd wanted. I pushed the thoughts aside.

Since Aunt Ingrid had been running late this morning and only downed a cup of coffee, she was famished when we got home. After I settled her at the table, I placed a bowl, bran flakes, milk, and sugar in front of her. During the drive she'd fallen silent—a silence that I took for reflection. The trying morning had drained her. She dumped flakes in the bowl and doused them with cold milk and four heaping tablespoons of sugar. She had a relentless sweet tooth yet her health was better than mine.

Go figure.

I ran a sink full of dishwater and began to wash the few dishes. Ingrid had enough money to manufacture dishwashers but she was too tight to buy one. She silently spooned bran into her mouth, her gaze fixed on the back of the box. Suddenly, she pushed the bowl away and slammed her open palm on the table. Silverware rattled and bounced. Startled, I whirled to stare at her.

Her belligerent tone echoed in the kitchen. "You're not feeding me this!"

I followed her accusing finger to the box of bran flakes. "Why not? Don't you eat bran every morning?"

The woman's face screwed into a coiled knot, her accusations distinct and emphasized. "I am not eating birdseed."

"Bird what?" I snatched up the cereal, my eyes scanning the offer on the back of the box: *Send three cereal box tops and the manufacturer would send a packet of birdseed.*

I sat the box on the table. "This isn't birdseed. I wouldn't feed you birdseed."

Ingrid's features turned into a hard line. "Birdseed."

"No, if you send in three box tops—"

"Birdseed!" She shoved back from the table and stalked out of the kitchen.

I picked up the box and reread the offer. "Three box tops. One packet of birdseed."

Sighing, I dumped the contents into the trash. *Birdseed.* She actually thought I'd feed her birdseed. What was I going to do about her? She was proving to be more of a challenge than I'd anticipated. How on earth was I supposed to leave on Monday when, slow but sure, I was starting to realize the unthinkable.

Aunt Ingrid might no longer be able to live by herself.

Early that afternoon, I was talking to Sara on the phone when Ingrid returned to the kitchen, every hair in place and a coin-sized dab of rouge on each cheek.

"Honey, I'll talk to you later. I think Ingrid needs something." I hung up before Sara could get in the last plea to "be sure and come home Monday."

Aunt Ingrid frowned. "Who's that?"

"Sara. Petey fell last night and had to have six stitches."

"Sara. Is that your daughter?"

Ingrid had met Sara once when Sara was two. Beth had another stroke and I'd flown back with my daughter, anticipating the worse. My aunt had rallied so Sara and I had left the next morning. Ingrid wouldn't recognize my daughter if she passed her on the street. Apparently she'd never cared enough to try to get acquainted.

It wasn't all her fault, I admitted in a fit of honesty. I'd not been very interested in doing the family thing either.

"Your daughter's mean to her baby?"

"No!" I tempered my annoyance. "Petey fell against the kitchen table."

She shuffled to the refrigerator and took out a container of water. "I have to go to the doctor."

"Are you ill?"

"No. You know doctors. They keep you coming back and back." She took a drink of the water and returned the pitcher to the shelf.

"Okay. When's your appointment?"

"1:30."

My gaze flew to the oven range. It was 1:15! "Today?"

"Of course today. Do you think I'd mention it if it were next week?"

"We're going to be late!"

"So? I've waited for him many a time."

Grabbing my purse and keys, I swung back and headed her toward the door.

"Slow down. We're not going to a fire."

By the time I settled her in the front seat and snapped the seat belt, her appointed hour was upon us.

I backed out of the driveway, and in my haste, knocked over a trash receptacle. It was going to stay down since I had no time to stop and put it upright. Gunning the car, I asked, "What's the address?"

She shrugged. "Never paid any attention. Just drive. I'll recognize the street when I see it."

She'll recognize the street.

I braked at every street corner. "Here?"

Ingrid shook her head.

"Here? Here?" The dashboard clock crept to 1:40.

I drove another fifteen minutes. She was making me nuts. My insides roiled; my hands shook as I gripped the steering wheel tighter. *Patience, Marlene.* She was aging and easily confused. Finally I pulled to the side of the road. Taking a deep breath, I turned to face her. "You don't know where the office is, do you?"

"I did." She frowned. "Do you suppose he's moved and not told me?"

I didn't suppose that. Not in a million years.

I made a U-turn in the middle of the street and drove Ingrid home, sans the doctor's appointment. She was still mumbling something about "I could have sworn it was a couple of streets back." He'd moved. That was it; he'd moved and not told her.

She turned accusing eyes on me as we pulled into the drive. "You should have known that he'd moved, Marlene."

The air smelled of rain as I stepped out onto the side porch. This was one day I was happy to kiss good-bye. Ingrid had gone to bed around seven, worn out from the day's events. I'd called the doctor and rescheduled her appointment. His office was two and a half blocks away—and no, he hadn't moved; been in the same building for twenty-five years. From the volume of the snores coming from the master bedroom, my cantankerous aunt was down for the night. At least I hoped so. Did she walk in her sleep? Wake up confused? Something else to worry about.

Now that I had her settled, though, I was ready to go back to Beth's house. I was looking forward to the peace and quiet. If I thought she'd needed me, I'd have stayed, but she'd been living alone for years. She could surely go one more night, right?

Uh huh. Right. And if something happens, then what?

My eyes automatically sought Vic's dark cottage, and suddenly I had the urge to see him—to talk to him. I knew I shouldn't. Vic was the past, and I had to do away with the past. He was getting on with his life, so I should too. Still, a visit wasn't exactly a lifetime commitment.

I slipped on my loafers, rehearsing what I would say when I just happened to drop by his office this time of night. I didn't have a dog or cat to explain a visit.

"Hi! I was passing by and saw your light." Or, "Goodness! I ran out for milk and noticed I needed fuel and the station was nearby—" No. Maybe, "Guess what! I figured you were working late and might want a sandwich!"

Then slowly but discreetly, I'd unload on him. About Sara's dependency, Aunt Ingrid's list of problems, my responsibilities and where they lay.

The streets were quiet when I drove the short distance to the clinic. I was struck again at how much Parnass Springs had changed. Oh, there were still familiar stores scattered down Main Street, and more businesses than I remembered, and they still "rolled up the sidewalks" at sundown, but new enterprises had sprung up. What I had once thought quaint was too provincial for words. Now it seemed restful. By the time I turned into the parking lot I had several viable excuses for being there—all plausible.

Be cool, Marlene. Detached.

A light shone in the back room. I drove around to the back of the building and spotted his truck—covered in thick mud. He'd been in some farmer's field today.

Seconds later I tapped at the back door. Tapped again. The door opened, and there he was. My Prince Charming, covered in mud from head to toe, his eyes and cheeks caked with reddish clay. My carefully constructed excuses flew right out the window. "I know I'm bothering you, but I need to talk."

"Sure, come in." He stood back and allowed me entrance to the dimly lit room. Cages littered the floor. Two kittens frolicked nearby. A lone hound sat beside a bench, head hung low.

"What's wrong with him?"

"He's lovesick."

I laughed. Who wasn't? "You're kidding."

"Nope. Gus's lady friend ran off with a neighbor's mutt and his owners can't get him to eat. I figured if he hung around here long enough he'd meet a new love interest. You know what they say; nothing like a new love to get over an old one."

The dog looked anything but romantically inclined at the moment. My eyes shifted to Vic's appearance. "What happened to you?"

"I've been waltzing with a cantankerous heifer all afternoon. She dragged me through every pothole and puddle in her pasture."

"Who won?"

"I did."

My mouth formed a moue. "Poor baby."

He calmly swiped a wad of wet mud off his jacket and smeared it the length of my nose.

I laughed and fished a tissue out of my pocket to scrub away the clammy substance. "Are you free to talk?"

"Not free, but reasonable." He started for his office, and I followed in his muddy boot tracks. The whole place was Vic. Comfortable. Warm. Caring and compassionate. Why had I let a little thing like genetics make me lose out on one of the best things God had ever given me? Look at Sara. She'd turned out beautifully. Why had I refused to let God handle my future, instead taking it into my own hands, only to make mistake after mistake? *Forgive me, Father. I thought I could do better. Instead I made a terrible mess of things.*

As I walked past Gus, I leaned over to give the rebuffed Casanova a reassuring pat. "Hang in there, buddy." I knew rejection all too well.

Vic sat down in his chair, mud and all. I winced when I saw the reddish gook mash into the dark fabric. At least I *hoped* the gook was mud.

"What's on your mind, Marly?"

Marly. I hadn't been called that in years. I shoved a pile of books aside and sat down. Office furnishings were sparse—and simple. Books, various periodicals, the usual jar of colored jelly beans. Vic had a crazy penchant for the candy. Gus wandered in, sniffed my shoes, then yawned and plopped down beside the doc's chair.

"Have you had dinner?"

He glanced at his watch. "I last grabbed something around noon. You don't happen to have a steak and baked potato in your pocket?"

"Afraid not. Just a sack of take-out trouble." My feeble idea of dumping on Vic pulsated guilt throughout my conscience. He'd worked all day, and it didn't take glasses to see fatigue rimming his eyes.

He stuck a pencil behind his ear, pushed back in the chair, and propped his boots on the desk. "Shoot."

I began with Sara, moved quickly to the roofers and plumber, and ended with Ingrid, the foot, and the new lawsuit. When I paused to catch my breath, Vic threw back his head and cackled, white teeth flashing.

"I fail to see what's so funny."

"You. You could always get into the biggest messes."

"True, but you always had the answers."

He sobered, his eyes softening with affection. "Not always."

My eyes acknowledged the silent condemnation. "Almost always."

"What's Noel's opinion?"

"Noel lives in his own world." That was absolutely true. Which world, I couldn't say.

He stared at me a moment, as if the past had suddenly invaded his mind. Long summer nights, stolen kisses beneath a vine-covered bridge …

"The foot problem will solve itself."

"How?"

"I'm not a lawyer, but I'd bet in the end, Ingrid has a right to keep the foot."

"And her failing health? I need to go home—back to Glen Ellyn, but how can I leave Ingrid with no one to care for her? I'm the last of the family."

"That's harder, but your obligation to care for Ingrid doesn't mean you have to stay in Parnass. There's a nursing home here, and another home that offers assisted living. Who knows, she might decide to cooperate."

"Ingrid?" I burst out laughing and told him about the birdseed and the wasted doctor's appointment. "You really think Ingrid could adjust to an assisted living facility?"

"She may have little choice unless you and Noel move back here."

"Sara wouldn't permit that."

He lifted a dark brow. "Who's the child in this relationship?"

"Sara, but—"

"But nothing. Sara doesn't make the rules; she's a grown woman with a family of her own. Your responsibility is to love and support her as she establishes her boundaries, not spoon-feed her."

I looked away. I loved my daughter and grandchildren more than life, but if I didn't teach Sara to stand alone, what would happen to her when I was gone? Noel was deceased—she had no brothers or sisters to help her. My shoulders slumped. She had no one but me.

And Pete. She has a husband.

Yes, of course, but that wasn't the same as a mother. I remembered how worried I'd been before she was born. Petrified she wouldn't be mentally stable. Afraid she'd be like Herman.

"I was lucky you know."

The admission slipped out. Sara was a sore spot between us, yet Vic, in the most illogical manner, seemed like a surrogate father, though he'd never met my daughter. He'd only been assured by me a hundred or more times that if I'd had my way, this child would never have existed. I knew how selfish that sounded, but I couldn't help myself.

"God has a way of handling our deepest fears." He crossed his arms. "I'd like to meet Sara someday. And Noel. Didn't you say he was interested in the transmission of infectious disease from animals to humans? I have a similar interest. We could have some stimulating conversations."

No, they couldn't, but even if it were possible, that's the last thing I'd have wanted. "My daughter has her hands full at home."

Vic shook his head. "I know we're beating a dead horse here, but why, Marlene? Why did you run away? One minute you were off to Chicago for nursing school, then all of a sudden you married Noel—who, by the way, remains a mystery. You're sure he exists?"

"Of *course* he exists." *Liar, liar, pants on fire!*

He fixed me with a stare. "I'm sure he does. You wouldn't lie to me, would you Marly?"

"Me?" I cleared my throat, praying for a way out. Vic helped me.

"So? Why *did* you run away from me?"

"You know why. I couldn't give you the family you wanted. I wouldn't have taken that chance, and I thought you deserved more."

He rubbed clay from the back of his hand, refusing to look at me. "And yet, you did marry. Didn't you worry about having Noel's child?"

The unspoken words were there. *Why him and not me?* For the first time I acknowledged to myself that I hadn't loved Noel the way I'd loved Vic. Had Noel sensed that? I hoped not. Could that have had anything to do with the way he cheated on me? My heart hardened. No. He made that choice. I'd not given him a reason to stray. To the best of my ability, I'd been a good wife.

Vic was waiting for an answer. I held my voice steady. "I told you, Sara wasn't planned."

His gaze skimmed me briefly. "I know of your fear. Why didn't you take precautions? You're a nurse. You know how babies are conceived."

"Noel must not have." That was a cheap shot, but nevertheless true. I was the one who didn't want babies, but Noel hadn't taken my concerns to heart—never had. Noel did what he wanted, and I couldn't stop him.

"He's a surgeon, isn't he?"

"He was. He's not in practice anymore." I didn't want to talk about Noel. We were treading dangerous ground, and I wasn't ready to go there. I changed the subject. "I ... I owe you an apology. I know what I said about children, and until I had Sara, I stood by my resolve. But once she was here—once her tiny hand curled into mine, I knew I loved her and would have missed out on the greatest thing in my life if she hadn't been born."

"You don't owe me an apology." Vic let the chair drop back to the floor, and I could practically hear a granite barrier snap into place. It seemed important to repeat my defense.

"Sara *wasn't* planned. I would have never agreed to a pregnancy—"

"Well." He smiled, an expression that didn't quite reach his eyes. "You did have her, and thank God she's fine. Now.

How about a tuna sandwich? I think the local café is still open."

I'd eaten earlier and hated tuna, but that didn't stop me from accepting the offer. He might still carry a load of resentment, but I'd take all the moments with him that I could get. After Sunday, those moments would be over.

Five

Lavender. The heavenly scent filled the house Saturday morning. Sunlight, warm and golden, slanted through my bedroom window. I stretched, going over the day's busy activities. Cemetery cleanup was always a big event that encompassed day and night. Around 6:00 p.m., work would cease and the town would gather for a picnic and then fireworks. Cemetery cleanup equaled the Fourth of July in Parnass Springs.

Today was going to be one of those warm days in mid-April, a day to be outside enjoying God's creation.

I yawned and then stretched again before rolling out of bed and heading for the shower. Ingrid didn't understand why I didn't stay with her. I'd misplaced my glasses and so far hadn't found them—I probably needed a keeper, but I'd lived alone for so long, I liked my privacy.

When I pulled into the cemetery, every parking spot was taken. I'd thought I'd be one of the first volunteers, but I was wrong. Already the two-acre plot teemed with activity. Men, women, and children manned rakes, hoes, and various other garden implements. I spotted Joe coming toward me with a super-sized box of Hefty lawn and garden bags tucked under his arm.

"Morning!"

"Morning." I eyed the box of lawn bags and the long pole under his left arm. "What's the stick for?"

"It's not a stick. It's a battery-powered leaf tamper."

"Battery-powered leaf tamper." I studied the long pole with a circular plate on one end. Another one of Joe's inventions, no doubt. "How does it work?"

Joe dropped the bag of Heftys, eyes shining. "Simple. Bag the leaves, turn on the tamper, tamp them down, bag more leaves, tamp. A body could get close to two hundred pounds of leaves in a sack if it's tamped down tight enough."

I nodded. "Who's going to carry the sack to the burn pile?"

Joe stared at the new contraption, forehead furrowed. "I don't do details—I just invent. We'll cross that bridge when we come to it." Flashing a grin, he picked up the lawn sacks and strode toward the Brewster plot.

I hauled implements and a gallon bucket to our site, and paused for a minute before heading back to pick up Aunt Ingrid. I knew I couldn't carry tools and manage her, so I'd decided to make two trips this morning. As I turned to leave, my eyes caught Herman's stone, covered in leaves.

Maybe it was a daughter's guilt—a daughter who had loved her dad and failed to show it as often as she should have. I was just beginning to realize how much I'd lost by not staying in touch with him. Overwhelmed, I knelt in the peaceful setting, gently brushing aside the weathered debris.

HERMAN EUGENE MOSS

Beloved son of Eugene, and stepmother, Ingrid Moss.

Herman had been Ingrid's child in every sense, though he was Eugene's son by a prior marriage. Years ago, forceps births were not uncommon. Eugene said Herman's birth was long and arduous. When it appeared that neither mother nor child would make it, the physician delivered the baby boy post-haste. Herman was notably slower than other babies his age, but around seven, he simply stopped developing. Whether the delivery technique was the cause for his mental state, doctors couldn't say for certain, and I had never wanted to chance that a rogue gene could be the cause.

As I brushed at the leaves, I could feel my eyes water. Allergies. Had to be. After all, I never expected a perfect life. How could I? But I knew others had it worse. I hadn't always made the wisest choices, but God overlooked my mistakes and gave me a healthy, beautiful daughter.

Once a therapist suggested that I refuse to count on anything because everything I'd counted on had failed me, but I'd preferred to think that I'd thrown away my rosy glasses and now viewed the world with an experienced eye.

But then, I'd been wrong before.

Ingrid was still puttering around when I stopped by her house. She moved from room to room, totally disorganized. Her higgledy-piggledy ways were driving me crazy.

"Almost ready," she called.

I got a drink of water and waited. She came into the kitchen muttering. "Hold on a minute. I need to check my bedding plants—I've set them out too early. I should have had better sense. I'll only be a minute." She moved to the side porch. A second later she called. "Marlene?"

"Yes?"

"Bring some water. There's a can in the pantry."

I found the can and filled it with water. Ingrid sprinkled the tender new plants, satisfied they'd survived the chilly night. "Oh goodness—roll up that hose, will you?"

I rolled up the garden hose lying on the porch and set it beside the outside faucet.

She moved back into the kitchen and paused. "I'll need a light sweater. Is this today's mail?"

"Yeah, I brought it in a few minutes ago."

She started to leaf through the pile while I went in search of the sweater. At this rate, it would be dark by the time we got back to the cemetery. When I returned, she handed the bills to me and motioned to the waste can. "Would you empty that, dear? It's full."

I laid the bills down on the counter and picked up the trash can, but then I spotted my car payment lying on the table. Everything I had was strung between Beth's and Ingrid's houses—I was always looking for something. Since I was going to be near the mailbox when I took out the trash, I may as well mail the bill. I reached for my purse and checkbook and groaned when I saw I was down to one check. My extra checks were in Glen Ellyn.

I went to get my credit card out of my purse and spotted the half can of Diet Coke I'd been drinking the day before. Wasteful.

Picking up the can, I carried it back to the kitchen to refrigerate it when I noticed the vase of spring flowers on the kitchen table. They needed fresh water or they'd be gone in no time.

I set the can on the counter and spotted my reading glasses. Thank goodness! I'd been looking for them all morning! I must have left them here last night when I stopped by. If I didn't put them in my purse, I'd misplace them again—but first I needed to change the flower water.

The glasses went back to the counter, and I filled a container with water and suddenly spotted the TV remote Ingrid had left on the table. I'd be looking for the thing sooner or later, but I wouldn't remember where it was. I should put it where it belonged, but first I'd replace the flower water—

I stopped, shaking off the mental fog. Good grief! I had to leave this environment. I was as ditzy as Ingrid! She had *me* confused now.

"Aunt Ingrid!"

She walked into the hallway. "What?"

"Are you ready to go?"

She tied the plastic rain bonnet around her hair. "I'm due at the beauty shop at nine thirty."

"The beauty shop! Ingrid, this is cemetery cleanup day. Did you forget?"

"I always have my hair done on Saturday. You know that, Marlene. I can't just up and cancel my appointment. I have to go. Betty Jean would be so upset, she'd give my standing appointment to someone else."

By now I'd loaded her into her car (which she insisted I drive) and I was drenched in sweat. Sliding behind the wheel, I started the car, trying to locate the gearshift. The Buick was an older model and had few accessories.

At ten forty-five, Ingrid was washed, curled, and ready to roll. Back in the car I buckled up. Joe would wonder what had happened to me.

Ingrid threw up a protective hand to shield her fresh do. "Roll up that window, Marlene!"

"Please, Aunt Ingrid, let's enjoy the fresh air." I cranked it up a notch to appease her.

We were nearly at the café when Ingrid spotted the car wash. "While we're out, would you mind running the car through the wash?"

"Aunt Ingrid." She was old and she had needs, but the cemetery cleanup was halfway over, and I still hadn't touched our family plots. "Can't we do that after the cleanup?"

"It'll be dark by then and I'll be worn out. Those fireworks go on forever. It'll only take a minute, Marlene."

I pulled into the car wash, and a young attendant ran out and explained that the change machine was broken. I counted out the coins and handed them to him, then eased the car into the long, narrow building. The car was nearly swallowed up when I thought to roll up the window. I reached for the button but couldn't find it. Frantically, I mashed around seeking one.

Ingrid glanced over. "What's wrong?"

"Where's the window button?"

"Button? There's no button."

The car had eased into the building. I could hear clicks and bursts of soapy steam. My throat closed as my hand slapped the door panel, looking for anything that would close the window.

Too late.

Water busted forth as if from a broken dam. A long, forked arm started down the sides of the car, spraying water. Ingrid screamed, throwing both hands up to shield her hair.

Water poured through the window. With Ingrid's screeches, it sounded like a cheap Friday-night Halloween fright movie. When the Buick finally hit the air blowers, there wasn't a dry thread on us or the car's interior. Ingrid's plastic rain bonnet fluttered to the floorboard and sank like a rock.

By then I'd located the window crank. With a lame grin, I rolled up the window. "Car's clean!"

Close to noon, I pulled back into the cemetery. Ingrid snorted when she saw the crowd. "Gets bigger every year. You think they've all heard?" She'd tied the rain bonnet flat to her head. She looked like a fool, but Betty Jean couldn't do her hair a second time that morning so Ingrid had to live with my mistake. And I had to hear her live with it.

"Heard what?"

"About the foot, Marlene. Eugene's foot! Sakes alive. Keep up."

"Oh. The foot."

"I hope *that* doesn't get around."

She had about as much chance of that not happening as a Q-tip had to grow hair. I got out of the car and snapped the trunk open. Minutes later I helped Aunt Ingrid across uneven earth. We'd had just enough rain to dampen the ground and make it nearly impossible to avoid mud, but I prevailed until I hit a mole run. Ingrid's left foot sank.

"You going to leave me here like this?" Ingrid demanded. "Help me!"

"I'm *trying*," I grunted. "Grab my hand."

I straightened, drew in a deep breath, and then maneuvered her free. *Move that mountain! Yes, Lord! Your child needs help!*

Finally, she moved forward, her right foot striking an upright tombstone shaped like a log with an angel slumped on top, wings folded. The stone face suggested a bad case of indigestion. What appallingly bad taste.

I left Ingrid beneath a spreading maple and paused to catch my breath, which didn't last long because I saw Vic walking toward me. You'd think after the morning I'd had, the sight of him wouldn't cause such open upheaval.

"Afternoon, ladies."

Ingrid nodded, her hand reaching up to touch the plastic bonnet. "Vic."

He caught my eye, and I prayed he wouldn't ask what happened to her hair. I managed a smile. "We're finally here."

Kneeling beside the lawn chair, he chatted with Ingrid. My aunt apparently earned, if not a vet's sympathy, then certainly his interest. I wasn't nearly so compassionate. It was all I could do to resist the urge to peel her out of that chair and shake sense into her.

Marlene, you're wretched.

I picked up my tools and started to work, leaving Vic and Ingrid to their conversation. For over an hour, I worked, peeling vines off our family's tombstones. Virginia creeper's strong, fine roots had dug into the granite, damaging the surface.

I'd worked my way back to Herman's site. Aunt Ingrid should have provided him with the best stone money could buy, but she was as tight as the bark on a log. I studied the plain stone, simple inscription, and thought about the statue the animal shelter wanted to erect. I was sure my adamant refusal took them aback. Was I being unreasonable? Was my unhappy past coloring my decision?

What if someone decided to tie a sanitary napkin around the statue's forehead? No doubt many in town still remembered the unfortunate incident when someone told poor Herman the thing was a sweat band. I didn't think it was funny—and Herman wouldn't have thought it funny if he had understood the tasteless practical joke.

"Looks like you're making progress."

I glanced up to see Vic leaning on a rake, grinning. The wind tousled his hair and stung his cheeks red. He looked so much like the boy I'd loved with all my heart and soul long years ago, that it nearly took my breath.

"Great progress. How about you?"

"Dad's been working me like hired help." He bent and pulled a stray weed. "Got time to split an energy bar?"

"Sure." I glanced over to check on Ingrid, who was holding court with a couple of peers. "What do you have?"

Vic studied the bar he'd fished out of his pocket. "I don't know. I picked it up at the convenience store on the way over. I hope it isn't one of those healthful things that tastes like cardboard."

I grinned and took the bar from him. "Hummm. I think you lucked out. It's loaded with white sugar, no fiber, and its carb count is off the chart."

He made a face. "Good thing I picked up an apple for you."

Bless his thoughtful heart.

We found a semi-clean spot beside a mound of filled trash bags and sat down. "How's the leaf tamper working?"

"I used it on one bag and then hid it. It's more trouble than it's worth." He uncapped a thermos and poured steaming coffee.

"Was Joe upset?"

"He would be if he knew what I'd done." He winked and handed the cup to me. "Have I mentioned what a beautiful woman you've become?"

I tested the coffee, trying to concentrate on the moment at hand, which wasn't supposed to be personal. "Have you had your eyes checked lately?"

"Yearly. You're beautiful, Marly. I always tell the truth."

Wow. He could *still* make my stomach turn cartwheels and land on my liver.

"How's Noel these days?"

Oh man. Just when things were going so well.

"You've never met my daughter, Sara, have you?"

He took a sip from his cup. "I haven't, but I'd like to. You need to bring her around sometime."

"She's one busy lady." I chattered on about Petey, Emma Grace, and Pete, hoping he hadn't noticed I'd switched subjects. He let me rattle on until I finally stopped, drew a deep breath, and returned to the earlier conversation. "You turned out pretty nice yourself."

"Have you had *your* eyes checked lately?"

"Yearly. I have near perfect eyesight with my glasses."

We sat in silence, enjoying the quiet reprieve. He'd devoured the energy bar in three bites and now lay back on the ground, resting. Blue jays chattered overhead. Someone had set up a large smoker, and the smell of burning charcoal drifted on the wind.

"Heard the town wants to dedicate a statue of your dad."

My heart sank. This town! You couldn't sneeze without someone handing you a tissue.

"Rumors fly, don't they?"

"In Parnass Springs? Like an eagle. Are you going to do it?"

"No."

"Figured you wouldn't."

"Not for the reason that you're thinking."

"Oh? What reason am I thinking?"

"You're thinking that I don't want to because I was … ashamed of Herman." What could have given him that idea?

Just because I'd cried on his shoulder, figuratively speaking, at least once a day when we were young.

"Why would I think you were ashamed of Herman?"

When he said Herman, in that reflective tone, it sounded strange. *Dad.* The word stuck to my tongue. I'd rarely thought of Herman as *Dad*, only as someone I wanted to avoid. I plucked a weed and turned it over and over in my hand. "Were you here when Herman ..."

"Got sick?"

"Yes."

"Sure. I visited him every day while he was in the hospital. I got special permission to take Butchie in to see him a couple of times."

I smiled, tears gathering in my eyes. "That was kind of you."

"He loved his dogs. The last Butchie died a month after your father—you knew that?"

I knew. Ingrid had written and told me about the dog's death. "Wasn't it unusual for Herman to catch a cold and die so suddenly?"

"His cold turned into pneumonia and took him quickly. It happens sometimes."

"He was fairly young, I guess. By today's longevity standards."

"Sixty-one is young. He just went to sleep, Marly, and never woke up. Ingrid made certain he didn't suffer."

Tears dripped off the end of my nose and dissolved into my apple. "I refused to dedicate the statue because I don't want to revive the past. It's just pointless to invite further controversy about Herman. It's too hurtful."

"Hurtful for whom?" He rolled over and propped his hand on his cheek. Dark eyes met mine.

"For Herman." That's who I was concerned about, right?

"Herman was happy. He loved the town, and most of them loved him. I couldn't count the number of times I saw him working alongside somebody in their flower or vegetable garden or helping paint City Hall or a public building. He stopped by my clinic almost every day and swept up for me or took care of a sick animal while I was out of the office."

White-hot heat flooded my face. "That was the problem. He was always around. Underfoot. Didn't that bother you? It bothered other people."

"Did it bother you?"

"No." I paused. "Sometimes, but I loved him, Vic. I'm beginning to realize how much, and I was family. He was my responsibility."

"Yours?" He chuckled. "He thought you were *his* responsibility, and he worried about it."

"Impossible. He was a child. He knew only childish things. It was my and Ingrid's responsibility to keep people from hurting him, and we tried. But as much as the people in this town loved him, we heard the whispers and saw the stares."

I could just see it now. If I let them put up a statue of Herman, the stories would flow.

"I remember the time Herman went to Marlene's prom and danced with all her friends. She must have been so embarrassed!" ... *"He molested that young woman."*

The ugly taunts I remembered well—too well. Herman was at peace. I wanted him to remain that way. No statue.

Vic reached over and grasped my hand. Electrical currents shot through me as I met his eyes, emotion tightening my throat. "You don't have to convince me. I knew how you felt about Herman."

"Did you?" I'd sensed that deep down he hadn't known, that he had questioned my feelings. My love for my father was obligatory, and yes, that love mixed with embarrassment had ruled my life. But I was over that now. I'd started to see Herman in a new light.

And no one, including me, was going to ridicule him again.

Ingrid tired shortly after the picnic and wanted to go home before the fireworks started. That was okay with me; I was bushed. I settled her, then went home and curled up on Aunt Beth's sofa, prepared to watch an old Hepburn movie. The cell phone interrupted my plans.

"Mrs. Queens?"

"Yes?" I'd expected Sara. This was a male voice, sort of gruff, not young.

"Winston Little."

"Ah, yes." And who was Winston Little? If I was supposed to remember him, I'd dropped the ball. Maybe Aunt Ingrid's mental confusion was contagious.

"Chairman of the statue committee?"

"The who ... what?" The statue. In my furor, I'd completely forgotten the statue.

"I've been looking forward to meeting you. We've much to talk about."

I couldn't think of a thing to say unless it was a declaration that they were going to build a statue of Herman over my dead body. I didn't care what Mr. Little wanted; I had a few wants myself.

"Are you free tomorrow afternoon?"

I searched for an excuse, trying to come up with a reason why I was occupied. I could say I was going to Joe's party, but that wasn't until evening. Unfortunately, I was brain-dead, and Mr. Little moved into the gap.

"What about now? I know it's getting late, but we can be there in a few minutes."

"Be where?"

"At your house—we'd be glad to meet you there."

And let them see the tattered, sun-rotted drapes downstairs, the stained ceiling that hadn't been replaced yet, the dripping faucet and cracked wallpaper; the rocks still crowding the living room. No way were they going to meet here tonight, after the day I'd had. "I'm sorry, but that won't be possible." Besides, I didn't want a meeting.

Mr. Little seemed to expect my objection. "I see. Well, we can move to plan B."

"Plan B?"

"I always have a plan B. In case I need a backup."

I had a hunch Winston Little would. "And what is plan B?"

"We'll meet at the shelter Monday morning. Is nine o'clock a good time? We have a magnificent meeting room. Just pull to the rear and park."

Before I could object, the man hung up. I stared at the wall for a couple of seconds before pulling myself together enough to replace the receiver in the cradle.

Sunday night I still hadn't cooled. I wanted to talk to Joe, but I didn't want to dampen his celebration. After forty years shepherding one town, he deserved the spotlight tonight. With few exceptions, the town turned out to help celebrate the pastor. Vic was chatting with Lana Hughes in a quiet corner. The sudden jealousy stunned me. He had every right to see Lana, and probably, if I were picking an ideal woman for the man I once loved more than life, Lana would be a top contender. But I wasn't picking his wife. I was grieving my foolishness while smiling, keeping a stiff upper lip, attending his father's retirement party, sipping punch, and trying to avoid the constant stream of advice bombarding me from well-meaning acquaintances.

"Don't blame you a bit for refusing the statue, Marlene." Joanie Miller, one of Joe's flock, winked. "I say, let sleeping dogs lie."

Woof, woof.

"Marlene, honey!" Shirley Lott, Joe's neighbor, cornered me at the punch bowl. "Everybody loved Herman. He was an angel among us. He'll never be forgotten. Erect the statue, sweetie."

Nodding, I smiled and moved on to seek privacy in a small alcove. I started when someone whispered in my ear. "How come the prettiest girl in the room is hiding?"

I turned and went into Joe's arms. "Oh, Joe, it's so hard."

"What's hard, honey?"

Straightening, I waved my hand, fanning away superfluous tears. I couldn't tell him it was excruciating to watch Vic with another woman. I was supposedly married to Noel. Why had I ever started—or worse, *continued*—the senseless deception? *Pride. Your pride, Marlene.* The day, the weekend, had been too much—too many unwanted memories to deal with.

Taking my arm, Joe threaded me through the crowd and out the front door. Flashes of lightning lit the west; a welcome breeze ruffled new foliage. He pulled his hankie from his pocket and pressed it into my hand. "Did you see Fred Faraday? I know he wanted to say hi."

I wiped my nose. The Faradays had been Ingrid and Joe's neighbors for years. Fred's motor scooter was his pride and joy. When I was little I used to say I was going to buy a scooter just like Fred's when I grew up. He'd taken me for rides around the block on long summer nights. I loved riding so much that I graduated to dirt bikes and motorcycles, and by the time I was fifteen, I knew how to ride a cycle as well as most men. Between Vic's and Fred's wheels, I was a born biker. "I haven't seen him, but I will."

"Want to rant?"

I sniffed, wiping at moisture in my eyes. "It's your celebration. I don't want to spoil it."

"You're my best girl. You'd never spoil anything for me." He took my hand and sat me down on the bench. "It's all this talk about Herman, isn't it?"

"I loved him, Joe."

He nodded, thoughtful now. "Of course you did. And he knew it, Marlene. But he also knew he wasn't the typical parent. And you knew he wasn't the typical father, and at times you felt cheated."

True. Cheated, distressed, and confused. Why had God picked me to be born to two simpleminded people who weren't capable of parenting? Who couldn't even blow their noses without help? Other kids had wonderful homes with fathers who didn't embarrass them with childish acts. Mothers who cooked pot roast and mashed potatoes. My mother ... well, I'd never met my mother. Never wanted to meet her. I knew practically nothing about her except the occasional overheard conversation between Ingrid and Beth. I knew the woman's family highly resented Herman and his perpetrated act on their helpless daughter. Maybe that's why they never sought grandparents' rights with me. Odd, though. My mother was their only child. One would think they'd have relished a granddaughter, a healthy child capable of giving and receiving love.

"The distasteful matter is over and done." Ingrid had repeated the Parishes' words to Beth, unaware that I was listening in the next room. "The child is dead to us."

That would be me. Marlene. Dead. Not exactly doting grandparent chatter.

I blew my nose. "Am I wrong, Joe? Should I let them put a statue of Herman on the animal-shelter lawn?"

"I think the gesture is appropriate, not meant for harm, but I suspect you don't want to reopen old wounds. Am I correct?"

"I'm not worried about my wounds; I've moved past that. I think I understand Herman and his ways more now than I did then, but I'm afraid the town hasn't changed. They might have loved Herman, but behind his back they whispered unkind things — things I heard and that he heard."

"Ah yes. Words are like swords. If only we thought before we spoke. Well, in the end you'll make the decision. He was your father."

"And Ingrid's stepson." Could I deprive an old woman of her memories? Her needs? I didn't see how I could. Joe shook his head. "That woman needs to stay out of this."

"Have you ever known Ingrid to stay out of anything? She'll be *paralyzed* for the rest of her life if that replica of Herman isn't sitting on the shelter lawn this fall."

Suddenly the bench we were sitting on tilted. My hand flew to my forehead as the world spun, and I realized all I'd eaten today was toast, a piece of fruit, and a protein shake. My blood sugar was going through the floor.

"Are you okay?"

I managed to tell Joe what was happening, and he took hold of my trembling fingers. "Come on. We need to get something solid in your stomach. You need to take care of yourself, Marlene. Vic's worried about you."

I let him lead me over to the food table. "What's he afraid of? I'll get hoof-and-mouth disease?"

"Heavens, no. If *that* happened, he could shoot you and put you out of your misery. No, I'm afraid the situation you're facing with Ingrid is far more worrisome."

Monday, I was up early, ready to do battle. I'd go to the meeting and make my position crystal clear. No statue. No way, definitely not. Herman had been my father, and I may have resented the fact, but that didn't mean I was going to let the town make him an object of ridicule. A statue. Something for pigeons to roost on and young hoodlums to deface. Nobody was going to make a mockery of Herman—not if I had anything to say about it. I reached for my toothbrush.

Dressed in jeans and T-shirt beneath a long-sleeved shirt to protect my bare arms from the crisp spring air, I headed for the animal shelter. I'd had to call Vic for directions. His last words shook me. "Be kind, Marlene. They're doing a commendable thing."

Right. Kind but firm.

The shelter wasn't hard to find. Very nice, very costly, with glass and marble accoutrements. Herman must have donated a hefty sum for the building. I sat in the car for a full minute before getting out. My reflection in the freshly cleansed glass of the building was anything but reassuring. Funny, when I worked at the hospital, I looked fairly savvy. Once I hit Parnass Springs, I'd seriously regressed. Right now I looked like Aunt Beth on one of her tackiest days. Apparently I should have taken more time with my appearance.

A small man with snow-white hair and a handlebar mustache met me at the door. "Mrs. Queens? I'm Winston Little."

We shook hands, and I was surprised at the firm grip. Two women sat at the glass table. The elderly woman who occupied the head of the table was dressed in a gray suit, a black fedora, a necklace of red beads, a pin shaped like a red rose fastened to her lapel, and rings on every finger.

I stared at her, fascinated. Had people in Parnass Springs taken to wearing hats? I'd not seen one in years, except on the heads of the female members of England's royal family. American women had fought their revolution, and we were, for the most part, hat free. She wore the feathery frivolity cocked at a rakish angle.

A second female lifted her eyes. "Lily Lippit, and this is Millicent Spencer. We're the remaining committee members."

Lily was the exact opposite of Millicent. Her beige suit with a pale yellow blouse blended into the woodwork. She had salt-and-pepper hair that curled in a short mop. I had to look twice to see if she was breathing.

I shook hands all around and took a seat, determined to dispense with the meeting as promptly as manners allowed. Winston adjusted his wire-rimmed glasses and looked over his notes. "Now, Mrs. Queens, we've given the matter extensive thought, and I believe we're prepared to make suggestions you'll favor regarding your father's statue."

Your father.

The words had been voiced so seldom, I barely registered the fact they were talking to me.

Millicent tilted her head and looked down her aristocratic nose at me. "You understand that we represent the shelter, as well as the town of Parnass Springs, Mrs. Queens. We believe we have a solid understanding of what the town desires."

Her white hair stuck out from around the hat, and her blue eyes zeroed in on me with all the intensity of twin beams of light. She reminded me of Mrs. Boswell, my fourth-grade teacher who had all the warmth and charm of an angleworm. Millicent and I were not destined to be bosom companions.

"That may be, but I believe that as Herman's . . . daughter, I do have something to say about the matter."

"That's why we're here." Winston folded his hands in front of him. "Millicent didn't mean anything out of line."

The fish-eye glance she cast in his direction plainly said she would say whatever she pleased, take it or leave it.

Lily offered a smile and dropped her notebook. She reached down to get it and straightened, a little flushed with the effort. "Perhaps you'd like to tell us what you have in mind."

"I have in mind closing this subject as of now," I said grandly. "I am not in favor of erecting a statue to my father, now or ever."

Winston gulped. "Oh, my. That won't do. That won't do at all."

"I assume you're not serious." Millicent iced over like a neglected freezer. "The town wishes to build this statue of your father, and we have the funds, so of course we will erect it. I can't imagine why you would object. It's a commendable and noteworthy effort to honor the man who funded our beautiful, state-of-the-art humane society."

I was so hot I could feel my eyeballs sizzle. "You will do no such thing. Not without my permission—which I'm not giving." I knew how the town had made fun of Herman—walking like him, talking—and spitting when they talked, like him. They might have meant the jests to be in fun, but they weren't humorous to me or to my family. I may not have been an ideal daughter, but I could protect Herman from hurtful people.

Millicent didn't back down. "Don't speak to me in that tone of voice, young woman. I'll have you know I drew the plans for that statue myself, with my nephew's assistance."

So she was an artist? Did that have anything to do with the flamboyant dress? "I'm sorry. The matter is not open for discussion."

She leaned forward, her heavily penciled brows pinned to her hairline, but before she could blast me, Lily stepped in. "I suggest that we take couple of deep breaths. Mrs. Queens, can you tell us why you object to the statue?"

Could I? I wasn't sure I could put my objections into words. I wasn't even sure I knew exactly what they were.

Since I'd come back to Parnass Springs, my attitude toward Herman had begun to change. Maybe it was living in Aunt Beth's house again, but the memories were coming thick and fast, and as I examined them, I was beginning to see that I'd viewed my life from a child's point of view. Herman *had* loved me. I knew that now. What's more, I was beginning to suspect that I'd loved him more than I'd realized.

Once he had taken me to the bridge to see the carnival lights. I hadn't known his purpose for dragging me off so late, but once there, I realized that he wanted to do something to please me. We'd sat and stared at the lights, talking little, but eventually his hand had crept over to take his daughter's. For once I allowed it—and it wasn't so bad.

The committee sat staring at me, like three little birds in a nest, waiting to be fed. I collected my thoughts.

"This is a difficult subject for me," I began. "We know what Herman was. There's no way to soften the truth: he was simple. I know you mean well, but I can't bear to see him made an object of ridicule again."

His childlike trust, his eagerness to help others, whether they needed it or not, would be tainted. He was gone. The tumultuous years were over. I didn't want to resurrect the dead. It wouldn't be fair to Herman, to Ingrid, or to me.

Lily leaned toward me. "We never planned to make fun of him. The statue is intended to show our deep appreciation. Herman's generosity touched hearts. He built the animal shelter and donated a large grant to the public library. We want to *celebrate* your father, Mrs. Queens, not mock him."

"Then you must respect my wishes." I knew what the older people in this town thought of my father. I remembered all too well. Clearly this committee didn't represent the town, but themselves.

Millicent twitched her hat to a more solid angle and brushed me aside. "I propose we move on with the meeting. Petunias around the base of the statue, in varying colors?"

No one brushes me aside. "I believe I've made my feelings clear. No statue."

Millicent bent forward. "Stubborn, aren't we?"

"Persistent—" I smiled—"aren't we?"

Lily wrung her hands.

My cell phone rang. I let it.

I pulled myself together and left the meeting. I should have been feeling pretty good. Triumphant. Righteous. But what was I feeling?

Deeply ashamed of myself. And I couldn't even begin to explain why.

Once safely away from the shelter, I called Sara back.

"Mom? What happened? I tried to call earlier, but your phone went to voice mail."

"Sorry. You caught me at a bad moment." I was smack in the middle of acting like a spoiled brat. I didn't feel like explaining the past thirty minutes; she wouldn't understand. "What's wrong *this* time?"

"Mom." She drew the objection out.

I was out of sorts, but there wasn't any need to take it out on my daughter. "Sorry, honey, but things are in chaos here. I've just had a meeting with the animal shelter committee. They want to put up a statue of Herman."

"A statue?" Her laughter trilled, as sharp and clear as a spring-fed brook. "That's hilarious."

"Yes, well. What did you need?"

"I've been thinking. As soon as you get home, we can redo the nursery. I found the cutest butterfly material. You can make a spread and curtains. Wouldn't that be darling?"

"Darling. If I knew how to sew. Don't buy the material yet, okay?"

"I already have. It's so cute, I was afraid to wait. I knew they would sell out if I didn't buy it now."

Okay, so I'd take sewing lessons. My social life was non-existent anyway. "Look, honey, I have to check on Ingrid. I'll talk to you later, okay?"

"Okay, Mom. Get some rest while you're there. Remember, I need you."

I arrived at Ingrid's around noon, expecting her to be upset that I was late. She did exactly what she wanted when she wanted to do it, but she expected everyone else to stick to a rigid schedule. I should have been at her house an hour ago.

She was waiting when I walked in the door. "I was beginning to think you'd had an accident."

"No accident. I had a meeting with Winston Little."

A curious light entered her eyes. "The committee. About time you met with them. Now. We have business to tend to. You need to phone the hussy and make it clear she isn't getting Eugene's foot."

I took a deep breath. "We have to do that today?"

"No need to put off until tomorrow what can be done today."

Easy for her to say. I walked to the kitchen cabinet and started opening doors. I didn't want to call the hussy. I'd had a morning of hussies.

"Where do you keep the antacids?" Attending the meeting on an empty stomach hadn't been a good idea.

I located the antacids and dropped a pink disk into my mouth before turning to the next ugly task awaiting me. Prue Levitt Moss. What did I know about the woman other than she'd moved in like a Sherman tank and mowed down poor Eugene's resistance until he'd succumbed to her charms—or at least that was Ingrid's version. Never mind that Eugene's charms had been easily seized by any or all females. Even staid and true Ingrid had been the recipient of Eugene's insatiable follies, but his final indiscretion broke her heart. I picked up the slip of paper with Prue's number scrawled in scarlet letters—Ingrid's less than coy method of tagging the enemy.

"I'm calling Hawaii, you know!" If that didn't shake sense into Ingrid, nothing would. In her opinion, long distance was used sparingly and for emergencies only. Hawaii was a distant planet with a hefty rate.

Ingrid's voice came from somewhere in the house. "Call anyway! And put the receiver on speakerphone!"

"Not a chance!" If I had to do this, I didn't want Ingrid interrupting.

I picked up the phone and dialed the number. Maui time? I had no idea what the time was there. Early morning, I thought. I'd probably get Prue out of bed and make her even less cooperative. A voice came over the line, "Hello?"

"Yes. Prue Levitt, please."

"Moss," a crisp voice corrected.

"Mrs. Moss," I cleared my throat. "I'm calling on behalf of Ingrid Moss. Do you have a moment to chat?"

Inane, Marlene. But how did you begin a conversation about a foot?

"Depends." Slight pause on the line. "Are you calling to say the foot has been exhumed and shipped?"

"No, Mrs. Moss." Island boars would spout pig Latin before that happened. "Ingrid has appointed me as her personal spokeswoman."

The woman's tone lifted. "She's passed?"

"No— " I glanced up as Ingrid walked past the doorway, surprised by the hopeful tone in Prue's voice. "Temporarily indisposed. She wants me to inform you that she has received your request to exhume Eugene's foot and have the article sent to you. She's placed the matter in her lawyer's hands."

Ingrid reappeared, motioning for me to cover the receiver with my hand.

"Excuse me." I covered the mouthpiece. "What?"

"Tell her I'm not shipping the foot. Period."

"I can't tell her that until we hear from Mr. Rexall."

"Doesn't matter what he says; the foot stays here."

I turned back to the phone. "You should be hearing something soon."

"Doesn't matter."

I braced for the inevitable. When two strong-minded women set their minds on one goal, hell hath no fury in comparison. "The foot belongs to me."

I repeated my message. "Mrs. Moss's attorney has the matter under advisement."

Ingrid blocked the doorway, pointing to the clock.

Prue turned as mean as a rusty barbed wire. "Now you listen to me, missy. If you and that aunt of yours think you're going to call me at the crack of dawn, get me out of bed, and keep me from my husband's—my devoted and *loving* husband's remains—you're sadly mistaken. I'm not asking for the whole body; the foot will be adequate. You would save us all a good deal of time and trouble if your aunt would see the futility of resistance."

Futility. Now *that* I agreed with, but then *I* didn't want the foot. As a matter of fact, I was having a hard time understanding why either of them wanted it.

Ingrid used her hand to make slashing motions across her throat. The long-distance clock was ticking.

"I have to hang up, Mrs. Moss. You'll be hearing from Mrs. Moss—"

"Don't hang up! Now you listen to me. Eugene was legally my husband when he passed. His folks insisted on burying him in Olathe, and I couldn't do much about it at the time, but all that's changed now. I'm living in Maui with my nephew and his wife—my *attorney* nephew. Do you get the drift?"

Get it? I was buried up to my neck in it. In an attorney-fee showdown, she was financially light years ahead. Then again, she hadn't seen Ingrid's bank statement. If the matter weren't so somber, a money shoot-out might be interesting.

Prue's voice crackled over the line. "You listen to me, dearie."

Dearie?

"You tell Ingrid that she can't send a fresh-faced-still-wet-behind-the-ears niece to do her dirty work. If she has anything to say to me, she needs the fortitude to say it in person!"

Ingrid jabbed at the clock.

"You go back to whatever it is you do, dearie, and I'll thank you to tell your aunt to fight her own battles. If I don't hear that the foot is being shipped within the week, you can bet you'll be hearing from my nephew."

"I'm hanging up now, Mrs. Moss. We'll be in touch." I hung up before she managed another zing with her venomous arrow. No wonder Ingrid got so bent out of shape when anyone mentioned Prue's name. *Dearie*, was it?

"Well?" Ingrid blocked the doorway, expression hard as a concrete mattress. "What'd she say?"

"She said no."

I dropped the number back in the wicker basket beside the phone. "She said her nephew would be touching base with us within the week."

"Humph. We have her whipped. She's scared."

"Yeah." The woman was quaking in her boots. "Does she have the money to fight this in court?"

After all, lawyers, even related ones, cost money. One hundred twenty-five dollars an hour! I couldn't get past that sum.

"She's got money; she's mooching off her nephew. She was in a car accident a few years back and got a chunk of money too. Must have been a pretty penny." Ingrid frowned. "Life's not fair. She got Eugene and all that money too. Now she wants the foot. Woman's never satisfied."

"You've got all the money you need."

"That's beside the point. I've never won anything."

"Aunt Ingrid, do you think this is the proper way for a Christian woman to handle this matter? Aren't we supposed to turn the other cheek—that sort of thing?"

"Prue's not Christian."

I sighed. *How* did I get in the middle of this situation?

By one o'clock, Aunt Ingrid had taken to a wheelchair. One moment she had been eating an egg salad sandwich at the kitchen table and discussing the weather, the next she was lying on the floor insisting she was paralyzed.

I scrambled around the table and hauled her off the floor, practically dragging her onto the sofa. Doctor Johnson arrived an hour later and spent a few minutes with Ingrid, then drew me aside in the kitchen. He didn't mention our earlier meeting involving the Coke display, and I was grateful.

"What's wrong with her?" She'd gone from striding around ranting and raving, to a total inability to walk. I'd never witnessed anything like it.

"Hysterical paralysis."

"What?"

"Your aunt has hysterical paralysis again." He said the words matter-of-factly, as if this was a common occurrence.

"Again? You mean she's had it before?"

Doctor Johnson nodded his head, tucking a stethoscope into his coat pocket. "Nothing unusual, Marlene. Has anything upset her lately?"

"Everything upsets her, doctor."

"Anything recently?"

"This morning. She's upset over her deceased husband's ... foot."

Thankfully the doctor didn't question the bizarre answer. "That's it, then. She periodically goes through these stages."

"Then she isn't paralyzed?"

"Oh yes, in her mind she is paralyzed, which makes it a fact. But physiologically? No, she's as healthy as you and I in most respects."

I stared at him. "How long will she stay this way?"

He lifted a shoulder, his expression sober. "Until she decides to walk again. Ingrid is a highly imaginative woman. I'll need you to bring her by the office tomorrow morning. I can run a few tests, though she had her yearly physical not two months ago, and everything checked out fine. Her cholesterol is a little high, and I started her on a light dose of thyroid medicine, but in general, her health is good for her age." He moved to the back door. "I meant to check her thyroid again this week, but you missed her appointment."

Oh sure. *I* missed it. "Her memory doesn't seem to be exactly intact—it isn't Alzheimer's, is it?"

He shook his head. "Some memory loss is to be expected at her age. I'm not concerned that it's serious at this point."

"She couldn't remember where your office was." I wasn't going to take all the blame.

"Tell you what, when you bring her in, I'll run some tests and see if there's anything for you to be concerned about."

Who needed tests? There was *plenty* to concern me, and Ingrid was merely one of my problems. Between my aunt, my daughter, statue committees, plumbers, and roofers, my stress level threatened to boil over. I was on the verge of erupting in an explosion that would make Mount St. Helens look like a Fourth of July sparkler.

"She's done this before. Don't worry. She'll come around in due time."

Don't worry? Easy for him to say. I closed the door behind him and leaned against the wood. Due time? My vacation was over come Monday.

The phone shrilled, and I grabbed up the receiver. "Yes?"

"Mom?"

Sara. Again! I slumped against the counter.

Ingrid needed bread and milk, and she'd lost the remote to the television. I'd searched and couldn't find it. She was forever leaving it somewhere. I hopped in the car and headed to the store, Beth's headstone on my mind.

I still hadn't phoned what's-his-name on Highway 86 and arranged for someone to redo the lettering. While I was at it, I might even redo Herman's stone. His was pretty nondescript for a man the town wanted to honor. Sara popped into my head—I'd sheltered her from the family, and now I regretted my decision to isolate her. She could help, be of comfort to me right now. Instead, I was fighting the battle alone. Our earlier brief conversation came to mind. I'd explained about Ingrid's sudden paralysis and my initial concern. She had concerns, too—primarily that I wouldn't be available to babysit the following Saturday night while she and Pete attended a charity function.

"First a foot, then a crazy ole aunt." Sara heaved a sigh. Totally put upon. "Your family is bonkers, Mom."

I stiffened, resenting her tone, ashamed of my daughter and her cavalier attitude toward her own flesh and blood. "Sara. They are my family."

"Yeah, but you've said the same yourself. They're all nuts."

"Different," I corrected. She was right. I had made careless remarks about my family. Since, thanks to me, Sara didn't know them, she had no way to understand their eccentricities. So why did the disrespect coming from my daughter's mouth anger me?

"Whatever. You *are* still planning on coming home next week, right?"

"That's the plan, and I'll be glad to keep the children if I'm home, but maybe you'd better line up a sitter just in case."

"Oh, Mom!"

"The Houston girl worked out nicely last month, didn't she?"

"She was okay."

"Then call her."

After dinner, Ingrid's phone shrilled. When I answered, I recognized Winston Little's voice. "Mrs. Queens?"

"Mr. Little."

"I hope I'm not disturbing you, but would it be okay to drop by tomorrow afternoon? I thought perhaps we could continue our discussion."

Was this a test? Was God giving me a chance to prove my faith? If so, I had a feeling I'd be tried and found wanting. Vic's words came back to me. *Be nice, Marlene.*

"I think we've exhausted the subject."

"I was hoping now that you'd had a little time to think about it, you'd view the situation differently. Herman *was* Parnass Springs. He imbued the milk of human kindness—the childlike innocence found in folks here. I beg you to please reconsider your objection, to at least take the offer under consideration."

I could hear sweat in his voice. Why was a statue of an artless man so important to Winston Little? To Parnass Springs?

We chatted another few minutes, and more out of desperation than honest reconsideration, I agreed to give the idea further thought. Given the situation, I knew any consideration of the shelter's request would be slight, but at the moment, I didn't have the energy to argue. When I hung up, I had yet another matter to keep me awake at night.

Did I subject the image of odd but lovable Herman to fallible humans, or did I allow my simpleminded father, whom I was beginning to see in a different light, to rest in peace?

I sat at the kitchen table and stared out the window. Memories of Herman flitted through my mind. We'd sat at this very table many a morning, eating breakfast. He'd come over here for his first meal of the day because he wanted to eat with me. He ... he ...

Wait a minute.

The man wanted to be with me.

Come to think of it, most of my memories involved Herman wanting to be with me, while I wanted to escape. Had I been kind to him? I wasn't sure. I only knew that for years I'd harbored a child's perception of what my life had been. Perhaps it was time to take a closer look from an adult perspective.

The doorbell rang, and I found Joe waiting on the porch, a bouquet of French lilacs clutched in his hand. "Here. Gathered them just for you. Melba loved them, and we've got a whole row blooming out back."

I buried my face in the dark lavender blossoms. "They're lovely." God had a way of sending what was badly needed. My eyes lifted to Joe, and it occurred to me that maybe God wasn't just sending me the flowers. "Come in. I'll put them in water."

He followed me to the kitchen where I filled a Mason jar from the faucet and arranged the blooms. "They smell so good." It was hard to be stressed with the smell of lilacs scenting a room.

"They're pretty, all right." He sat at the table, and I poured him a glass of iced tea before I picked up mine and sat across from him.

We sat in silence for a minute before he said, "You left early this morning. Looked like you were in a hurry."

This morning? Had it only been this morning when I'd set out on an ordinary day?

"Oh . . . the new animal shelter wants to put up a statue of Herman. I had a meeting with them."

He nodded. "Knew they wanted to do that. What did you think of the animal shelter?"

"It's nice." More than nice; I knew that. Herman would have burst his buttons over the accomplishment.

"Town's rather proud of it. Real state-of-the-art facility."

I nodded. New York probably didn't have any finer.

"He did it for you."

He. Herman. "If he was going to do something with his money, I guess an animal shelter would make sense. He loved animals."

"That he did. Never saw him without a Butchie on his heels. When one died, he got another, but the name never changed." Joe grinned. "Makes it real easy to remember. Herman had a lot of love to give, Marlene. He loved this town, and he loved you."

I nodded, the lump in my throat too big to speak around. "I'm beginning to understand that."

"I tried to make you see it when you were younger, but it was hard to say too much without hurting your feelings. Didn't want you to stop confiding in me. I figured you needed me back then."

"I'll always need you, Joe. You've been a blessing in my life. I think in some ways you've been the father I never had."

He shook his head. "You had three fathers, Marlene. God, Herman, and me. Herman wasn't like other fathers, but his love could never be faulted. Fact is, other than God, I don't know anyone who had more unconditional love for you."

I got up from the table. My relationship with Herman was so—confusing. Maybe my attitude had been detached, but *I* lived the life, not others. Joe didn't understand. No one did. A memory flashed through my mind. Herman picking flowers from the city boxes in the park. He'd presented them to me, as if they were a precious treasure. Tears burned my throat. Where had that come from? How many other things had I forgotten?

Joe finished his tea and stood up to stretch. "I'll be getting along." He paused. "Marly—I know life's pressing in on you right now. I'm here when you need to rant."

I smiled, blinking back tears.

He patted my shoulder. "That's what friends are for. Don't forget you have people who care."

I often forgot; the reminder was nice—and needed.

Six

One thing became more evident than my change of heart about my father: I should never have promised Sara I'd be back so soon. The snare confronting me would take a month, maybe even two, to untangle. My little blessing was anything but sympathetic when I phoned her after Joe left.

"Mom! You promised!"

"I know, darling, and I'm sorry. I need another week. Who knew Aunt Ingrid would take to a wheelchair? And the roofer is behind and can't get here until next week. Aunt Ingrid can't oversee the repairs. One more week, Sara. You can manage, can't you, sweetie?"

Cat screeches in the background drowned out our conversation.

"Petey! Put the cat *down!*"

I winced, holding the phone away from my ear. My daughter's morning sickness apparently had strengthened her lung capacity.

"Mom?"

"Yes?"

"Come home. I can't handle this."

Oh, but you will, my darling. Your desire to have a large family means sacrifice. Yours, and quite possibly Pete's, if the worst happens and your family medical history is passed down. I shuddered at the thought.

"I feel abandoned."

"You're the most cherished daughter in the world. One more week, Sara."

"But I'm *sick.* I spew five times a day, Mom. I've changed my mind about a big family. If I live through this pregnancy, I promise you, this is my last one."

Where had I heard that before? Oh yes, with each of Sara's first two pregnancies. How quickly one forgets.

"Battle Hymn of the Republic" filled the room. Aunt Beth's doorbell. I told Sara I'd call her later, and when I opened the door, I was humming the opening notes of the tune. My song died an instant death when I saw the head of the animal-shelter committee, Winston Little, standing on my doorstep. This man kept awful hours. The cheery little figure with the snow-white mustache whipped off his hat, grinning.

"Marlene. So sorry to disturb you at this hour, but I was anxious to continue our prior discussion."

I peered over his shoulder to see if his shadow, Lily Lippit, accompanied him. She didn't. Millicent was missing too. God was smiling on me.

"Well, now." He cleared his throat, shuffled his feet. "I'm afraid we left our prior conversation up in the air so to speak."

"Regarding Herman's statue?"

He nodded. "Now, Marlene—"

I pointedly consulted my watch. "Winston, I don't want a statue of my father put on the animal-shelter lawn."

"But my dear, your father's generous donation built that shelter. It's only fitting that his image be immortalized."

"No."

"Oh my." Winston fished a hankie from his coat pocket and mopped his forehead. "Mind if I step in for a moment?"

I stepped back, allowing him entrance, though I would rather have admitted a mongoose. I'd said all I wanted to say about the statue. No. A double dozen times no. Let others think I was too embarrassed to allow my father's public image; I knew my real reason. Respect. I respected Herman too much to subject him to more mockery. My childhood memories had nothing to do with it.

Winston wandered into Aunt Beth's parlor. He stood for a moment, his eyes roaming the unorthodox room. I tried to see it through his eyes. Rocks. Big ugly stones littered every table and corner of the room. I'd carried out what I could, but the parlor looked like the bottom of the Grand Canyon. I tiptoed through the room, trying not to put my weight down. I motioned to the sofa, a hideous orange with some sort of putrid purple stripe. "Have a seat."

"Now, Marlene— "

"No, Winston."

He sat down, crossing his stubby legs. His pants hiked a good three inches above his black nylon socks. Tiny, once-black hairs covered parchment-colored flesh.

"It's not my intention to twist your arm, but you really must give this matter more thought." He wiggled in the chair, clearly antsy. Enough already. They had their new animal shelter, why did they insist on more?

"Winston." I sighed. "I don't wish to be troublesome, but I really don't want a statue. Herman is gone—at peace. I want to keep it that way."

"Oh my, my." He mopped at his neck with the hankie. "In that case, I must be frank. The statue *must* be erected."

I slid to the edge of my chair. "Who says?"

"Because . . . well, to be honest, Ingrid demands that it be built."

I came off my seat now. "She *what?*"

"Oh, please—she can't know that I've told you." He fanned his perspiring face. "She'd have my job for certain. Herman was her stepson, and you know the clout Ingrid carries in this town. If she wants a statue—and she is funding it—we'll put one up. But it would have been nicer if you had cooperated. So much nice—"

"This is an outrage! I *won't* have Herman subjected to further ridicule because of Aunt Ingrid's whim. He was *my* father."

"And Ingrid's stepson, and if she says statue, we say 'how big?' "

I argued for over fifteen minutes before Winston took flight. We were at an impasse. Clearly Ingrid's wishes superseded mine.

I stole a glimpse of Winston hotfooting it to his sedan, still wiping his neck.

The very audacity of Aunt Ingrid going over my head. *No* statue.

End of subject

Period.

I'd bought a little more time, but days were passing. The roofer still hadn't showed up, the animal shelter committee had come again, and I barely escaped coming to blows with Millicent, which had given Lily a fit of the vapors. Aunt Ingrid was paralyzed, and Sara had called six times in the past two days. I'd kept count. Six.

And the one person I did want to see pulled into Ingrid's drive around nine that night. How often did that happen? The day had gone so badly, God must have decided I needed a break. Vic swung out of his truck carrying a bouquet of roses so huge he had trouble managing them. They'd cost someone the equivalent of a January utility bill.

Did Aunt Ingrid have a secret admirer? The mere thought of Ingrid with a serious suitor induced a giggle as I opened the screen door to greet him.

The bouquet landed unceremoniously in my arms. "For you."

"Me?" I stared at the fragrant floral offering, astounded. "Why for me?" Two bouquets of flowers in one evening. What was going on?

"It isn't my birthday."

"No, but considering the week you've had so far, I figured you might need them." He grinned, reaching in his pocket and popping a jelly bean into his mouth. The Stetson and the plaid western shirt made him even more cowboyish, a trait I'd never particularly admired in a man until now. He was cute enough to put any woman on point.

"Vic." I lowered the roses, overcome with gratitude. "How did you know about my problems?"

One dark brow lifted. "You think news of hysterical paralysis doesn't spread like wildfire? Oh, and Sara's called half a dozen times."

"How did you know about Sara?"

He winked. "Intuition." He inclined his head to the flowers. "Spotted them in the flower shop on my way home and knew Noel would want you to have them."

Ingrid's voice bellowed from the bedroom. "Marlene!"

My eyes locked with Vic, eyes that knew me better than I knew myself. How could I have walked away from him regardless of my fears? "I'm right here, Aunt Ingrid."

"Is that Vic's voice I hear?" Her victim tone was unmistakable.

"It is. He stopped by for a few minutes."

Vic called. "How are you, Mrs. Moss?"

Our gazes held.

"Oh, not so good, Victor."

"Sorry to hear it! You take care of yourself!" He nodded to me, eyes still holding mine. "Try and salvage what's left of the evening."

"Thanks. I will." I clutched the roses to my chest and watched him walk to his truck.

Noel would want you to have them.

I closed the door feeling as low as a flat frog in a dry well. Vic would never forgive me when my lies surfaced.

Tell him—go after him and tell him now. Clear the air. Then, if God wills, rebuild from the ashes you've made of your life—

"Marlene!"

I clamped my eyes shut. "Yes, Aunt Ingrid?"

"I need help."

"On my way!"

I searched and found a glass vase, filled it with water, then dumped the contents of a package attached to the bouquet into the water. I'd had a bad day, but Ingrid had had a worse one so I carried the flowers into her bedroom and sat them on the dresser.

Her eyes lit. "Are those for me?"

"They're yours to enjoy." I rearranged her pillows, straightening the tousled spread. "What did you need?"

"I need to use the bathroom."

"I'll help you into the chair." Once she was aboard, I wheeled her to the bathroom adjoining the kitchen. When she made no attempt to move, I realized I'd become her nurse and caretaker.

Five minutes later I backed out of the room with the chair and closed the door for her privacy in time to hear the doorbell. I glanced at my watch. Eight o'clock! Who could it be now? When I went to answer the summons, there stood a man who looked like a character out of the movie *Deliverance.*

Good heavens, *now* what?

"Your neighbor said I could find you here. You call for a roofer?"

"Yeah. Days ago. Let me get a flashlight." People in Parnass kept the weirdest hours.

I trailed the young man over to Aunt Beth's, where I proceeded to point out by flashlight beam the various spots needing attention. Appearance notwithstanding, he answered my questions and seemed knowledgeable about shingles and soffits.

Time slipped away as I spent more than half an hour discussing the job before the man left.

Ingrid bellowed my name when I walked into the house.

"What?" Good grief. Did she think I was Job?

"Come in here!"

"Come in where?" I scoped out the rooms and couldn't find her anywhere. "Where are you?"

"Where you left me!"

I left her in the—I bolted to the bathroom and tapped.

"Get in here!"

I cracked the door and looked in. My aunt was sitting on the commode exactly where I'd left her. "Is something wrong?"

The look she gave me would have fried eggs. When she spoke, her words spilled from gritted teeth like acid. "I can't get the wheels to roll."

I looked at the commode, then back to her. "Wheels?"

"This chair won't roll!"

Great day in the morning. She'd sat for over thirty minutes thinking she was in her wheelchair. I returned to the kitchen, got the chair, and pushed it back to the bathroom. After wrestling her into the chair, I pushed her back into the kitchen. "I'm sorry, the roofer came and I lost track of time."

"Wheels wouldn't roll," she grumbled. "Shouted your name over and over and you wouldn't come."

"I'm sorry." I pushed her to the table and locked the wheels into place. "What would you like?"

"I'd like to go to the bathroom." She crossed her arms and stared straight ahead. "And sister, you'd best hurry."

Around ten o'clock, I fled Ingrid's in my rental car. I needed time to myself, away from Ingrid, away from my cell phone, which I had turned off, away from the hassle and pressure since I'd returned to Parnass Springs. I was weary of being at everyone's beck and call. I needed space.

With no particular destination in mind, I drove until I reached City Park. Serenity beckoned; I slowed and turned in.

Years ago the park had been a refuge. I used to come here and swing, pushing the little wooden seat higher and higher, pretending I could soar away from Parnass Springs and my life. I had to slip off without Herman knowing. He liked to swing too, but his cheerful chatter would interrupt my despondent thoughts.

Looking back, I could see the situation was never as desperate as I'd felt. Why had it taken me so long to start seeing my life through an adult's eyes?

The swings were empty at this hour. My gaze roamed the deserted area. Would the therapy be as effective today?

I parked the car and got out, then wandered to the grassy knoll. As far as I could see, crime was non-existent in Parnass. The town was one of a few left where a woman could go swing in the park at night and not fear for her safety. Tall floodlights lit the area bright as day.

When I approached the row of swings, I saw none other than Miss Lily Lippet, from the statue committee. What was she doing here, sitting on a bench by herself at this time of night? She had on a pair of jeans and a long-sleeved, navy blue T-shirt—attire not nearly as intimidating as her no-nonsense business suit. She gave me a tentative smile. "Ah … good evening, Mrs. Queens. Lovely night, isn't it?"

"Mrs. Lippit, yes, it certainly is. I wasn't sure it was you."

"You were busy trying to figure out which swing you wanted."

Had I been that transparent? I blushed. "I'm afraid I've never gotten over my love of swinging. It helps me relax and get my thoughts straight."

Her lips curved into a sweet smile. How could I ever have thought she was mousy? She was more alert, calmer tonight.

She shook her head. "I understand completely, though I always preferred the slide."

"You go down the slide?"

Colored tendrils crept up her neck. "Oh my, no." She hesitated. "That is … well …"

"You *do*?" I could not believe it. I glanced at the high slide. I wouldn't go down that thing on a dare. "You really mean it?"

"Sometimes, but only if no one is around. I suppose it really isn't proper for a woman my age to be so frivolous, and I wouldn't want Millicent to know about it. She has such firm opinions about everything, and she'd be sure to think it wasn't appropriate. I'm always careful to wear slacks though. One must preserve propriety."

"Oh, yes, one must indeed." I was determined not to grin.

She smiled. "You're thinking I'm too old to play on the slide?"

"Of course not." But I was. I sighed. I was too old for the swings, too. Childhood was a long way behind me, and I couldn't go back and start over, no matter how much I'd like to. God is the God of second chances, but that doesn't often include the opportunity to go back and right a serious wrong. The moving finger writes and moves on. I'd read that somewhere, and it certainly described my life.

Lily laughed. "Mrs. Queens …"

"Please, call me Marlene."

"Marlene. I can tell from your expression that you think a woman your age shouldn't be swinging either. Don't you know age is just a frame of mind?"

A frame of mind? She had to be kidding. "Oh, I think it's more than that."

She shook her head. "The body ages, whether you do or not is a choice."

Like I had a choice? The events in my life had worn me down, changed me from a young girl to a woman older than my years. Evidently Lily's life had been less problematic. I kept my voice calm, denying her comment. "We don't always have a choice."

She reached out and patted my hand. "Listen to me, my dear. Three years ago I was diagnosed with cancer. I had surgery and treatments, but for a while I didn't expect to live. And then one day I was praying about it, having a pity party, I suppose you'd say, and it came to me that I wasn't dead yet. I could use my remaining time to enjoy what I had and be thankful for it, or I could sit there and feel sorry for myself. I decided to live every day I had left."

And here I'd been thinking she didn't know what suffering was. Her problems made mine dim in comparison. "I'm sorry, Miss Lily. I trust you're recovering?"

"In remission and feeling fine." Her eyes twinkled. "I've done a lot of things since then. Nothing big or exciting, but little things I've enjoyed."

"Like what?" Suddenly I needed to know her secret. How she knew what was important and what wasn't.

"Well, I waded in the Parnass Spring one day last summer, took off my shoes and socks and walked right in. Caught a frog too. And I climbed on General Hooker's horse on the American Legion front lawn."

"You didn't! I always wanted to do that when I was a child."

She laughed. "Me too. I grew up here in Parnass Springs, just like you, only I'm many years older. I finally decided I wasn't getting any younger and I'd never ride that bronze horse if I didn't put away my fears, so one night around this time of evening, I drove down to the American Legion Hall and climbed right on. Just sat there and looked at the night sky. I could see the Big Dipper, so clear, like God hung it just for me."

"You're lucky someone didn't catch you."

"God caught me, but he didn't mind."

I bent closer and whispered. "What else have you done?" What deep dark secrets lurked in Lily Lippet's adventurous soul?

"I dropped a water balloon from the top window of the shelter. Just barely missed Winston. I felt bad about that."

"About dropping the balloon?"

"About missing him."

We shared a smothered giggle.

"Miss Lily, you were so quiet when I first met you. I had no idea you're such a hoot."

"Well, you see, Millicent was there. She's a wonderful person, organized and efficient, but a bit judgmental. Her staunchness makes it uncomfortable to be around her sometimes. She disapproves of so many things."

"She'd not approve of dropping water balloons."

"Oh no, or riding bronze horses or going down the slide, either, I'm afraid." Melancholy entered her eyes. "I feel guilty."

"Because you do those things?"

"No, because I enjoy them so much." She deftly changed the subject. "I knew Herman."

"You did?" I didn't remember her from my childhood days.

"I worked in the five-and-dime. He used to come in and buy bubble gum from me."

Ah yes. I'd forgotten the bubble gum and the massive pink bubbles he used to blow. "Did you like him?" For some reason it was imperative for me to know. If anyone had sound judgment, it would be this woman.

"Of course I liked him. Herman was a special boy. I believe you were too close to the situation to fully understand, but he had a gentle personality. He was always eager to assist."

"Whether you needed help or not."

"Yes, sometimes. I understand your feelings about the statue, but I do wish you'd give it more thought. It means a lot to the town."

"That's what I don't understand. Why would anyone care one way or the other?"

"Because he was one of us. And that shelter is a wonderful building we could never have afforded if it weren't for Herman. It didn't cost us a thing."

Part of me said go ahead and build the statue, but something within me hung back. If only I knew which argument to listen to. *God, I need guidance and wisdom, more wisdom than I have ever possessed.* I glanced at my watch. "Ingrid will be wondering where I am."

"I've enjoyed our visit." She cocked her head, grinning. "Remember, Marlene. You can live your life acting your age, and be bored to tears, or you can do something silly once in a while, just for the pure enjoyment of it."

"Age is just a matter of mind."

"You got it. If you don't mind, it doesn't matter."

I laughed and turned to go.

"Marlene?"

I turned back to see what Lily wanted.

"The swings are usually empty this time of night if you want to come back."

"Thanks. I might do that, Lily, I just might."

Halfway across the park, I turned and looked back. Lily was climbing the ladder of the slide. I slipped behind a tree to watch. When she reached the top, she carefully positioned herself and shoved off, hands lifted to the sky, unbound hair flying. Her laugh rang out, as joyful as an enchanted child's.

I walked to my car, thinking hard. Lily was onto something. From now on, I was going to enjoy every moment God gave me. Live life with gusto.

Just one problem: true gusto and joy came from a clean heart and soul.

What are you going to do about that, Marly?

Seven

I scrambled eggs and bacon Tuesday morning, in lieu of the birdseed cereal. At this rate, Ingrid's cholesterol would be off the chart, and that would be my fault too.

She spoke around a mouthful of bacon. "Heard any more from the homewrecker?"

"Not a word. We'll probably hear from her attorney nephew though."

That seemed to give her pause. "Well, he can talk to J R if he has anything to say. That's what I pay him for."

Lawyers. I could live on the man's pocket change. Ingrid held out her empty cup, and I rose to fetch the coffeepot. I had to get her back on her feet, but short of tipping her out of that wheelchair, I didn't see how I could accomplish it. Woman was as stubborn as a cockeyed mule.

The phone rang and I reached to answer it.

"Mrs. Queens? R J Rexall. I've been doing some research into the … uh … alleged foot ownership."

"And?"

"Well, it's a complicated issue. I don't believe I've ever run across one like it before."

Trust Ingrid to come up with an unsolvable quandary. "So who owns the foot?"

He cleared his throat. "Mrs. Moss can contend that the foot is not an asset of the estate but rather a completed gift. However, the third Mrs. Moss, Prue Levitt Moss, given enough money and time, can continue to fight the case. I do believe, though, a judge will reach the conclusion that Ingrid owns the foot."

R J Rexall had done his homework. I appreciated his effort, and the conclusion was sure to make Ingrid happy. I glanced at my aunt. But by the preset scowl on the woman's face, it appeared unlikely this would end the dispute, and a judge *could* rule for Prue Moss.

The attorney continued. "Ultimately, I would say we can take this matter as far as your aunt wishes to pursue it, but in all good conscience, I must warn that it will be a long and costly fight. Perhaps the two women should sit down and try to reach an amicable solution, even if it means moving the deceased body and severed limb to a common grave that both parties could visit."

Ha. He didn't know Aunt Ingrid. Or for that matter, Prue Levitt Moss. Both women had enough money to burn a wet mule, and at their ages, they had nothing to lose by spending themselves dry just to prove a point.

"Thank you, Mr. Rexall. I'll talk to my aunt and see what she wants to do." I hung up and turned around to find the room empty. Ingrid could move that wheelchair when she wanted to. She was seriously starting to get on my nerves, but she couldn't run forever; she had to face the truth sometime.

So do you, Marlene.

I was caught between two selfish, self-centered women—Sara and Aunt Ingrid. Three, if you counted Prue. But Prue Levitt wasn't my problem. Sara and Aunt Ingrid were, and right now I wanted to shake both of them.

What a lovely Christian attitude. Still, I had a feeling God understood my dilemma since he'd *put* me here.

God did? He's not the one who made Sara overly dependent. Or who made promises that should never have been made about only being gone a week. Or who caused Aunt Ingrid's maladies. And he's certainly *not the one who has lied to everyone all these years.*

Right on every count. *Sorry, Lord. I'm getting as bad-tempered as Aunt Ingrid.*

Speaking of whom, I found her in her bedroom thumbing through a magazine. I squinted. *Cat Fancy*? Since whe had she been so interested in cats?

"That was R J Rexall."

She turned a page, ignoring me.

I cleared my throat. "The man knows his business. Perhaps you should listen."

"Don't need to listen. My mind's made up. I'm keeping the foot."

"You know Prue won't give in that easily. She'll take it to court."

"I can handle it. Bring it on." She glared at me, as if the whole thing were my fault. "Woman thinks she can just send a telegram and I'll bow and scrape. If that's what she thinks, she's way off base."

"This could get very expensive. Lawyers don't come cheap, you know."

She shrugged and turned the page. "It's for a good cause."

"Sure it is." Besting the homewrecking hussy would rank right up there with giving blood. I sighed.

My cell phone rang, and I stepped out on the porch for privacy.

"Mom?"

"Yes dear, what is it?" What minor crises had her in a snit now? What would she do if something bad ever really happened? Didn't she have friends? One other brave soul to help her out?

"Mom, I just thought of something."

"Uh huh."

"Wouldn't it be cute to paint a mural on the nursery wall? It would make the room absolutely special."

Sure, if she had someone who could do it. I was a nurse, not an artist or a seamstress. And with my job, a new baby on the way, two small grandchildren, one full-grown, helpless daughter, and a paralyzed aunt, I had all I could handle, thank you.

"Exactly what did you have in mind?"

"I'm praying for a girl. A pink and white castle set on a hill, banners flying, and clouds overhead, and a long, winding road with a knight on a white horse riding up it. Wouldn't that be the most fabulous thing?"

Possibly, and completely out of my talent range. "It does sound adorable, Sara, honey, but be realistic. I'm not an artist. If you want something artistic, you'll have to hire someone to do it."

"But, Mom—"

"I'm serious Sara. You may have to get by with something simpler."

"Oh, Mom! When are you coming home? I need to talk to you."

"We're talking now."

"You know what I mean. When will you be *here*?"

I hesitated. "Well, that will depend on Ingrid."

"Mom! I need you too."

Oh, honey, think of someone else for a change.

"Marlene!"

"I have to go now, Sara, Ingrid's calling."

"Mom! Don't hang up."

"What is it, Sara?"

"Promise me you'll be home by next week."

I sighed. "No promises, Sara." I ended the call.

Progress, Marlene. Maybe next time I'd see if I could get by without answering the phone or responding to Ingrid's summons. I was getting a little tired of being pulled apart like a wishbone.

The plumber finally arrived when I was cleaning up breakfast. I'd almost given up hope. I followed him around as he checked the ancient plumbing, jotting notes in his tattered spiral notebook. Finally he stopped. I held my breath, waiting for the final verdict.

"Faucets need to be replaced."

"All of them?" That couldn't be right, could it? Water came out of them.

"Yup."

"They still work."

"Yup. Won't for long though."

"Why not?"

"Getting old."

Well, so was I, and I was still serviceable. "The faucets stay. What about the hot water heater?"

"Yup, that needs to be replaced too."

I sighed. I figured the faucets would be overlooked in lieu of decent linoleum, which the kitchen didn't have. I would receive the sum of Beth's estate, but a lifetime of pinching pennies had left me with a master's degree in Thrift. Besides, I still had to do something about the rocks in the living room. It made my back hurt to think of them.

We finally agreed on what needed to be done, and he left in his old pickup truck with Kelo Plumbing written on the side. He promised to be back tomorrow. I wouldn't hold my breath.

During the early afternoon, I left Ingrid napping and drove to the local tile-and floor-covering store. I picked pretty blue and white linoleum for the kitchen, patterned in squares, reminiscent of Dutch tiles. The clerk checked her schedule. "Let's see, we can be there on Friday, will that be all right?"

"You can't make it sooner?"

She shook her head. "Sorry, we're booked until then."

I sighed. "Sure, Friday will be fine." I wasn't sure how that would work out, but anyway, I'd still be here. I paid for the purchase and left.

Driving by the covered bridge on the way home, I noted frenzied activity. I slowed the car and watched a carnival crew set up concessions and hoist heavy cables. The carnival had arrived early this year! A stiff wind blew from the north, ruffling the workers' thin Windbreakers. On impulse, I rolled down the window and sniffed the air, thinking I could smell cotton candy, candy apples, and popcorn.

Right then and there I followed Lily's advice. I promised myself a treat—the first I'd had since coming to Parnass Springs—unless I counted the flowers from Vic. Tomorrow night I'd go to the carnival. By myself. I'd eat one of those candy apples and a bag of popcorn and maybe a corn dog lathered with thick mustard, and I'd remember the good God had put in my life, because the good far outweighed the bad. I'd take care of Ingrid's immediate problems. Get her settled with a home companion, list Beth's house, then return to Sara and my life in Glen Ellyn. It should be easy enough. I just had to focus.

Right, Marlene, focus. Like I was good at that.

Rain fell overnight, and by the following evening, the soggy ground had turned into a swamp. A cold wind blew off the pond adjacent to the bridge. Late April in the Ozarks. Warm one day, cool the next. April showers brought May flowers.

Ingrid sat in her wheelchair, crocheting after dinner. "You surely don't intend to go to that carnival in this kind of weather," she said. "And what about evening service? Joe will wonder where you are."

"I thought I'd go after services." I didn't know why she was so concerned with my plans.

She'd been suspiciously absent all day, and I figured she was hatching up some new plot to hinder Prue. The phone had remained silent during the afternoon; Rexall was awaiting Ingrid's next move, and even Ingrid didn't know what she'd do, but she'd have a plan soon. I knew there would be no last-minute reprieve, no phone call from Sara inviting me to stay until my work was completed.

Like I really expected one. My daughter was waiting me out, and I knew it was a matter of time until I caved in to do whatever she wanted.

You're a big pushover. I knew it and resented it, but I hated confrontation. Maybe that was why my life had taken a downward spiral when Noel walked out the door. Not that it had been perfect until then, but I'd gotten away from Parnass Springs and its memories, which was what I'd thought I wanted at the time. Now that I was back, the accomplishment only sounded pathetically immature, but I'd made a lot of foolish mistakes.

Living a lie had hardened my senses, but I was scared at the time, insecure, wanting to avoid confrontation with Vic and Aunt Ingrid at all costs. Neither reason was good enough to continue the ruse, but how do you undo a lie of such proportions? Every year it had grown and taken on a life of its own. Every year I'd dug myself in deeper until I was in a bottomless shaft and couldn't see daylight.

Aunt Beth was gone, but Aunt Ingrid was still in good verbal condition. I didn't want to hear what she'd have to say about my deception. Her words would be caustic and to the point. Even worse, I'd have to face Vic and Joe and their knowledge that I'd lied.

Rain pattered against the kitchen window. Bent over the sink, I wiped steam off the pane and peered out. Everything drooped with moisture. Raindrops glistened on the forsythia bush, its shiny green leaves soaking up the spring shower. Shivering, I rubbed warmth into my forearms. Ingrid's house was also damp; she refused to turn up the heat, fearing large utility bills. Outside the temperature was chilly, but not uncomfortable.

Ingrid still refused to discuss Rexall's advice; she ignored me when I tried to talk about it. Then again, maybe she'd gone deaf. She didn't mention it, but by now, nothing would surprise me.

I put on a heavy coat and gloves, and wrapped a scarf around my neck. I glanced in the mirror for a last-minute check before taking a twenty out of my purse, then letting myself out the back door. Mist, as fine and light as a bridal veil, created a circled haze around the streetlights. The night seemed cloaked with mystery—a good night to be out, even if I had no one to share my adventure.

After services, I made the brief drive to the carnival ground, the colorful lights reminding me of my high school days when we skipped classes to watch the brightly lit rides go up. Teachers looked the other way or were busy themselves, gawking at the activities that gave the small town a holiday-like atmosphere.

This was a first for me: attending a carnival alone. I'd felt alone many times in my life, but never so much as now, walking through the near-empty grounds. Huddled vendors beckoned from concession stands, inviting me to throw a ball or break a balloon and win a stuffed toy. The rain, falling in a light mist didn't seem so mystical now, just wet. I huddled deeper into my jacket. Most folks stayed home tonight.

Most folks were smart.

Loud music blared from the roller coaster but few occupied the metal cars. I fished in my pocket and took out the twenty. I wouldn't ride. I'd eat.

A couple of minutes later, I bit into steaming batter smothered in mustard, letting the exquisite taste of grease and cornmeal bolster my spirit. I'd forgotten how much better things tasted outdoors.

"Marlene?"

I looked up, my mouth around the corndog, and saw Vic and Lana Hughes coming toward me. I choked, removing the batter-fried dog from my mouth. I wiped mustard off my lips and swallowed. "Hey guys." I'd assumed since he wasn't in church tonight that he'd been working. Instead, he'd played hooky.

Vic grinned, busted. "What are you doing here on a night like tonight?"

I held out the dog. "Eating!" I grinned and greeted Lana. Her hair was a lovely shade of blonde, carefully styled, makeup just right—not too much, not too little. I had a hunch she looked the same going to bed or getting up.

Perfect.

We engaged in typical small talk, but I couldn't keep my mind on the conversation. What was the extent of Vic and Lana's involvement? He hadn't mentioned her in our talks now or over the years, but likely there were many things he'd not mentioned. I wasn't the only one who neglected to say things.

"Where're you headed?" Vic lifted his Stetson and ran a hand through thick hair. He'd matured—gotten so ruggedly charming. In his youth he'd been cute. Now he wore his forties like a fine suit, his pure masculinity drawing women's eyes.

He was successful and focused.

My seesawing personality resembled a balloon, whipping willy-nilly, hither and yon, to and fro.

I'd been certain that when Julie died, he'd fall apart, but eventually he'd risen to the tragedy and overcome it. How did he do it? How did he stay calm in the middle of life's storms?

His faith, Marlene. He'd always been steady in his belief that all things happened for a purpose. What ever happened to your *faith?*

I returned to the question at hand. "Oh, I'd not planned to stop, but I saw the lights— "

Another lie, Marlene!

And it was time to stop. Now. "Actually, I saw them setting up yesterday and decided to come. I think I'll eat one more corn dog and then go home."

Lana laughed "You can't go home! There'd be nobody left. Come with us."

I glanced at Vic. "I shouldn't . . ."

"Why not?" He reached into his shirt pocket and drew out a handful of jelly beans. "Bean?"

"Thanks, no."

He popped a couple in his mouth. "Better come with us. We were on our way to ride the Ferris wheel." He extended an arm, and as quick as that, they talked me into staying. With Lana on his right and me on his left, Vic ushered us to the big wheel with the multicolored lights and the blaring music. The deserted ride looked like it needed a customer.

We marched to the base of the ride and waited while Vic purchased tickets. A blue metal car jerked to a halt, and the operator loaded us into the wide seat he'd wiped clean of rain.

As the wheel lifted and soared above the carnival grounds, the pond came into view. High above the ground I detected raindrops falling, creating rippling circles on the glassy surface. Much like my life. Each new day, creating rippling, widening circles . . .

Awareness of Vic sitting beside me crept into my conscience. Did he feel it—the emotional thread that continued to connect us after all these years? If he'd known that Noel was out of my life, had been out of my life for a long time, would things be different now? Would the emotions licking through me like wildfire affect him in the same spine-tingling, yet worrisome, way?

I'd never know. That's the problem with lies. They turned into snares. Steel bonds. Barnacles that latched onto your life and never released.

Below us lay a sea of rides: the Octopus, Round Up, Rock-N-Chairs, Paratrooper, and the Moon Bounce. My heart was bouncing itself as our car reached the top of the Ferris wheel and halted. The wind whistled through our hair, and a handful of raindrops splattered against my face, but I didn't mind. An imprecise creak sounded somewhere in a car beneath us. Colored lights glistened off the pond, and the glassy image reflected the tall round wheel blinking magnificently in the rainy night. With the almost deserted midway below us, we seemed separated from reality. I loved it.

I wanted to look at Vic so badly it hurt. No one said anything; we sat in the car and I gazed around, reveling in the beauty of God's creation. Such a perfect blend of light and the Master's surrounding creation forging a calming peace within my soul.

The wheel bumped. The car swung. I noticed Lana reached out to grasp Vic's hand. Small gesture, but what I wouldn't give for the same self-indulgent privilege.

The ride started up again, and the car swung out over the ground in a dizzying whirl, swaying back and forth. Damp air whipped my hair, and the sound of feminine laughter—was that mine?—blended with Vic's deep timbre and Lana's lilt. The incredible freedom I had missed for years tore at me, making me laugh so hard I had trouble catching my breath.

Around and around we went, and I wanted the experience to never stop.

But it did. All too soon it was over. We climbed out of the car, rearranging our damp hair.

At Vic's insistence, we ordered three forks and shared a hot cinnamon roll. I could have eaten a whole one. And another corn dog. Carnivals brought out the pig in me. By the time we left the grounds, we'd agreed to come back late in the week, the three of us, and tackle that interesting-looking Paratrooper ride. Who said you had to be young to have fun?

We said good-night at the entrance gate, but Vic insisted on walking me to my car once Lana was safely in hers.

So she hadn't ridden with him.

I was ashamed at my surge of relief. It was none of my business whom he dated.

I unlocked the car door and switched on my headlights. Vic braced an arm on the open driver's car door, waiting until I snapped my seat belt in place.

"All set." I looked up, then away. He was too close now, my feelings too raw to risk his gaze. Did he want me to look at him? Of course not. He thought I was married, and Vic would never overstep such a boundary.

"It's been fun." His deep voice rattled my senses.

"It's been a blast." Did I show my age or what? *Blast.* The proper slang would be *sweet,* but I wasn't thinking clearly. Nothing unusual when Vic was around.

At least the passing years hadn't changed everything.

"Yeah." He straightened. "A blast. Drive carefully."

"I have all of a mile and a half to go."

"I know your driving."

I shrugged, recalling the first night I'd pulled into town. He would have to wonder, wouldn't he? "I'll be careful."

"A lot can happen in a mile and a half." His eyes met mine as he closed the door. I drove out of the parking lot watching him disappear in my rearview mirror.

Time sprouted wings. Thursday rolled around faster than a freight train. I called my boss, and he encouraged me to take the whole month off; I wasn't sure if that was a compliment or something else to worry about, but I grabbed the invitation.

As I dressed, I braced for what I knew lay ahead of me that day. I'd made up my mind to see Herman's gift. The animal shelter. Really see it this time. Not drive up to the back of the building and ignore everything I could.

Mixed emotions colored any excitement I might have had regarding the new building. The old one had been little more than a garage converted to hold homeless animals until they were claimed. If not claimed, Nick Henderson drove to Columbia and put the animals in the county shelter.

I applied lipstick and evened the color with the tip of my finger. Better that the Butchies were honored than Herman. Those dogs were the reason Parnass Springs's animals had a home. Herman might have built the shelter to honor me, but I knew my father's love for his dogs. The Butchies were his family.

An hour later I stood in front of the sparkling glass and brick building in awe of the structure. Green lawns and rows of flowerbeds blooming in variegated colors stood out around the low, sand-colored building. The area was clean, neat, and attractive. No wonder Joe wanted me to really see it. Herman would have been overjoyed with his accomplishment.

I dashed unexpected moisture gathering in the corners of my eyes, confused at my sentimentality. Years ago sentiment hadn't come so easily. Little girls didn't understand little boys. Herman loved to tease me. Aunt Beth said it was because he loved me so much, but at the time I'd not felt loved, but humiliated.

A memory drifted through my mind, and suddenly I was a third grader again.

"Marlene loves Billy ..." Herman danced around me, holding his teddy bear in his arms.

"I do not!" I shoved him, knocking him off balance. He fell flat and burst into tears.

Billy helped a sobbing Herman up.

I pushed Billy away and grabbed Herman's arm. "Here." I wiped my father's nose on his handkerchief and stuffed it back into his pocket. "Now stop crying."

He didn't. He'd bawled and bawled until someone called Aunt Ingrid to come and get him ...

I pushed the memory away, wiping my eyes. I'd been so dogged about blotting out those years. But had I really? Love seeded with emotion—emotion I still didn't know how to handle—hounded my life. I hadn't known how to deal with my child-father, and I did so many things wrong. If only I could go back and set things right, but life didn't work that way. I sniffled as another memory swam up through my subconscious. My father dancing around as Vic came to the door.

"Hey Vic! Marly fixed her hair just for you!"

"Shut up, Herman!" I tackled him and we fell in a tumbled heap at Vic's feet. Arms and legs flailed. Vic broke us up, me sobbing and Herman filled with confusion. Later Herman approached me, eyes sad. "Are you mad at me, Marlene?"

"No, Herman, but stop telling boys that I like them or that I fix my hair specially for them."

"But you do!"

"But I don't want them to know it!"

I shoved him, and he shoved back, and . . .

Enough, Marlene. I dropped down on a park bench, watching a squirrel scamper up a tree, then jump from limb to limb. Native African tribes often believed that the souls of their ancestors were in animals. Was that Herman, lunging from tree to tree, joyful in his innocence?

No, I was a Christian, albeit a disobedient child, but I didn't believe that, although I remembered his love for all animals. Since returning to Parnass Springs, it seemed I was drowning in memories. Beneath the embarrassment and resentment, ran a strong thread of love. I'd been a child then, with a child's mind and reasoning. Time had brought a new perspective. Working with patients over the years had brought a new understanding of challenges. I'd grown more thankful for my health and less critical of others' handicaps.

Was he coming? I watched the gym doors, praying that for once my father wouldn't insist on coming to a school chili social and parent meeting. I deliberately hid my note concerning the event in hopes that even Aunt Beth wouldn't find it, but she had.

"Your father enjoys these meetings, Marlene. Just relax."

"But he'll embarrass me."

"No one ever died from embarrassment." Her lips tightened. "You should be ashamed of yourself, young lady. Your father is a good man."

He was not *a man. I swung my legs back and forth, listening to sound of the heels of my shoes strike the metal folding chair. He was a dumb goofus.*

Aunt Beth reached over and squeezed my knee.

"Ouch!"

"Stop kicking."

Chair legs scraped and I heard Herman's voice. "'Cuse me." His big feet tromped on others' as he maneuvered his way down the row of seats to drop down next to me. He grinned. "Hi, Marly."

I refused to acknowledge his entrance. He'd embarrass me; I knew he would.

The meeting started. Peggy Wiser stood up and made her introductory remarks, then asked if there was any new business.

I mentally groaned when Herman stood up and offered his news.

"Marly wet the bed last night. It got all over her doll, and I got to help Aunt Beth wash it off and change the sheets!"

I wanted to die. To just sink into the floor and die. Why did he do this to me? I hated him! Hated him!

A shudder rippled up my spine.

Marly. Herman had called me Marly first—not Vic. Why had I blocked that out of my mind? How could I have had such love and protection and yet felt such utter dread for my father? Would God forgive me for the thoughts I'd had? Mean thoughts, wishes that I'd never been born—that *he'd* never been born. In retrospect, I saw what he was doing. He wasn't trying to embarrass me, he was *proud* of me, trying his best to share my life.

No wonder my life had turned out so badly. God was paying me back for my sinful ways.

I stood and paced. *Stop it, Marlene. You know better than that.* Indeed, I did. God's Word was clear. If we confess our sins, he is quick to forgive ...

I paused. But did confession necessarily lift the consequence of sin from our lives? I was still paying for an unrepentant sin, for lying to Vic and Joe and Aunt Ingrid. And even though I knew that in my father's mind he'd tried to be the best dad he knew how to be, I'd harbored resentment toward him. Could it be ...?

Was that the real reason I'd refused to have Herman's image placed on this lawn?

I sat up straighter, the notion like a physical blow. No. I wasn't that petty or unkind. I'd loved Herman.

And you were ashamed of him.

I was ashamed of his *actions*, not of him. There was a difference, wasn't there? True, I wanted—longed for—a traditional father, but after awhile I knew that wasn't possible. You were allotted one birth father, and though I couldn't pick him, God had given me Herman. I didn't pretend to understand God's ways—didn't pretend to know why my birth had to be more a burden than a blessed event—yet I believed he had a plan for my life.

Of course, I still had no clue what that plan was. But I was starting to see something.

I had a little holy housekeeping to do. It was time to get my own house in order before I tried to fix someone else's.

Sitting in the peaceful silence, a second truth became clear to me: I shouldn't prevent the town from honoring my father. When I left Parnass Springs this time, it would be for good.

When Aunt Ingrid passed, there would be nothing to bind me to this place, no reason for me to ever return. My convictions were sound; I didn't want Herman ridiculed, but if the shelter could convince me they would oversee the statue and retain its dignity, then who was I to deny my father this acknowledgment?

I slid off the bench, more optimistic, as though an anchor had dropped from around my neck. My foot encountered something on the walk and I paused, lifting my heel to inspect. *Squirrel droppings.*

Scraping the goop off on the edge of the sidewalk, I sighed.

Squirrel yuck. Right in the middle of my holy housekeeping. God's sense of humor grounded me.

Eight

Ingrid was lying in wait when I stepped into the house, now apparently ready to discuss my earlier conversation with R J "What'd Rexall say about my countersuit?"

I draped my coat and purse on the hall tree. "He didn't mention the suit, but I think you should reconsider. It's not biblical to sue anyone."

"I didn't start this—Prue Levitt did."

"You know, Aunt Ingrid, this issue has clearly gotten out of hand. Eugene would roll over in his grave if he knew what you were doing."

"Like I'm going to worry about Eugene." She sniffed. "He didn't worry about me."

"Even more reason for you to let the matter drop. The past is over. The Bible says 'do unto others as you would have them do unto you.' "

You mean like telling them the truth?

Ouch. Good point. But I was talking about Aunt Ingrid here, not myself.

"You're taking Prue's side?"

"No!" I turned, taking a deep breath. "I'm taking your side. Look at you. You're paralyzed from stress. Is a foot worth your health?"

She waved a dismissive hand. "My time's about up anyway."

"Nonsense."

"While we're on the subject—" she handed me a thick folder—"here's my trust and burial plans. I want Joe to sing 'Shall We Gather at the River' at my services, and I don't want Mattie to play the organ. Get someone else. My plot is next to Eugene's foot. Don't bury me anywhere but there. And oh, you mentioned something about getting Herman a new stone?"

"I have to call about that, and I need to have Beth's redone. I'm not happy with the work."

"Order me one when you call; a double one with both Eugene's and my name on it."

"You can't do that, Aunt Ingrid."

"Do what?"

"You can't have your name and your ex-husband's name on the same stone without Eugene's permission." I didn't know the law, but I thought that was a bit presumptuous, even though Ingrid had never remarried.

"How do you propose I get Eugene's permission?"

"You don't! He's *gone!*" Good gravy!

"Is there some law against having my ex-husband's name on the stone?"

"I don't know. How would I know?"

"I have Eugene's permission."

"How do you conclude that?"

"He took a vow to me till death do us part. Some legal paper doesn't change that. He parted. I'm still here, and I want his name on my tombstone."

"Okay." I reached for a pad and pen. "Here's what I'll put:

'Here lies Eugene's foot, the only part he allowed Ingrid to keep.'

'Here lies his ex-wife, Ingrid. Stubborn as a mule.' "

I waved the paper in front of her. "Is this what you want friends and strangers to read?"

She rolled her eyes. "Fine, but leave out the stubborn as a mule part."

I slapped the pen back on the counter. Some days it didn't pay to get out of bed.

After lunch I made several calls. To the monument company, where I ordered a new stone for Herman and a new inscription for Aunt Beth. I didn't bother ordering Ingrid's stone. Knowing her, she'd change her mind overnight. "Consistency" wasn't in her vocabulary. The second call was to the animal shelter.

"Mrs. Queens!" Relief hummed in Winston Little's tone. "I am so glad that you've called."

"I've reconsidered, Mr. Little. If the shelter wants to put a statue of Herman on the lawn, I won't object."

"I can't tell you how happy I am to hear your decision!"

"I'd like one thing though. Will you order a statue of Butchie as well, and put him at Herman's heels?" That way the two would be immortalized together—Herman would love it, and the multiple Butchies deserved it.

"Certainly! Marvelous suggestion!" I could tell by Winston's tone that he was beaming. "Ingrid said if we just gave you a little time you'd come around."

"Oh she did, did she?" White heat seared my cheeks.

His tone dropped to apologetic. "Well, of course, like all of us, we want only the best."

"I can't believe Ingrid would be so manipulative!" What was I saying? The woman was a *born* manipulator. A natural talent.

"Well ... er ... you know, your aunt wields a great deal of power in this town." I could almost hear a smile surface on the other line. "But since you've agreed, there's no problem."

No problem? It seemed to me like we had a big problem. She had treated me like a child and ignored my feelings. I was ticked.

"I'm sorry, Mr. Little. In view of this new information, I may have to rethink my decision."

"Oh dear!"

"I won't be here to maintain the integrity of the site. I'll have to call you later." I hung up. The sound of my uneven breathing and the ticking clock filled the kitchen. This was the last straw. I'd have it out with Ingrid right now. Regardless of how she felt, I would have something to say in the matter.

Whirling, I shouted. "Aunt Ingrid!"

I marched through the house ready to do battle. Herman was Ingrid's stepson but he was my father. My aunt might rule Parnass Springs, but she didn't rule me, and I refused to be pushed around. Hiding out in her bedroom, was she?

My cell phone rang, and I jerked it out of my pocket.

"Mom?"

"Can't talk right now, Sara—"

"Mom. You have to come home. I'm losing the baby."

I cried most of the flight home early Friday morning. How could I have left Sara to take care of two toddlers under the age of three? I allowed myself the reasonable excuses, but I'd failed as a mother and I knew it.

My son-in-law met me at the airport and drove me to Chicago Hope Hospital where Sara had been admitted. When I walked into her room, my daughter was sitting up in bed, pale, but smiling bravely. "Oh, Mom." She dissolved in my arms, weeping.

"It's okay, honey. I'm here." I shrugged out of my coat and dropped down on the side of the bed. "I'm so sorry, Sara. I should have been here."

"It's okay. False alarm. The baby's fine." She sat up, sniffed, and blew her nose.

The welcome news almost took my breath. "You didn't lose the baby?"

"No. Thank God." She grinned at Pete. "We were pretty scared there for a few hours."

The mad rush to book a plane, the frantic scramble to get someone from Ingrid's church to stay with her, the flight, and the emotional wringer I'd been through left me sagging. I moved to the chair and sat down.

Sara frowned. "I can go home this morning—you okay, Mom?"

"Just tired, honey. Incredibly tired."

"I'll bet. Pete, why don't you take Mom to the cafeteria and get her something to eat? It'll be a few hours before the paperwork gets done here."

Pete led me to the hospital cafeteria where he got me a hot coffee and a ham sandwich. I was so exhausted my head spun.

"What happened?" I finally managed when I leaned back to catch my breath.

"Sara woke up from a nap and was having some discomfort. I decided it was best to let her doctor determine if it was anything serious."

"Who has the kids?" I cupped my hands around the mug, relishing the warmth.

"A neighbor." He checked his watch. "I need to phone and check on them. Sara should be released within the hour. I have patients waiting at the office." He glanced at me. "A friend brought over our other car just in case. Can you drive Sara home while I go in to work?"

I nodded, still numb. All this rushing and worrying was too much for me. I was relieved that Sara and the baby were fine, still . . .

He pushed back from the table, draining his mug. "How was your vacation?"

"Lovely."

"Thanks, Marlene." He dropped a cursory kiss on the top of my head. "You're a peach." He turned to walk away, then turned back. "You'll need to get the kids the minute you get home. The neighbor seemed a little antsy when I talked to her earlier."

I nodded. Check. Get kids. Neighbor antsy. Welcome home, Marlene.

Petey and Emma seemed glad to see me. Nancy Billings, the neighbor, seemed even happier. "Hey, Marlene. Good to have you back. Sara's sure missed you."

"I missed her too. Thanks for taking care of the children, Nancy."

She sobered. "Did she lose the baby?"

"No. False alarm."

Petey clasped his arms around my legs, knocking me off balance. "Me-maw, where *haf* you been?"

I glanced down at him. This beautiful boy was my first grandchild. How could I have left him? Emma toddled toward me. "Me-maw. Me-maw."

I scooped her up in my arms. "Me-maw's home. Did you miss me?"

She nodded. "Uh-huh."

Petey yanked my pants leg. "I chased the cat."

That wasn't good. In Nancy's house the cat ruled. Nancy's Tommy was huge, gray, and overweight. If Petey chased the cat, Nancy must be beside herself. I glanced at her. "Tommy all right?"

"Shut up in the bedroom. Poor thing almost had a nervous breakdown. Don't believe he'll ever be the same."

"Petey, you shouldn't chase the cat. Tommy's too old to run."

He flashed a dazzling smile. "I wanna to."

I nodded. Took after his mother. "I'm sorry, Nancy. First chance I get, I'll bring Tommy a catnip mouse."

She nodded, a frown creasing her forehead. "He'd like that. He's under the bed, and I can't get him to come out. Just sits there shaking and staring into space."

Yeah. I knew the feeling.

"Yes, well, he'll settle down as soon as we leave." A twinge of irritation pricked my conscience. Petey was just a little boy who was used to playing with his cats. I reached down and took his hand. Emma's chubby arms clasped around my neck. "We have to go, Nancy, thanks a lot."

"I'm really glad you're home, Marlene. Don't run off again."

"No danger of that. I'm here to stay." The thought made me want to cry. Never see Vic or Joe again? I said good-bye to Nancy and led the children across the yard to the house where Sara, and work, waited.

Sara's housekeeping skills had gone by the wayside with Emma's birth. When I unlocked the front door and ushered my daughter inside, I resisted the urge to ask if there'd been a burglary. I wasn't sure if the chaos was the result of bad housekeeping or if the house had been ransacked in their absence.

Sara headed straight for the sofa, features pale. I dropped Emma's diaper bag on the floor and herded Petey to his bedroom.

"I don't wanna take a nap!"

"I don't wanna make you! So give us a both a break and go nite-nite without a fuss."

Emma bucked in my right arm, bursting into tears.

"It's okay, baby. You're going nite-nite too."

"Haveta kiss mama." Petey bounced out of the youth bed, and I caught his shirttail before he escaped.

"Later. Momma's resting now."

While the weary household napped, I picked up the clutter and started a load of wash. The results of my absence were duly noted. Sara was behind in her chores. Cereal had dried on the high-chair tray. A Cheerios trail snaked through the downstairs' rooms.

Home. You had to love it.

I made a grilled cheese sandwich and a cup of tea. My blood sugar was doing cartwheels, so I stuffed the sandwich down, keeping an ear tuned to the children's bedrooms. The past twenty four hours' events had worn them out and they slept soundly.

When my cell rang, I snatched it up and hit the button, then remembered to switch the ring to vibrate. Joe was on the line. "Just checking on you, Little Marlene. How's your daughter doing?"

"She's okay, Joe. False alarm."

"Well, praise the Lord. We've all been worried about her. I stopped by Ingrid's earlier and she was asking if I'd heard anything."

"Is Ingrid okay?"

"She's a tough old bird. She'll do fine, but she's driving Mrs. Henkins up the wall."

She'd drive a drill sergeant up the wall. What was I going to do about her? Mrs. Henkins lived four doors down and she'd agreed to step in during the emergency, but I still had no long-term solution for Aunt Ingrid's care. During the flight home I'd done some soul searching and didn't like what I'd unearthed.

Me. Or the woman I'd become.

Raising Sara, struggling to make ends meet, I'd never stopped long enough to think, but the past ten days had allowed me a glimpse of the real me. A daughter that had failed her father. A niece who had little patience for her aunt's needs. A mother who nurtured her daughter's overdependence.

But most of all, a woman who willingly continued to live a lie.

I didn't like that woman very much.

"Marlene? You there?"

"Sorry. I'm here."

"You're coming back, aren't you?"

No. I wasn't coming back. I knew at that moment I'd never go back. I'd arrange to have Aunt Ingrid flown here.

She could stay with me until her paralysis lifted. The change would do her good, maybe even enhance her life. I'd list Beth's house with a realtor and appoint someone to oversee the needed repairs. Joe would look after Ingrid's home until we could decide if the move was permanent.

Leaving Vic a second time would be the hardest, but he would continue his life, move on, and maybe eventually marry Lana. They made a great couple.

So why did I feel like crying?

Me—I'd stay in Glen Ellyn where I belonged, help raise my precious grandbabies, and be the mother Sara wanted. Lord knew I'd failed Herman; I would not fail my daughter.

"I won't be back, Joe."

"I'm sorry to hear that, though I know your place is with family." Regret filled his voice.

"Joe ..." Could I do this? The person I needed to tell wasn't Joe, but he was the only person who might understand.

"Yes?"

"Noel is dead. He walked out on me when Sara was a toddler. I've raised her alone."

Silence.

"Did you hear me, Joe?"

"I heard you."

I swallowed, my heart pounding. "Noel ... Joe, he didn't die recently—he's been dead."

"I know. He died in Utah, in a skiing accident, if I'm not mistaken."

"You ... you ..." I closed my eyes as shame swept over me. Joe knew. He knew about Noel. And if he knew, then Vic had to know too. Joe would never have kept a secret like that from his son.

"Vic knows." Joe confirmed my unspoken thought.

"Oh, Joe." Sara's kitchen walls closed around me, and I couldn't breathe. The tight band crushing my heart threatened to buckle my knees. Was I having a heart attack? I shifted in the chair, blindly groping for my water glass. I took a sip. Then another.

"Marlene?"

"I'm here." I swallowed. "How long have you known?"

"Awhile—maybe two months. Why would you feel you had to withhold the truth from us. From me?"

A question for which I had no definitive answer.

"When Noel ... left me, I was scared. I didn't know where to turn. Sara was small, and we still didn't know for certain that she would be all right—mentally, that is. I'd never done anything right in Aunt Ingrid's eyes, and Aunt Beth couldn't have helped even if she had known. And of course, there was Vic. I ran away from him and Parnass Springs ..." What a fool I'd been. What a fool I was. "How ... did you find out?"

"Vic read an article your husband wrote on the transmission of bird flu from animals to humans. He was puzzled when the article referred to the late Dr. Queens. With a little research, he found out why."

Closing my eyes, I did what I should have done years earlier. *Dear God, forgive me for this horrible lie! Forgive me for all the years I've misled, confused ... I am so very sorry. With your grace, I will never knowingly tell another lie.*

"Marlene?"

"Yes, Joe." I dashed tears from the corners of my eyes. "I'm sorry. Vic has been so *civil.* He's never hinted that he knew."

A pointed pause. Then. "Yes, he has been civil, Marlene, but I suspect it's all an act. I suspect that on the inside, he's furious. He's playing a game, waiting to see when—or if—you'll tell him. We've talked many hours about why you would continue the deception. I prayed mightily that while you were here you'd come and talk to us, tell us the truth. I'd have understood. More than once I've backed myself into a brick wall with no way out."

No more deceit, Marlene.

"I had a way out. The truth. But I chose not to take it. Vic had his life together. Aunt Ingrid never needed anyone, and Aunt Beth was doing fine on her own. I didn't want anyone to know what a disaster I'd made of my life—not when it seemed at the time that my whole life had been confusion."

"Little Marlene, don't you know God does not expect perfection from you or me? He expects our best, which often falls short of our expectations. Always know there is no problem that you can't bring to God, or to me, for that matter. Neither of us will ever turn you away."

I grabbed my napkin to catch the hot tears. Every word he spoke drove a nail into my black heart. I believed what he said, yet I'd chosen to live long years in turmoil and guilt. And Vic knew. He'd played along the entire time I'd been in Parnass Springs, never mentioning my lie. My face was as hot as the electric sandwich maker sitting on the counter as I remembered the chances he'd given me to confess, and how I had evaded them.

"What will you do about Ingrid?"

Between sniffles I told him my plans to bring her to Glen Ellyn, relieved to change the subject.

"She won't want to come, you know."

"It's either she comes here or I move her to assisted nursing, and I don't think she'd want that either." I'd have Sara, my job at the hospital, the grandchildren, a new baby, *and* Aunt Ingrid to run after. Could I keep up?

"Well, I can help with Beth's house and overseeing the repairs. I can even list the house for you and fax papers to sign, but seems we have a new problem."

A new one? I couldn't imagine such a thing, not after the past fourteen days.

"What's that?"

"Herman's statue."

"That isn't a problem. Aunt Ingrid tried to manipulate me into erecting it, but I'm still considering the matter."

"Humm . . . interesting. Well, it seems your birth mother's parents think it's a given."

This time the uneasy silence came from my end of the line. He couldn't have said what I thought I'd heard, could he? My birth mother's parents? Like in grandparents? Like in the people who never wanted to see me?

"You heard me say your birth mother's parents—"

"I heard you." My ears buzzed. Why on earth would my birth mother's parents object—or want any say in the matter? Joe again read my thoughts.

"They got wind of the proposed statue, and they've gone to the town council to oppose. They feel their family, their daughter, has been through enough with the circumstances surrounding your birth. At this moment they're trying to get legal permission to protect their daughter from further embarrassment. The whole town knows what happened between Lexy and Herman."

"The project *is* halted," I argued, still trying to make sense of the interference.

"But Ingrid won't give up the fight. She already has Rexall on the case, and he's filed for a hearing."

"You must be kidding."

"I wish I were. I have a feeling all Hades is about to break loose around here."

In the ensuing calm, a new, more troublesome thought occurred. Understandably my birth mother's parents would be concerned about their daughter. And if their concern continued, that meant she was still alive. No one had ever encouraged me to seek her out. Somewhere in or near Parnass Springs lived a woman who'd given me life, a woman I'd never laid eyes on. I shook my head, trying to clear the mental fog.

"I hate to say it, Marlene, but it's quite possible you'll have to come back. I have a hunch this hullabaloo isn't going to go away overnight."

I had the same hunch, and the thought struck terror into my heart. Not only would I have to face Vic's condemnation, but now I would be forced to defend my father's right to be immortalized on the animal shelter lawn against a set of grandparents I'd never known. My father's rights? I shook my head. Clearly I was losing it.

After I said good-bye and hung up the phone, I sat there staring into space. I'd had too much information dumped on me to absorb it all. Vic and Joe knew all along I'd been lying. Why didn't they say something? How could they abet me in my crime?

Well, one thing was for sure, I was going back—a decision that would be as popular with my daughter as poison ivy. I'd tell her as soon as she woke. No use putting it off.

I put in another load of laundry and fixed myself a cup of tea, plotting my strategy. Half an hour later, when Sara left the living room sofa for her bed, I sat down on the edge of the king mattress and folded my hands in my lap.

"Joe Brewster called."

She closed her eyes. "What did he want?"

"Well, it seems there's been a complication."

"Ingrid? What's wrong now?"

"Not exactly Ingrid, though I suppose it does concern her. It seems my other grandparents are determined to prevent the statue from being built."

My daughter opened one eye. "That's good, isn't it? That's what you want."

I'd thought it was, now I didn't know what I wanted. I only knew I didn't want these people who'd ignored me for all of my life, never wanted me or acknowledged my existence, ganging up on Ingrid. Something in me wanted to fight, although I wasn't sure exactly what I was fighting for.

"Mom? You're not *really* going back there, are you?" Sara pushed herself upright, eyes wide. "Mom! You can't leave again!"

"Oh, Sara, you can manage without me." She was in perfectly good health. It's not like I was leaving an ailing child.

"No, I can't. I *need* you. Mom, what if I lose this baby while you're gone?"

Sure, Sara, lay a guilt trip on me. "Anything can happen, but if you have problems, I'll hop a plane and be back within hours. I still have unfinished business in Parnass."

"But I wanted *you* to help get the nursery ready. You know, paint the room and make curtains. And I thought maybe you could make a mobile to hang over the crib."

And pigs could fly. "Be reasonable. Have you ever known me to make a crib mobile? I'm not a crafty person."

"You could learn. Besides, you've always told me I could do anything I really wanted to."

And I'd thought my advice had been in vain. My daughter, God love her, hadn't done much more than she'd had to do all her life, but she'd been saving my advice to hand back to me when she had something in mind for me to do.

"That's a cliché, Sara, and here's another. You can't teach old dogs new tricks."

"You're not old. I know you could learn to sew curtains. They're just straight seams."

And where did my daughter get that gem of information? She'd never held a needle. Now she's an expert on sewing curtains? "I'm sorry; if you want to redecorate the nursery, you'll have to hire someone to do it for you. It's not in my line of expertise."

Petey wandered in, rubbing sleep from his eyes. "Wanna go chase the cat."

"Not today, darling," Sara said. "It's not nice to chase the cat."

"I want to."

"Well, maybe tomorrow, all right, sweets?"

I interrupted. "Don't promise him he can chase the cat tomorrow. Nancy doesn't want him doing that."

Sara shrugged. "He'll forget about it by tomorrow."

I wouldn't bet on it. I slid off the bed. "Dinner is ready to put in the oven an hour before Pete comes home. I've got to go check my house and water the plants."

Life would go on; Sara would survive without me whether she knew it or not. I'd give her another day to absorb the news. She'd come around. We were only talking about one more week.

Nine

"You *can't* be serious! You're actually going back! I thought this weekend would make you wake up and see that your family is here, with me and the kids and Pete." My daughter sat on the bed watching me pack on Sunday night. I had an early morning flight back to Missouri, and I'd talked until I was blue in the face, but Sara wouldn't budge.

"You'll be fine, Sara, you have Pete."

"But I *need* you. I'm not well."

I could tell her we didn't always get what we wanted in life. Instead, I gentled my news. "Look, you can get by for a while longer, and I'll call every day. I have to find someone to care for Ingrid. You don't expect me to forget about her, do you?"

"You did once."

I was getting pretty tired of the snide reminders. I shut the suitcase and pretended I didn't hear her remark.

Sara's eyes narrowed. "Is there something you're not telling me, Mom? What's in Parnass Springs—something you're not telling me, that's pulling you away from us?"

Yeah, there was something all right. Vic. But Sara didn't have anything to worry about. He had to be utterly over me after the way I'd lied to him.

"The only thing holding me there is Aunt Ingrid's condition, and this statue controversy."

"I don't see why someone else can't look after your aunt. What about that Joe person? Seems to me he's a good sort—you talk to him enough."

Was that resentment? Jealousy in her accusation? *Oh, Sara. What have I done to you? Made you an emotional cripple, not only with me but the world?* My lie had gone on too long. It had to stop. And now.

I took a deep breath and plunged. I told her the truth.

The lie.

The deception her mother had carried on since Sara was two years old. Her eyes widened in disbelief.

"Why would you lie about Daddy to a family you detest?"

"I *love* my family, Sara. I simply have mixed emotions about their sanity."

"Apparently they don't have any."

For the first time in my life, I slapped my daughter's cheek. She sprang back, holding a hand to the smarting injury, eyes condemning. But before she could spew her anger at me, I jumped in.

"You are speaking about my family, Sara. In the future, you will address them with respect."

She glared at me. "You don't."

"You're right. I didn't use to. But that's going to change. Right now. I was wrong to talk about my family the way I did. And I was wrong to shield you from them. They may not be perfect, and yes, my childhood was less than ideal, but they are my family, Sara, and I will uphold and respect them. And right now, they need me more than you do!"

I picked up my bag and walked out, leaving a sulking daughter to no doubt wonder what had happened to her once-sane mother.

For once, though, I didn't care. My daughter had to grow up sometime. And now couldn't be a better time.

The weather had turned considerably milder in Columbia, Missouri. Spring had sprung; the sky was a clear, bright, cloudless blue, and everything was blooming—I sneezed—tiny pollen danced in the air as I left the plane Monday morning. I had a different rental car this time. The guy in charge stared at my driver's license for what seemed like an inordinately long time. Who could blame him? The last time I'd rented a car from him, I'd brought it back pockmarked from hail damage and with an ugly scratch across the front bumper caused by playing tag with a stack of hot Coke cans.

I approached the city limits of Parnass, thinking it would be different this time. No trying to sneak into town, though I still dreaded facing Vic. That would be the hardest thing I'd ever done, and I'd done a few hard things lately. Would he forgive me for my idiocy? Only God knew, and he wasn't talking.

I drove straight to Joe's house. When I pulled into the driveway, he came out to meet me. Later we sat at his kitchen table, and he explained what had gone on the past few days. The news wasn't pretty.

Lexis Parish's parents had caused quite a stir by filing to stop the statue. Aunt Ingrid rose to the occasion by filing to stop them from stopping her. It seemed my wishes were wheat chaff. My head whirled, trying to take it all in. Joe pointed to a copy of the morning news folded to the editorial columns. "I'd suggest that you don't read them. Most will hurt your feelings, and the others will infuriate you, but you should know the town's in quite a snit."

I picked up the morning paper and scanned the first letter.

How can Parnass Springs think of erecting a statue of a mentally retarded man! Is this how we want to portray our lovely little town?

I pitched the paper aside. Hateful rant!

Joe sighed. "Town's in a real uproar. Real divided about the situation all of a sudden. Some remember Herman fondly and think it's a great idea. Others think talk will get around about the town's division over the statue, and curiosity seekers will flock here to see the uproar. Course, that would mean business for the shop owners, and folks come here all the time anyway to see the covered bridge." He shook his head. "Don't see what all the uproar's about."

I buried my face in my hands, gritting my teeth. I couldn't let the town turn Herman into a sideshow, yet who better to personify humanity and the goodness found in an innocent heart than my father?

Sometimes it was good to go back to one's roots, but going back to mine had stirred up an emotional maelstrom.

Was my birth mother blissfully spared the brouhaha? Rumors probably couldn't touch her, though I really didn't know anything about her life. It struck me that no one would object to a healthy, mentally sound young man or a young woman, like Sara, having a statue erected to honor them. The problem was that Herman had been what he was and some people couldn't accept that.

People like I'd been.

Wouldn't you fight for Sara in this situation?

Of course I would. Suddenly my hackles rose. Who was this town or my birth mother's parents to interfere? They'd never shown an ounce of concern regarding me, or made any effort at grandparenting duties. Why step up now and focus the spotlight on an incident that happened forty-three years ago? Their reasoning and overdue concern was absurd. Only I, and Ingrid, should determine Herman's legacy. We'd lived the crisis too.

I wanted to ask Joe about Vic, but pride laced with remorse wouldn't allow me. Joe had said he was furious. Who could blame him? I doubted Vic would ever trust me again. "Have you talked to Winston Little?"

Joe nodded. "He's eager to do battle. That's an outstanding animal shelter and it means a lot to the town. Winston appreciates what Ingrid and Herman have done for Parnass."

"The shelter is nice, but I don't want a statue if people resent it. I couldn't stand someone defacing it in some way."

"Don't worry about that. Feelings are running high right now, but once a consensus is reached, they'll settle down. They always do."

He was trying to make me feel better, but emotions ran deep when people chose up sides. This could cause a permanent split in the community, and that was the last thing I wanted.

"Will Vic talk to me?" I had to know; the uncertainty was eating me alive.

Joe's tone turned evasive. "Well, he was talking when you left town, wasn't he? Suppose he still is. We haven't discussed the matter."

Men. Women would have talked about nothing else. "Looking back, I realize how foolish I was, but it seemed like nothing ever went right for me. Vic was so happy with Julie, I couldn't bear to tell him my problems."

"He would have understood if you'd given him a chance."

"I know that, but I was young and wounded. Noel just walked out, leaving me with nothing." I stopped, overcome by it all.

Joe bent and patted my hand. "You've had a rough time, haven't you?"

I sniffled, reaching for a tissue. "I had a hellish time. I worked long hours; we went without food and proper clothing at times because Noel was late with child support. I was lonely and scared; Sara missed her daddy. Looking back, I see now that God got me through it. I can see his mercy and grace, running like a scarlet thread through every uncertain moment. When I needed him, he was there, just like you always said he'd be."

His gaze searched me. "So, are you going to fight for the statue?"

"I guess you find that surprising."

He shook his head. "I know the real Marlene. You only remember the bad times, and that's human nature, but you shared good times with Herman too. I always knew you loved him. You just had to grow up enough to realize it."

"I must have been a slow grower."

He grinned and reached for a pint jar of green granules. "You need some of my new plant food. Mixed it up myself this morning."

"What's in it?" I backed slightly away from the noxious-looking stuff.

"Secret recipe—guaranteed to make your plants bust into bloom overnight."

"Have you tried it yet?"

"Poured some on Gladys Burwell's petunias. Didn't tell her about it, though. Want to surprise her."

Smart man. I'd driven past Gladys's house on my way here, and her petunias looked sort of whacked out. If Joe had any sense, he'd hide that jar of fertilizer before Gladys planted him.

I let myself into Ingrid's hallway. "Aunt Ingrid?" The house was silent; Ingrid's crocheting lay on the sofa arm.

Mrs. Henkins, the kind soul who'd been staying with Ingrid, appeared in the kitchen doorway, suitcase in hand. "Thank goodness you're back." She brushed past me on her way out.

"Wait, I'll get you a check—"

"Send it through the mail." The door slammed, and I whirled and lifted the curtain to watch the elderly lady high-stepping it down the drive. I stared after her, thunderstruck. Where would I find anyone to replace her? Aunt Ingrid was too well known in this town.

Sighing, I turned back when the lady in question rolled into the living room.

She glanced at me, her features impassive. "'Bout time you got home."

"Have you given Mrs. Henkins a hard time?" Do birds sleep on guy wires? The smell of black burning rubber came to me as the woman peeled out of the drive.

"*She* gave *me* a hard time."

I set my bag down on the floor. "Aunt Ingrid." Might as well continue the day on its downward spiral. "I have something to tell you."

She interrupted. "Guess you know that your birth mother's folks have filed a legal paper. They say we can't put up Herman's statue."

She wasn't listening.

"People say a lot of things—some not always true."

"Lot of ugly stuff in the newspaper editorial columns. I'll fight them on this."

The problems surrounding my aunt were endless. Whatever made me think I could solve them? "What's our next step?"

"R J didn't say. Just said to be at tonight's town council meeting. The Parishes will be there with their attorney."

At least R J was still with us. I stared at the vacant fireplace, void of ashes, and then said something I never thought I'd say. "We'll fight them on this."

Her brows lifted.

"You and me. Herman built the shelter, and he should be recognized for his charitable contribution."

Her look was anything but convinced. "You're on my side?"

"We're family." My kin may be nuttier than a Payday candy bar, but they were *my* nuts and nobody was going to run over them, the Parishes included.

"What did you want to tell me?"

Time to fess up. "Noel is dead. He left me when Sara was a toddler. I never told you because I thought you'd tell me it was my own fault for running away with him when I was young. For leaving Vic ..."

She shrugged. "Good. Never cared for Noel anyway. Any man who refused to bring his family around to meet kin wasn't worth a lick of salt. Don't think we didn't notice that he never came to visit with you—not that you came that much, but his absence was duly noted." She whirled to wheel off. "Fix me a cup of soup. Old Lady Henkins can't boil a decent cup of water."

My tensions deflated. I'd had my explanations ready, braced for her questions, and now this. Poof. Nothing. Yet what did I expect from a woman who had never expressed affection. I swear, that woman ...

Wait a minute.

I frowned. I never knew she didn't like Noel.

That evening I was in Beth's bathroom touching up my makeup. I needed to eat something, but it'd been such a hectic day and I'd grabbed periodic snacks. My blood sugar wouldn't let me get by with junk-food surfing. I'd have to get something balanced after the town council meeting. I could not continue neglecting myself this way; I had to follow doctor's orders. The hairs on my neck stood up as my eyes moved to the bathroom window where Aunt Ingrid's curious features appeared against the pane, her hands cupped on both sides of her eyes, peering through the glass.

Why couldn't the woman just ring the doorbell like any normal visitor?

I moved the curtain aside and lifted the window. "Yes?"

"How soon will you be ready?"

"Five minutes. Do you need help?" I leaned over the sill to see how she'd managed to reach the window. She'd wheeled flush to the house, and now she balanced her toes on the chair's metal steps to see inside. Her window peeping technique was an accident waiting to happen.

"Sit down!" I fired the request out like a drill sergeant's command.

Ingrid sat.

First time she'd ever listened to me. I yanked the curtain shut, ran a little gloss over my lipstick, and then turned off the bathroom light. By the time I locked the front door Ingrid was waiting beside the car.

I paused, keys in hand. "How did you get out of your house?" There was no handicap ramp. She had to roll down concrete steps. Could she do that?

She sniffed. "A body has to devise ways when she's on her own."

Theatrics. Still I was skeptic. Just how *did s*he devise a way to get the wheelchair and herself down those steps? Was it possible my theatrical aunt could walk when she wanted?

"I was on my way to get you." I unlocked the rental car, then turned and helped her out of the chair and into the passenger seat. By the time I'd stowed the chair in the trunk, Ingrid had managed to snap her seatbelt into place and tie the rain bonnet around her head. There wasn't a cloud in the sky, but she'd be prepared if a monsoon hit Parnass Springs.

"Drive slow. We're not going to the circus."

"Yes, Aunt Ingrid." If I sped, it wouldn't be because I anticipated a fun evening. The town meeting would be anything but fun. My thoughts turned to the coming fracas.

Vic would be there tonight. How would I face him?

Simple. I'd look him straight in the eye and confess that all these years I'd been lying up a storm. Something he knew—had known for a long time and never mentioned. That made it even worse. He'd stood back and watched me make a complete fool of myself.

Suddenly every reason I'd ever manufactured for my deception wouldn't fly.

Fine. So I'd wait and let him confront me about my lie.

That's it. I'd go along as if nothing had happened—never mention Noel or my private life unless he brought up the subject. Once I got this statue thing settled, I could go back to Glen Ellyn and conduct Aunt Beth's and Aunt Ingrid's business from there. I'd avoid his phone calls—never have to subject myself to the humiliation.

In time I'd convince Ingrid to drop thoughts of an inane lawsuit against Prue, and hopefully persuade her and Prue Levitt Moss that a foot was not worth wasting a fortune on. While I was at it, I'd sway Ingrid into a homebound caregiver service. And my life would fall into a nice, serene pattern.

Are you there, God? I'm going to need a lot of help on this.

Even as I sent the prayer heavenward, a sense of hopelessness swept over me. My solution wasn't the best or most Christlike way to handle my problems, but I didn't want to face Vic—*couldn't* face him. Yet even I knew that was improbable. One way or the other we'd talk about it. And most likely, civil tones would be lacking.

I backed out and drove off, anticipating a circus.

Parnass Springs City Hall seated fifty people, give or take a few metal folding chairs. The hot, airless community room connected to the police station, and tonight every light in the room blazed as citizens piled in for the meeting. A long line of windows faced the north; someone had opened a couple to allow a sultry breeze to clear a perpetual musty odor. Even with the windows opened, the room's air turned stale quickly. I held my breath, hoping my allergies wouldn't kick in. The seats were filling up fast.

I pushed Ingrid to the front row and made her comfortable before I took the folding chair beside her. A few people paused to say hello, names and faces I vaguely recalled. Most were respectful toward Aunt Ingrid, but curious eyes turned on me, Herman's daughter. Probably wondering how I'd turned out. Not too good, truth be told, but I was a work in progress.

With God's help, I was going to tell the truth, the whole truth, and nothing but the truth, whatever the consequences.

As the room continued to fill, I turned in my chair to look behind me, amazed that so many would have an opinion about Herman. He was always around, the editorials claimed. In the way, some accused, while others said he was courteous and helpful—a familiar theme. I wouldn't have thought most in attendance would have cared one way or the other about the town impaired. That they did, surprised me.

My eyes skimmed the room and paused on an older couple just entering. My gaze focused on the woman's hand, long fingers with salmon-colored nail polish. The diamond on her left hand was understated but classic. Silver-white hair cut in a fashionable bob made her age impossible to judge, but I pegged her somewhere between her late seventies and the grave. The impeccably dressed man gently ushered her into a seat and then sat beside her.

For a moment our eyes touched, and then his moved away. I knew intuitively that he was my grandfather. My grandmother leaned over and whispered something in his ear and he nodded. Did they recognize me? Had they ever once seen me—maybe a picture? Maybe driving by Aunt Beth's house hoping to glimpse their grandchild, a child with their blood running through her veins?

How cold and disconnected were these people? My emotions ran amok. I'd never had grandparents. As a child I would lie in bed at night and pretend that I did; that Grams or Pops (that's what I'd named them) would pick me up after school and I'd go to their house and eat cookies and play ball in the backyard with Pops. I'd even told my closest friends that Grams had knitted me colorful scarves and warm mittens for cold winter days. My friends called me nuts.

You don't have a Grams and Pops! You got stupid Herman!

Yes, just stupid me and stupid Herman. These people hadn't accepted him then, and I didn't accept them now.

I turned in my seat, focusing on the podium, pushing reminiscences aside.

"What time is it?" Ingrid fanned a hankie. "The room's hotter than a smoking pistol." A breeze blew through the open window, but not strong enough to overcome the body heat of the crowd. We were packed elbow to elbow. If it got any hotter, we'd be dropping like flies.

I glanced at my Timex. "A few minutes before seven."

Vic walked in the side door with Joe and a second man. I hastily averted my eyes, pretending to search for something in my purse. When I looked up, the acting mayor was standing over me. So much for deception. I managed a weak grin. "Hi."

"Is Sara okay?" His tone was neutral, but that was Vic. He wouldn't cause a scene here.

"False alarm."

His eyes touched mine briefly.

"I thought you might have called and let me know."

"About Sara?"

"About leaving."

"I'm . . . sorry. Would you have wanted to know?"

She didn't think so.

He turned and continued to the front of the room.

I must have looked confused because Joe reached down and took my hand. "Good to have you back, Marlene." We chatted a few minutes about the meeting topic before Vic called the hall to order.

The acting mayor glanced at his watch. "Let's settle down and get started."

I still wasn't sure I was ready for this.

The crowd quieted when Vic stepped to the podium. Standing in front of the group, he absently searched his shirt pocket, then pulled out a pair of glasses and put them on. I'd never seen him in glasses. The poignant aging process touched me.

"Okay, now. We're gathered tonight to hear concerns about the animal shelter's proposed motion to erect a public statue in honor of the shelter's benefactor, Herman Moss. I believe R J Rexall will speak for the Moss family, and . . ." he peered at his notes, "James White will speak on behalf of Mr. and Mrs. Parish and their daughter, Lexis."

Lexis. Lexy Parish. My birth mother.

"Following R J and James, Ben Staid will represent the town's position. I'll open the floor for comments following the attorney's presentations. Gentlemen, please keep your comments brief and to the point."

Ingrid fanned harder, her color heightened in the warm room. I pressed closer. "Do you need a glass of water?"

"I'm fine."

She didn't look fine, but I knew better than to argue with her. Any hint that she needed to leave would bring out the mule in her nature.

James began on behalf of the Parish family; his argument was succinct and concise. "The Parish family adamantly objects to a statue of Herman Moss. The public display would dredge up a painful past, one best left alone, regarding their daughter. Lexy Parish is still living, and though she will spend the remainder of her life in an assisted care health facility, Grayson and Ann Parish feel that their daughter, Lexis, is unable to defend herself. As her court-appointed guardians, the Parishes are acting in their daughter's behalf on this matter."

I fixed my gaze on a vase of cut flowers, conscious of curious looks. Most in attendance knew the Parish family had ignored my existence. How dare they put me in this position. Ingrid, of course, ignored everyone, her face an inscrutable mask. I tried to match her aplomb, knowing I failed miserably.

R J stood up. "The Parnass family has been a pillar stone of this community. Many families sitting here tonight have been touched by Ronald Parnass and his generosity. He founded Parnass Springs. He built the covered bridge that allowed faster, safer passage of supplies, supplies our ancestors sorely needed.

"Many of us knew Herman and his peculiar peccadilloes. Nevertheless, the man's eccentricities were understandable." He paused, squinting up at the rapt audience. "But he wasn't understandable to all. That's why we're gathered here tonight, to sort through any objections and to try to reach an amiable solution. A statue is stone; granite, marble, whatever. It isn't town doctrine. It's one simple way of remembering someone for a noteworthy act. So then, why are we concerned about one clump of marble? Herman Moss left a legacy; because of this man, homeless animals—creatures that have no spokesman other than us—have a home. They have a clean bed, fresh water, excellent medical care, a kind word." He paused, adjusting his glasses. "How many of us would not race to put up a statue to the person who, when we needed it most, offered a kind word? Excellent medical care. A clean bed. Does it matter if the person who did this didn't go to Stanford or couldn't define the theory of gravity?"

He glanced up, fixing his eyes on the audience. "Who among us is worthy of marble? Or granite? Herman Moss did a notable act; it is the Parnass family's contention that he be honored with a statue on the animal shelter lawn. Thank you."

I fished in my purse for a tissue to fan my face. Perspiration ran down my neck as R J took his seat.

Ben stood up. He studied a yellow legal pad, and then cleared his throat. "I always hesitate to involve myself in cases like these. I knew Herman—knew him well. He was a good soul. He gave us a glimpse of heaven when those brown, trusting, doelike eyes pierced our being.

"Herman was simpleminded. He often did and said things that made us shake our heads or run in the house and slam the door and thank God we hadn't been given his care. We need to consider this as we realize that Parnass Springs is increasingly growing into a tourist site."

He flipped a page and his eyes scanned the information. "Last year alone we had over eighteen thousand visitors to view the bridge. Strangers find our town 'quaint' and 'different,' and we'd like to keep that image. Now many will say, 'Who would know Herman was simple?' A statue won't proclaim the man's mentality, and our answer is 'That's true.' Those opposing the memorial will argue that the statue should enhance and personify the town. Herman's bigheartedness is noteworthy—but to the extent of a statue? Some argue not. Who can forget the scandal between Herman and Lexy—two mentally challenged teens? Who among us needs to be reminded of that time in our town's life that brought chaos and division?

"The town suggests that a small plaque on the side of the building is adequate. Herman, though loved by many, doesn't imbue the spirit of Parnass Springs and its people ..."

I glanced at Ingrid. Ben's summation had to be hard for her to hear. We'd experienced the town's perspective first-hand, but to hear it openly stated, hurt. Though Ben didn't or wouldn't state it, the point was clear: Was there one here who wanted a statue of the town's simpleton on the shelter lawn?

My face burned as Ben continued. If I'd known how humiliating this was going to be, Ingrid couldn't have dragged me here with a team of wild horses. I reached for my aunt's hand when the summaries ended and Vic opened the floor for comments. I had a hunch this wasn't going to be easy on either family.

One by one, those for Herman stood up. I was amazed at how many there were. More people had liked him than I'd expected. How had I missed the love these people had for my father? I'd been too blinded by my own embarrassment to see the way he'd been accepted. Not a comfortable assessment of myself. I wiped moisture from my eyes.

Jack, the local grocery store owner stood. "Herman was a good man. He'd come by the store and sweep up for me nearly every day and wouldn't take a penny for his work."

Hank owned the cleaners. "Herman was a little boy; never meant anyone an ounce of harm. He used to come by the shop and sort hangers for me. Tie them in neat bundles and store them in the back room. Good fella, that Herman. He loved cherry popsicles."

"Good, yes, but always underfoot. I had to run him off my porch twice a day." This came from Virginia at the flower shop. "One afternoon he picked every pansy in my front bed and brought them to me in a mayonnaise jar. I knew it was a gift, but people remember Herman for what he was: not all there."

Virginia glanced at Ingrid, then away. "Ingrid tried to make him fit in, but he … just didn't. Then the outrageous scandal. I'm sorry, Marlene and Ingrid. You're good folk and you can't help what the Good Lord trusted you to raise, but the indignity was hard to live down. What other folks said hurt. We do care for our own, and we don't let the likes of Herman run loose to be a threat to our young daughters. Do we want a reminder of those terrible accusations, that Herman molested this young innocent child, every time we drive past the animal shelter? I agree with the Parish family. Let sleeping dogs lie." She sat down.

A few days ago, I'd have cringed at her words. *Molested.* What an ugly term—yet wasn't that the common thought, even in my mind? Or it used to be.

Now the objectors just made me angry.

Virginia didn't know it, but she had just heightened my determination to fight. Herman had not run the streets or threatened young girls.

Ingrid shifted in her chair, her expression tight as a coiled snake. I patted her arm. "Do you want to leave?"

"No." Her features set like cement.

Amazingly, I agreed with her.

Vic spoke up once in Herman's defense, but other than the brief remark, the Brewster men kept silent. Maybe Vic felt that as mayor, he shouldn't take sides, but I knew I could use his support. Both men wore a solemn demeanor. Of course, neither Joe nor Vic would fight for me now. I'd lost the right to their defense. The acting mayor took notes, but not sides, while others stood and talked, some for fifteen minutes to make a point either for Herman or against him. My nerves were raw. Perspiration stood on Ingrid's upper lip, and twice I saw her wipe tears.

By the time Vic closed the floor I was choked with anger and resentment. It took all my willpower to keep from standing up and defending my father. These people hadn't known him. They thought they had, but only Ingrid and I had really known the man with the child's mind. He'd been an integral part of our lives. And yes, more people than I'd expected had defended him and I was grateful for them, but the opposition stung—more than I had expected.

The only thing agreed upon in the three-hour meeting was the right to disagree. By the time Vic dismissed the meeting, it was well after ten o'clock, and Aunt Ingrid and I had been put through a handwringer.

There were a few well wishes as I pushed Ingrid's chair to the back of the room. Some reached out to pat her shoulder or take her hand. Others looked ashamed, or defiant, not meeting our eyes. I skimmed them with contempt.

Winston Little approached. "Evening, Marlene. Ingrid. You folks doing all right?"

Aunt Ingrid took his hand. "It's always good to know who your friends are." She didn't bother to lower her voice, and I was proud of her. My family may be different, eccentric, but they didn't back down. Neither would I.

The hall buzzed with conversation; some weren't content to sleep on the controversy, to rethink their opinions. I spotted Vic threading his way toward me, and I picked up speed, determined to avoid him at all costs. At least for tonight. I'd had enough for one day. Ingrid's chair hit a bump and stopped. I tried to shove the wheel over the obstacle and couldn't. I shoved harder. The wheel thumped and Ingrid groaned. "Marlene!"

"Sorry, Aunt Ingrid." Vic was closing in fast; I had to get out of here. I shoved hard, and the chair cleared a lady's handbag that had fallen into the aisle and shot forward, taking me with it. I concentrated on steering through the throng gathered inside the doorway.

"Where's the fire?" Ingrid demanded.

"No fire. I just want to get home." She didn't have any idea how badly I wanted to get out of this place.

Between the rows of chairs and the prospect of escape, I suddenly slackened my retreat. Grayson and Ann Parish had reached the door at the same time. The older couple stood transfixed, their eyes set on me. For the longest moment of my life, we stared at each other. Ingrid, for once, kept quiet.

I didn't know how to break the silence. The words weren't there. Would they turn their backs on me?

"Marlene?" Grayson broke the awkward stillness.

"Yes. Mr. and Mrs. Parish?" Pops and Grams; they looked exactly like the people in my dreams.

His eyes softened. "Yes."

What did one say to grandparents they'd never met, barely knew existed? The man standing before me personified my childhood dreams; distinguished, grandfatherly, with benevolent blue eyes. Eyes that now assessed me. I'd have bet those eyes twinkled on Christmas morning and birthdays. Hadn't he ever wanted to see me? What kept them away? Pride? Anger? Or other all-too-human emotions that constrained our lives.

For the life of me I couldn't look away. I drank in the sight of Pops, tucked away the memory of my grandpa in a safe place, a place where not one single soul could rob me of the joy of the moment. Ann hovered in the background, her timeless features unreadable.

Grayson extended a hand, large, soft to the touch. "You're a lovely young woman." He turned and drew his wife to his side. She reached out, and I took her hand. It was thin. Frail. I sensed hesitancy, an almost imperceptible tremble. She was nervous. So was I.

"Ann. It's nice to meet you."

"Yes … the same." She glanced at her husband, then back at me. "You have Lexy's eyes. So warm and liquid."

The observation stunned me into silence. I drew a sharp breath. "This is my Aunt Ingrid. I'm sure you've met." Yes, they'd met. How inane of me.

Impersonal handshakes followed the introduction. History colored the exchange, making the moment even more self-conscious. I was grateful Ingrid didn't speak. I didn't want to guess what she'd have said.

Vic reached me and intervened. "Mr. and Mrs. Parish. How good to see you."

"Dr. Brewster."

Grayson Parish had impeccable manners. The hall behind us had grown silent, everyone engrossed in the drama that was taking place before their eyes.

The acting mayor relieved me of the wheelchair. "If you'll excuse us?"

With a courteous nod, Grayson stepped aside. As quickly as they had begun, the long overdue introductions were over. The jackhammer in my heart slowed to a more normal pace. I took a deep breath, tamping down emotions best expressed in private.

"That had to be uncomfortable." Vic pushed Ingrid to the parking lot and I trailed behind.

"Those were my grandparents, Vic." It seemed important he understand that. *Grandparents.* I held the word in my heart. After all these years, I had finally met them.

"I know. Are you okay?"

"I don't think so." Turning, I glanced over my shoulder and caught one last glimpse of the Parishes walking through the parking lot.

I had my mother's eyes.

All sorts of emotions filled me: elation, resentful curiosity, longing, fear. Who were these people who looked so ordinary, so pleasant? Nice people didn't make an innocent child pay for others' mistakes.

The past flooded back. They hadn't wanted me. Still didn't. I was something they'd tried to ignore, to live down. Beth and Ingrid had raised me. They were my family.

"Want an ice cream?" Vic's inquiry pulled me back.

Suddenly I was drained, I'd emotionally hit rock bottom. All I wanted to do was go home, go to bed, and sleep for days.

"We have ice cream in the freezer." Ingrid sniffed. "No use paying for something we have."

Good old practical Ingrid. Yet she'd saved me from facing Vic—from what likely would have been an ordeal. On the whole, I'd had enough tribulation today. Enough for a lifetime.

"We'll pass on the ice cream."

He didn't argue; I didn't expect him to. Some things didn't need an explanation.

Ten

Vic helped me load Ingrid into the car. We each avoided meeting the other's eyes. Tension hung between us. The door closed behind him, and Ingrid rubbed her hands together. "Quite a meeting."

"Too loud." And partisan. I'd never expected it to be so divisive.

"The Parish family hates Herman."

That was natural, but they didn't know him. I wasn't excusing his actions; only his inability to reason like an adult. "Didn't they ever ask to meet me?"

"It was a hard time for everyone, Marlene. They had their daughter to think about. No one blamed them for not wanting to take on the additional burden of raising a child."

"But you and Beth took it on."

Ingrid stared out the window, passing car lights illuminating her features. "I would have taken you in a second, but Beth and I knew it was better that I raise Herman and she raise you, especially under the circumstances."

"Did the Parishes object?"

"At first they suggested abortion, but later they admitted they couldn't take a life. I made it plain that Beth and I would raise you; we would absolve them of all responsibility."

"They could have put me up for adoption." That was one viable solution. So many couples longed for children when they couldn't have their own. It had never occurred to me how much I owed Beth and Ingrid, which made my neglect all the more odious. "Did they consider that avenue?"

"Oh, it was mentioned, but R J told them we'd fight, and they gave in, as long as we promised to take you."

"And they never wanted to see me?"

"No. You belonged to Herman."

"I belonged to Lexy too."

"They didn't see it that way." She rubbed her forehead. "Maybe it was partly our fault. We didn't encourage them to come around. There were too many hard feelings."

My birth. Not exactly a time to break out the gold, frankincense, and myrrh.

Ingrid patted my hand. "None of this was your fault, Marlene. It was an unfortunate situation. We did the best we could."

I leaned and kissed her cheek. "I'm just beginning to realize how much you and Beth did for me. I've not done a good job of showing my appreciation."

She frowned. "No need to get mushy."

No, Ingrid wouldn't get mushy. I'd never acknowledged it before, but we were more alike than I'd suspected. I noticed her eyes were shiny with tears. I'd bet mine were too.

I settled her for the night and returned to Beth's house, which was beginning to feel more familiar. Even the rocks in the living room didn't bother me anymore. I fixed a cup of tea and carried it out to the porch swing, my nightly ritual now. Lights burned in the windows of Vic's cottage. I pushed the swing with my toe, the rusty chains squeaking with each forward motion.

Vic.

He'd been pleasant tonight, but distant. A barrier stood between us. Or maybe it was always there and I hadn't noticed.

I needed to talk to him, but what could I say? I stared at the lighted windows. Was he thinking of me tonight? Were his thoughts friendly? I retreated to my earlier decision: I'd wait and let him make the first move.

My cell phone rang. Sara.

"Mom? Did you make it back okay?"

I blinked. When had my daughter ever started her conversations by asking about me? "Just fine. Why?"

"I just wondered. How are you—you're okay, aren't you?"

"Fine, sweetie. Has something happened?" Not the baby ... *Please Lord, not the baby.*

"No, I love you, you know. A lot."

She clicked off after a few minutes of chatting, leaving me to stare at the phone in disbelief. Was that my daughter or an imposter? I suddenly found a wry grin forming. I'd lost control and struck her. Remembering the incident, shame filled me. It wouldn't happen again, and I needed to apologize to her.

Waiting for a phone to ring was like waiting for water to boil. You couldn't hurry it. Tuesday morning, the instrument remained silent. It wasn't like Vic to let something like my colossal deception pass without comment. He'd known I'd been lying for a couple of months. Why was he letting me stew in my own juices? To torture me?

Because he no longer gives a rat's nest.

That had to be it. He didn't care enough to challenge my deception. My perceived insight into his psyche hurt, yet I knew he had every right to ignore me. We'd had the world by the tail during our youth, but I'd destroyed our relationship when I took my life, and his, into my own hands.

How could I have ruined something so beautiful?

Water over the dam, Aunt Ingrid would say, and she would be right.

I pushed the kitchen curtain aside and stared out at the rainy day. Widening puddles stood in Ingrid's drive; street gutters overflowed with heavy runoff. Even Sara was acting weird.

"How are you mom?" I still couldn't get it out of my head.

I let the curtain drop into place. I'd come over to see what Ingrid was doing and found her napping and the house a dank tomb. I wandered around, then decided to make a peach pie for dinner. Peach was Ingrid's favorite. I wasn't exactly Martha Stewart in the kitchen, but I could bake a decent dessert.

Flipping on the basement light, I descended the narrow steps. I'd always hated coming down here when I was a kid. Ingrid piled everything she'd accumulated the last forty years in the cellar. The place needed a good cleaning.

I located the shelf of canned peaches and started back up the stairs, pausing on the first rung. My eyes traveled the musty-smelling room—old bicycles, trunks, boxes upon stacked boxes. Eugene's workbench still sat in the corner, tools in place.

Poor Uncle Eugene. I remembered him as an odd but lovable sort. We'd play dodgeball in the driveway and occasionally

I'd help with one of his carpentry projects. One Christmas we made thirty wren houses and gave them to everyone we knew. I'd bet if I looked closely, I'd still see some of those bird houses in neighbors' trees.

Ingrid always badgered him, demanding that he come to dinner, cut the grass, fill the bird feeders, weed the flower bed, oil the lawn mower, paint the shutters, fix the roof.

I knew she loved him, but Ingrid had always been Ingrid, determined to be in charge. Eugene hadn't seemed to mind... Or was that the reason for his desperate search for acceptance, why he seized upon so many women? Why he'd run off with Prue? She didn't seem any more agreeable than the wife he'd already had. Had Ingrid's constant list of chores been a way to keep her wandering husband at home, where she could keep an eye on him? I'd been too young to understand back then, and time had dulled my perception of reality.

I recalled the way he'd look at me, eyes twinkling. "Want to go get a soda pop?"

Off we'd go, with Ingrid's voice bellowing from the open window. "Eugene! The car is filthy. And I can't see a thing out of these windows." Uncle Eugene needed two extra hands and one less prison guard.

I set the jar of peaches on the step and headed back down, eyeing one large camelback trunk I'd never noticed before. What secrets did Ingrid store in that chest?

Locating the latch, I lifted the heavy lid with an air of anticipation. Junk. I picked up stacks of moldy old clothing and set them aside. Discarded items my frugal aunt couldn't bring herself to throw away. My eye caught the corner of a cigar box, but I continued to dig deeper through old clothing, surprised at the items Ingrid had kept.

I rocked back on my heels. Beth and Ingrid had money, lots of it. They'd inherited it from their parents and handled the money judiciously. If rumor was true, the two women had more than quadrupled their funds over the years through investments and shrewd real estate transactions. They never spoke of their wealth, and if I asked, I was told it was none of my beeswax.

That's why I hadn't gone to them during the troubling years of Sara's childhood. I knew they would refuse to help, citing my impulsive marriage. I could hear Ingrid now: "Don't come to me with your problems. You made your bed, now sleep in it."

Aunt Beth would have said, "I told you so."

I wasn't there when Aunt Beth's will was read. I knew her holdings were tied to Ingrid's and nothing would be settled until Ingrid passed or my aunt agreed to sell off mutually owned property and allow me to settle Beth's estate promptly. She'd held out for two years, and I still didn't know why she'd suddenly grown willing to comply. The gesture was unlike her, but maybe, with Beth gone, she realized that years were passing and she wouldn't live forever.

Ingrid had been grasping, stingy, and reluctant to spend more than she needed for her own use. Beth had been the town bag lady, scuffling along in worn-out shoes, carrying her grubby tote bag. She'd been a fixture at local garage sales, rooting out the free boxes, bringing the most forlorn items home with her, whether she had a need for them or not. I'd sorted through piles of discarded bits of junk in the last weeks, all to be hauled away.

I folded the clothing and placed the items back into the trunk, willing to leave them for another day. I was about to close the lid when the cigar box caught my eye again. Digging deeper, I pulled the box from the heap. Worn, time faded. Someone had taken a crayon and drawn what looked to be a fire truck with a large bell on the side. I studied the childish rendering, my gaze shifting to the bold lettering.

HeRRmaN

Herman's earthly treasures.

Was it right of me to invade my father's private world? Would the intrusion be unfair, even callous, considering Herman's mental state?

Or was I entitled to know what went on in his mind, what he valued most here on earth. I pushed aside a stack of magazines and sat down on a rickety wooden chair. After a moment, I carefully opened the box. Inside, Herman's world quickly materialized: a shiny agate marble; a soiled and tattered piece of twine—one that undoubtedly had gone wherever Herman had traveled. I held up a yellow hair ribbon that once belonged to me. Herman brought it to me the day I started kindergarten. I remember Aunt Beth questioning him about how he'd acquired the trinket and he said he'd found it. Turned out he'd taken it from a girl at Sunday school. When asked why, he'd said, "It would look prettier on Marly."

An eraser.

A red Duncan yo-yo.

A piece of tablet paper with a large red heart with the initials, H. L.

A baby tooth in a baggie marked *Marly.* Various pictures of me: blowing out birthday candles, tumbling with kittens. A faded picture of Butchie standing beside the large mimosa tree in Aunt Beth's front yard.

A lacy white handkerchief with "Lexy" embroidered in pink thread. *Lexy.* My mother. I held the handkerchief, my mind racing with intriguing thoughts. Had Herman had a boyish crush on Lexy? Had that fascination gotten out of hand?

In the bottom of the box I found a ring. Cheap, Cracker-Jack quality.

Sighing, I closed the lid on the box, thinking how sad it was to hold a man's entire life in my hand, yet the items here represented what God intended men to be: childlike, trusting. Loving.

Sitting there, I suddenly realized that man, when given a full IQ and educated, was sometimes more mentally challenged than Herman had been. I understood why I was so embarrassed by Herman's attempts at fatherhood—my reaction was typical enough. Even my resentment wasn't all that mysterious. I was fallible. I had hurt because Herman wasn't like everyone else.

What I couldn't explain then, but knew better now, was my love for this child-man, this man who was more like a puppy—a defenseless puppy—than a parent. Had I even once shown him compassion? Unconditional love? I couldn't recall a single instance. He hadn't required hugs and kisses; he was happiest when we played ball or roller-skated, most content when Butchie and I went to the park with him.

My whole life had been avoidance—avoidance of Herman, avoidance of difficult adult choices, like childbearing and divorce.

Avoidance of Vic.

Even after I'd fled Parnass Springs, married Noel, and had Sara, I'd still continued to run, to evade God's plans for my life. I should have known my rebellion would bring upheaval upon upheaval. I hadn't known then what God wanted of me, I'd second-guessed him, and he'd allowed me to have my way. He gave free choice, didn't he? But my choices had been far from his. And now I, and others, were paying the price.

It was high time to rethink my life. I closed the trunk and took the cigar box with me. I couldn't let it go.

It was all I had left of my father.

Rain drops spattered the windshield as I drove into the cemetery. Was there a more depressing place on earth than a cemetery on a cool rainy afternoon? I got out of the car and zipped up my slicker, then hiked across soggy ground. A north wind cut through the thin vinyl. Aunt Beth would call this weather Blackberry Winter—one of the last cool spells before warm weather came to stay. Across the fields and fencerows, blackberries would be in bloom, their white blossoms hinting of the dark, juicy fruit to come.

Herman's headstone lay there, bleak, small, and unimportant. I stood in front of the grave, uncertain where to start. Confession would be as good as anything.

Clearing my throat, I began. "I'm sorry, Herman. I'm here to ask for your forgiveness. For all the times I made fun of you so I could be one of the kids, for all the times I embarrassed and hurt you. I showed disrespect, when in my heart I loved you—but I never told you so."

I fought back tears. "There were so many things I didn't tell you, Dad. Things like I got married. My husband walked out on me and left me with a two-year-old child, Sara. He was a bum, but a bum with a silver tongue and a brilliant mind. Sara's your grandchild. You met her once when I came home to see Aunt Beth after one of her strokes. Of course you didn't know she was your grandchild. I don't think I said over two words to you during that short visit. I'm sorry; I'm so sorry for all the times I failed you. I was a different person then—young and self-centered. Thought-I-knew-it-all Marlene. But I was the one with problems.

"Like Uncle Eugene used to say, I couldn't see the forest for the trees. Well, it took awhile, but I see those trees, Dad." It was getting harder to hold back the emotion. "I know I'm not the only person with problems, and whatever they are, I can't outrun them. Believe me, I've tried and failed. I have to face them head-on and that's not easy.

"You never knew—or maybe you did know about Vic and me. I loved him." I hugged myself. "I loved him so much it hurt, but I knew I couldn't give him children. I couldn't or wouldn't because I was scared. Scared that my child would be like you, Dad. Now I realize there are worse things than having a childish mind, like having an adult mind but a child's behavior. That's me, Dad. Adult-challenged. I've tried to solve my problems on my own and made a big mess of my life. I've finally decided I can choose to be happy or I can choose to be a martyr. I can choose to let others validate my happiness, or I can make my own."

I looked up at the gray sky. "I'm thinking on this cool, chilly spring day that I'm going to choose to be happy—to choose to be responsible for my actions and not lay blame to them. I think, Dad, that maybe I'm starting to grow up."

Tears finally coursed down my cheeks as I dropped to my knees beside his grave, cleansed, like the Sunday morning I'd been baptized, dipped in water made whole by the grace of God. Could Herman hear me? Would he ever know that the daughter he loved, loved him back?

I think he did. If not back then, he certainly knew now.

On the walk back to the car I passed the remainder of the family plots. I spotted Eugene's foot's grave. In the past, the story had meant nothing to me but a rather bizarre tale from an even more bizarre family. Suddenly I knew he could use a word of encouragement too. Poor Uncle Eugene's remains were being fought over like two hens squawking over the same kernel of corn.

What would he think of this disgraceful fight for his foot? Not much, I'd guess. The Eugene I'd known wouldn't have approved of spending good money on trivial pursuits. Eugene had been a giver, not only of his time to women—all women—but deep inside the man's perfidious soul, goodness lurked.

I recalled when a tornado had once cut a large swath through the county. Eugene had barely slept for days as he went about helping the victims restore order to their lives. I'd watched him stack cases of bottled water and canned goods in the trunk of his old Chevy. Then he invited me to drive the storm-ravaged neighborhoods and distribute the gifts. The distribution made an impression. And since the drive ended in an ice-cream cone for me, I enjoyed the time I spent with him immensely.

"Thanks, Eugene." I brushed my hand across his marker.

On the way home I stopped by the market for fresh ground sirloin. Ingrid liked meat loaf. Adding mashed potatoes, green beans, and peach pie would make my curmudgeon aunt all smiles this evening. I longed to ask Joe to dinner, but I wouldn't, not without Vic. And I wasn't going to invite trouble.

Yes, it was my place to go to him, but I hadn't matured quite that much.

As plans often are, mine were altered when I ran into Joe at the market. He was leaving as I was walking in. He paused, his eyes skimming my muddy clothes and rain slicker. "You been pig wrestling?"

"Nope. Conscience wrestling." I grinned. "Funny, but I was just thinking about you."

"You were?" He winked. "Women. I attract them like flies to watermelon rind."

"Before your head swells and your hat doesn't fit anymore, I hasten to tell you that my thoughts have no romantic intonation."

"None?"

"Not even a tiny bit. They're more gluttonous in nature."

"Dinner!"

"Meat loaf. Ingrid's house. Five-thirty." I might as well have said he'd won the lottery.

"You're on." He smacked my hand in a playful high five. "Can I bring anything?"

"Can you cook?"

"Can't fry a decent egg."

"Then please attend with an empty hand or dish."

The unspoken words hung between us: what about Vic? Not including Vic in the invitation was equivalent to not brushing my teeth in the morning. In the past he hadn't needed an invitation, but Joe must have known the silent war waging between us. Thankfully, he let the prickly moment pass without comment.

"Well . . . I'd better get Mrs. Kelp her milk. Her arthritis is acting up and she didn't want to get out in the damp air."

He walked off, and I continued into the store, suddenly feeling less buoyant. Without Vic, the dinner was just . . . food.

Late Tuesday afternoon the house swam in the fragrance of pie baking in the oven and meat loaf browning on the rack. The persuasive aromas drew Ingrid from her lair. She rolled into the kitchen around four, her lap full of the afternoon mail. "We having company?"

I peeled potatoes and rinsed them under running water. "Joe's coming over around five-thirty."

"What about Vic?"

I pretended to be absorbed in filling a pan with water. "Haven't talked to him."

She sniffed the fragrant air. "Is that peach pie I smell?"

"I thought you might enjoy one."

"Hope you got enough sugar in it." She picked up a stack of letters and leafed through them. Her fingers slowed as she held an envelope up to the light, squinting. "What's that say, Marlene? I don't have my glasses with me."

I dried my hands and reached for the letter, eyes drawn to the Maui postmark. In the upper left-hand corner, *Claybridge Law Firm* jumped out. Prue Levitt Moss had volleyed the ball back into our court.

"It's from Prue's lawyer."

"Open it."

Oh brother. Why didn't she leave me out of this? Wasn't I trying to change, become a decent, upstanding, Christlike role model?

I picked up the letter opener and neatly slid the blade beneath the flap. The firm's letterhead had a Lion's face emblazoned across the heading. I scanned the body text.

Dear Mrs. Moss:

I am writing on behalf of my client, Prue Levitt Moss, concerning the status of her late husband's foot.

While Mrs. Levitt Moss is sympathetic to your feelings on the matter, she was Eugene Moss's legal wife at the time of his death, which gives her the greater claim of ownership. Mrs. Levitt Moss has been patient, but this situation cannot be prolonged. If she has not received notice that the foot has been exhumed and shipped, she will be forced to take further legal action. It is not my client's wish to cost you your life's savings, but her grief for her late husband will not allow her to give up her quest for ownership of said foot. We will expect to hear from you by return mail. If you do not respond to this letter within thirty days, we will be forced to take action.

Respectfully yours,
Derek Claybridge, Attorney

Ingrid chortled. "Ha! Call R J and read the letter to him. We'll fight this to the Supreme Court!"

I stopped her. "There's no need to involve your lawyer in this and cost you yet another legal paper to file." I moved to the phone. "I'll take care of it."

"You?" Ingrid shifted in her chair.

"Me." I glanced at the clock realizing that it was the middle of night in Maui. I'd have to call in the morning—and Joe would be here any minute.

Ingrid's lower lip jutted like a tenacious bulldog. Clearly she wasn't convinced I could handle the matter. "You best call R J"

I'd best do a lot of things, but calling R J Rexall wouldn't be one of them.

I'd put a stop to this nonsense, pronto.

Ingrid sulked during dinner; I knew I'd upset her by not letting her lawyer handle the letter, but in this instance, the case was pretty clear cut. The two women could haggle over the foot until the cows came home, but like it or not, Ingrid was Eugene's legal wife and heir when he lost the foot. According to R J, Ingrid had been right all along—the severed appendage was a completed gift, so to speak. Ingrid owned the foot—for whatever comfort that might bring. If Prue wanted to fight in court for body remains, and have Eugene's bones flown to Maui and reburied, then she could have a case, but I had serious doubts the woman had the fortitude to carry out the mission. Even with an attorney nephew and accident settlement lining her bank account, there had to be a limit to the amount of money she would be willing to spend. With Ingrid out of the picture, the haranguing would lose its appeal.

"Marly—" Joe shoved back from the table and patted his belly straining over his belt—"even my Melba couldn't bake a better peach pie."

Smiling, I dipped my spoon in the syrupy pie dish. "High praise, sir, and I thank you."

He leaned to get a paper sack sitting on the counter. I'd seen him carry it in and wondered what he'd brought. Nothing to eat, I hoped. "Got something to show you ladies."

Ingrid the Discrete muttered. "Not another one of your foolish inventions. You nearly killed Mattie with your last one."

"It didn't hurt her—speeded her up a bit, but didn't hurt her." He took a pile of nuts and bolts out of the sack and laid them on the table. Then out came an odd-looking robotic frame.

I peered at the strange assortment. "What is it?"

"A glass robot."

"Glass? That's aluminum—or—what's that stuff Erector sets are made of?"

"Don't know, but it's neither. It's hard plastic, and it's not a 'glass robot,' it's a Glass Robot."

I turned my palms up.

Enthusiasm brimming now, Joe hurriedly assembled his newest creation. In moments, he set the hard plastic on the kitchen floor. "Now, be prepared to be astounded." His gaze roamed the table. "This your best china, Ingrid?"

She sniffed. "Certainly not. Everyday stuff— "

He picked up a coffee cup and smashed it to the floor. Ingrid and I gave a collective gasp. Glass shattered and flew in opposite corners of the floor.

"Joe Brewster!" Ingrid's features mottled. "Have you lost your mind?"

"Don't get upset. I'll buy you a new cup—saw one like it at Wal-Mart last week. Now ladies, keep your eye on the robot." He flipped a switch and noise exploded. Stiff-legged, the robot moved across the floor pulling up shards of glass. Huge hunks and pieces sucked into the frame.

"Is it magnetic?" I shouted above the clattering roar.

"No! I put a souped-up, one-horsepower vacuum motor in it!" He beamed. "Ain't she a beauty?"

The robot skimmed the floor grabbing broken glass like a Hoover. The concept was sound—what woman didn't dread the thought of broken glass and tiny invisible slivers found weeks later? Now I got it! It wasn't a glass robot, it picked up glass—ergo, a Glass Robot.

Ingrid's attention followed the invention, eyes round. "Great day in the morning, Joe. You might be onto something this time."

"Watch." He smashed a water glass, and the robot whirled and attacked the debris.

"This is great!" I called above the din. "But the noise—it's so loud!" You couldn't hear yourself think. Women wouldn't allow the gadget in their households unless it ran quieter.

"I'm working on that!"

Ingrid blocked his hand with a stern look when he reached for another glass.

Glass hitting hard plastic beat a rhythm. The robot made a wide sweep of the kitchen, then turned on a dime and darted through the kitchen doorway. Springing to our feet, Joe and I followed behind. Ingrid trailed in the wheelchair. The invention had picked up speed. RPMs revved. The thing was moving fast now. Paper clips, ballpoint pens, Ingrid's crochet needles—all stuck to the metal plate on the front of the robot.

Ingrid went ballistic. "My needles!"

The robot moved down the hallway, attracting anything in its path. It caught the hem of Ingrid's lace cloth covering a hall table and jerked it loose. A lamp toppled and shattered.

Wheeling, the robot sucked glass. The device was almost comical looking with the remains of three ballpoint pens and at least a dozen paper clips stuck to its surface. The android headed down the hallway.

Ingrid waved her hands in the air. "Turn the thing off, Joe!"

The inventor lunged for the robot, but it disappeared behind a chair. When it emerged, black hairpins and a gold chain had been added.

I dodged Joe, trying to catch the pesky little creature that suddenly had taken on a life of its own. Joe grasped it. The motor roared. Smoke filled the room.

"Shut it off!" Ingrid pounded her hands on the arms of her wheelchair. "It's smoking up the curtains and ceilings!"

"I'm *trying!*"

I wouldn't have believed that one small mechanical machine could dispense so much smoke! The room boiled with the stuff. I coughed and covered my nose, eyes burning.

"Shut it off, Joe!"

"I'm trying! Blessed switch is faulty." The sound of frantic clicks, then I saw a trail of blue smoke fogging down the hallway as he rushed out of the house carrying the invention.

Standing in a blue haze, I listened to the slamming front door. Then silence.

"Aunt Ingrid?"

"What."

"Are you okay?"

"I can't see my hand in front of my face. Wish the old fool would keep his inventions to himself."

I smothered a snicker. If it wasn't a foot plaguing her, it was a hand.

This poor woman couldn't win.

Later I took a pill for a migraine and then fixed Ingrid a cup of hot chocolate. I'd aired the house and the smoke finally cleared, though a distinct rubber scent hung in the air.

"Never saw anything like it," my aunt groused. "A glass-sucking robot."

"Actually, I think Joe's brilliant. Just needs to work out a few kinks."

"Humph. You always did favor the man."

"Yeah." I poured hot cocoa into a cup. "You know, Aunt Ingrid, I've been thinking. I never understood why God gave me Herman. I loved him, you loved him, don't know many who didn't love him."

I knew a lot that were embarrassed by him, that had been made crystal clear of late, but most were fond of him. I sat the pan down and wiped milk dribbles off the counter. "I used to go to Joe with my problems. You knew that."

"I knew."

"I needed someone. Someone to listen and understand my concerns, a surrogate dad. Joe filled a niche in my life."

Ingrid toyed with her cup. "I know you resented the fact that Herman … well, Herman wasn't like most dads."

I carried my chocolate to the table and sat down. It wasn't often Ingrid made me privy to her thoughts, and I planned to take full advantage of the moment.

"My going to Joe didn't mean I didn't love Herman." God might not have given me a traditional father, but what he hadn't supplied naturally he'd sent by proxy. Joe had been my confidant, my father figure, and an ally in most every situation, except with Vic. Having two children, one biologically, the other theoretically, had not been easy for the kindly pastor. Before I'd left Parnass Springs for the last time, it was imperative to me to come to grips with my heritage. To embrace it. To forgive myself.

"No, I know you loved my boy."

We shared a contemplative silence.

"I worry that Herman didn't know. I never told him." Except for this afternoon.

Mist suddenly filmed my aunt's eyes. "I was never certain what Herman knew. I know he loved you. And Butchie. Dogs in general."

"Yeah." I thought of all the dogs Herman had owned over the years. They were his soul mates—he connected to them in some way.

"Do you think Herman really knew?"

Ingrid stared at her saucer. "That you loved him?" She was silent for a minute, and then she nodded. "I think he did. Fetch me my Bible."

I brought the worn tome and she turned to a section, then read aloud. " 'Do not forget to entertain strangers, for by so doing some people have entertained angels without knowing it.' "

I swallowed hard. "Do you believe in angels?"

"Herman was an angel. You know that." Ingrid's tone had gentled.

"I do now."

"Some folks have different views of angels. The Bible portrays them as fierce individuals who deliver fiery messages from God. Others believe they're loving and sent to watch over us."

"What do you believe, Aunt Ingrid?"

"I believe there's much the good Lord doesn't have to explain. Angels are one of them."

We sat in the kitchen listening to the clock tick and rain patter on the roof, lost in memories.

Once we started to talk, we couldn't stop. We talked and talked, sharing our deepest feelings. Ingrid spoke of when Eugene had left her—of her shame and confusion.

"Liked to have killed me. I knew about the women, of course. You can't hide anything in this town, but he always came home to me. Then one day he didn't come home. I kept waiting, thinking he couldn't have left, but he was gone. That woman was poison, a thief, taking what was mine."

"The same happened to me."

She stared at me in silence for a moment. "Your man left for another woman?"

I nodded. "Yes. Just like Eugene left you."

"When?"

"Sara was two. At least Eugene left you money; Noel took everything we had. He was supposed to pay child support and alimony, but checks were always late and we struggled."

"You could have had him thrown in jail."

"I could, but he was Sara's father. And I didn't want him in our life again. At that point I didn't want him near me or Sara."

She frowned. "Always knew he wasn't any good. Sounds like you've had a hard life. Why didn't you come home, here to me and Beth? We'd have taken you in."

"I wasn't sure you would, Aunt Ingrid." Our eyes met. "You never asked about Noel or my life. I thought you were glad to be rid of me."

"Never asked because I didn't figure it was my place. Beth never asked?"

"Never."

"My sister was an odd sort. I know she loved you—loved you like her own."

Was Ingrid softening? Starting to change? "She never mentioned that."

"Pity."

Yeah, a real pity. Three simple words would have meant a lot to me during those dark years.

"Well, you should have stayed here and married Vic."

Couldn't argue with that reasoning. "It's easy to look back and see what we should have done."

She chuckled. "Hindsight's clearer than foresight. Vic know about Noel's death?"

I nodded. "He found out recently through a magazine article Noel wrote before he died. I should have told him all these years, but I didn't."

"I expect he's angry?"

I shrugged. "I've been avoiding him since I got back. On the surface he's the same old Vic, but beneath that calm veneer he has to be furious with me."

"I'd say he has a right."

I couldn't deny that. Still, he could call and give me a chance to explain.

You could call him, Marlene.

For some reason, I couldn't bring myself to do that.

When I finally looked at the clock, I couldn't believe the time. Nearly 4:00 a.m. I'd spent all night having a heart-to-heart talk with Ingrid, of all people.

Today I'd try to talk some sense into Prue.

Lord, I'm going to need some help here. Since I'd come back to Parnass Springs, he'd been leading me in some very strange paths. What would today bring?

Then again, maybe I didn't care to know.

Eleven

No Hawaii *Aloha?* No *Aloha kakahiaka!* (Good morning!) Hardly.

When Prue Levitt Moss picked up the receiver that Wednesday morning and recognized my voice, an Alaskan Express blew across the miles between us.

I explained that I was calling to discuss the recent letter. Prue informed me to contact the Claybridge Law Firm and hung up.

I redialed, aware of Ingrid's frantic eye on the clock.

"It's long distance." She pointed to her watch.

"My cell phone's dead, Ingrid." I'd gladly pay the charge in lieu of R J Rexall's fee; I would be short and to the point, while R J would take several reams of legal papers to say the same thing in lawyer ramble.

I tapped my fingernails on the cabinet, picturing Prue standing, hand poised over the instrument, debating. If she was like everyone else, she had caller ID.

The phone rang once. Twice. I absently hummed the refrain from a song, "*. . . three times a lady . . .*"

Prue picked up.

I snapped to attention. "Don't hang up on me, Mrs. Moss, because I'll only call back." I motioned for Ingrid to keep her cool. She looked faint, her eyes rolling money signs. *Long distance,* she mouthed.

Prue was talking. "Whatever you have to say, you can say through my attorney."

"I know the proper procedure and that my call is highly irregular, but I can save you and Ingrid many hours of time and angst if you'll hear me out."

A perceptible sigh came over the wire.

Seizing the lull, I dove in. "Please be assured that I sympathize with your concerns, Mrs. Moss. Losing a . . . loved one is never easy and your particular case is distressing, but I sense that you're a reasonable woman. Your letter contends that you intend to carry this case to the highest court— "

"I do indeed. The Supreme Court if necessary."

Over a foot! Give me a break!

Resting my hip against the counter, I shut my eyes. I didn't want to be mean to the woman; Eugene had caused her heartache. Her nephew might fight the case in her behalf for years, but the outcome would be the same. How did I make her see reason? I breathed a quiet prayer and carried on.

"Mrs. Moss?"

"I'm here."

"May I suggest a possible solution to this problem?" The subsequent silence lent hope. At least she was considering the offer.

"I'm listening."

"There isn't going to be a winner. Even if you win the case, you'll be out thousands of dollars transporting Eugene to Maui. Then there'll be the burial plot, a stone. On the other hand, my aunt . . ." I paused. Ingrid was counting every word, eye on the clock's second hand. I slapped my hand over the receiver. "May I have some privacy, *please*?"

"Why? The call concerns me."

"That's why." I shooed her into the living room. Giving me a short look, she wheeled and rolled off. "Three minutes—no more. My phone bill will cost me a fortune."

Free to speak candidly, I returned to the discussion. "Prue, may I call you Prue?"

"You may call me by my name. Mrs. Moss."

"Mrs. Moss. May I speak candidly?"

"You need to speak through our attorneys. That's what we pay them for."

"Granted, but what I'm going to say is free and not one legal paper involved." Surely she could appreciate the service. I waited for the click on the other end of the line. When I didn't hear one, I continued. "Eugene lost his foot in a hunting accident many years ago. At the time he was married to Ingrid, so in the eyes of the court, ultimately, the foot belongs, or is a completed gift, to Ingrid." I heard fumbling noises like Prue was about to slam the phone in my ear.

"Wait! Please hear me out!"

More rattling. Then, "Go on."

"You, on the other hand, were Eugene's legal wife at the time of his death. I'm not certain what took place at the time ..." My brain turned over every detail I'd heard about the dispute, and to my surprise, my facts were accurate. Prue agreed with my account of the story.

"I didn't have the funds to bury Eugene at the time. His parents did, and they wanted to bury their son near them. Eugene left his money to Herman."

"I understand, Mrs. Moss. My husband walked out on me and left me with a two-year-old child to raise. It wasn't a happy time in my life. I'm sure we shared mutual fears."

An emotional catch filled her tone. "I wanted Eugene with me."

What did Eugene have (other than a missing foot) that attracted so many women? It wasn't steadfast loyalty; he'd proven that many times over. Good looks? Never. But the man was a salesman and charismatic to the core. Evidently what he did best was sell himself. I'd never seen the fascination, but then I had been a child, immune to the fatal attraction.

I did recall Beth talking about the time Ingrid discovered Eugene and Prue's peccadillo. She packed all his clothes, drove to his office, and set the three bags inside the door. When the secretary frowned her confusion, Ingrid stated, "When you see Eugene, tell him he's moved."

But then he'd showed up and sweet-talked Ingrid into letting him move back in. Temporarily, as it worked out. Ingrid still loved him.

"Ingrid is aware of your deep devotion to Eugene and she sympathizes." Not exactly a lie. Ingrid wasn't made of stone, as I'd discovered during our long talk. "So here's what I propose."

I was taking a big chance of inflicting irreversible harm. Prue could clam up and keep the case alive and in the court system for years, but "nothing ventured nothing gained." How often had I heard Aunt Beth express the old saying?

Dead silence on the other end of the line.

"Mrs. Moss?"

Silence. She had hung up on me. *Marlene! Now you've done it; Herman's statue wasn't enough of a boiling cauldron, now you've got Prue on an even bigger warpath.*

"Marlene! Are you still on the phone?"

I didn't answer Ingrid's bellowed question, just dropped my voice. "Mrs. Moss . . . are you still there?"

Silence.

I leaned over and tapped the receiver on the kitchen counter, then raised it back to my ear. "Hello."

"What's all that racket coming from?"

"Sorry, I wasn't sure if we were still connected." One excuse was as good as another, I guessed. Now if I could just keep her on the line.

"Marlene! I'm coming in there!"

I was running out of time. "Okay, here's my plan. Drop the lawsuit that's costing you time and dredging up painful memories. Eugene was a great man, but he loved women—all women. You know that, Ingrid knows that. He loved you, I'm certain of that. But he loved Ingrid, too, so you ladies can fight until the moon falls out of the sky, but in the end, you'll both be not only financially strapped but emotionally whipped."

I knew I had her attention. "I propose that you and Ingrid make peace. I know that won't be easy, and it doesn't have to be accomplished overnight. It took the Lord six days to create the world; you and Ingrid can take all the time you need. With the money you save, you can take a relaxing cruise around the world. Enjoy life."

"What are you suggesting? That I forget that I had a husband, never be allowed to visit his grave, grieve his loss?"

"No, not at all. I'm suggesting—no, I'm *inviting* you—to share Eugene. Here in Parnass Springs. Ingrid is a wealthy woman; she has the power and the funds to bring Uncle Eugene here and bury his remains with his . . . foot. Drop your suit, allow her to bring Eugene here, to Parnass Springs, and every Memorial Day you can fly to Missouri and honor your husband."

"That's ludicrous. Why would I spend good money to fly to Missouri once a year when I could have Eugene here?"

"Would you do it if I sent you a round-trip ticket every May?" The offer would mean overtime work for me, but it would be a blessing to do something for these two women to put them out of their misery. And my hair. Besides, Prue had money. I was counting on curiosity to prompt her to pay her own way—maybe coming more than once a year. After all, she had past ties to Parnass. She lived a short distance from town when she met Eugene and fell for his winning ways.

"Oh ... I don't know ... I'm not sure ..."

"I don't need an answer today. Just think about it." My eyes fixed on the clock. I'd been on the phone five minutes.

"Mar*lene*!"

"I'll call you over the weekend, Mrs. Moss. Please pray about your answer." I hung up. I didn't know what Prue must think of my hasty departure, but Ingrid was about to birth a cat.

This was the woman who had more money than the Kennedys. And she was screaming about a few dollars!

My aunt rolled into the kitchen. "What'd the old witch say?"

"She isn't an old witch; Eugene hurt her, too, Aunt Ingrid."

"You're taking her side! You're just like my sister. When I needed her most, Beth wasn't there."

"I'm taking sanity's side. Aunt Beth never betrayed you. She was put between her sister and a very dear friend. Beth didn't orchestrate Eugene's infidelity."

I understood better than I wanted. In my own pride-driven fallacy, I'd thought Noel would change if he wanted to. Who was at fault in that relationship? Me, for running away and marrying a man I didn't love, running from my past, shutting God out of my life, going it alone, and asking nothing of anybody? Or Noel, who took what he wanted and walked away when he tired of it? Looking back, I realized I'd expected his faithlessness, and he'd not proved me wrong. Maybe I'd even encouraged it.

I made Aunt Beth and myself a cup of hot tea and sat down at the table. We had a long talk before us—one I didn't relish. Prue might be softening, but I had serious doubts Ingrid would be the voice of reason.

"I have something to discuss with you."

"I'm keeping the foot."

"That's fine."

She eyed me over the top of her spectacles. "Am I going to like this?"

Probably not. When had she ever liked anything that wasn't her idea? "Give it a chance, okay?"

Ingrid's expression settled into the familiar stubborn line. "I'm making no promises."

"Just listen, that's all I ask."

As I explained my solution, her lips tightened, her expression hardened with every word. "Why should I spend my money to move Eugene here? If the *hussy* wants him moved, let her do it."

"She doesn't plan to move him, just visit the foot. It would be nice if you'd consent to move him—all of him—here. Then Eugene would be ... intact." A whole man to fight over, per se.

"I'm keeping the foot."

"If you'll go with the plan, you'll have both Eugene *and* his foot. You're always complaining about having to take flowers to a foot." Ingrid wasn't really listening to my efforts for peace.

"And why would that woman ever show her face in Parnass again?"

"Doesn't she have family here? I thought she was local."

"Got a sister. Nice woman. Nothing like the hussy."

"Then she can come back for a visit and pay her respects at the same time."

"What's in it for me?"

God, give me strength.

"A truce. Money not spent on attorney fees." I studied the wheelchair, about to say *health*, but changed my mind.

Her chin tilted. "I can afford to pay a lawyer."

"I know you can, but why would you want to make R J Rexall a rich man?"

That stopped her, but not for long. "Foot still belongs to me."

"Forget the foot. This is not about the foot. I'm talking about having *all* of Eugene brought here!"

"You don't have to shout, Marlene. I'm not deaf."

"I'm sorry. What do you think about my plan?"

She wheeled the chair toward the door. "I'll think about it."

Well, that was progress of a sort, I guessed.

Midmorning, I went to the park. Ingrid had kept me busy since I'd been back, but today I had some heavy thinking to do. So I headed for the park, hoping the swings would be empty. If Lily was there, maybe I could talk her into switching from the slide to the swings.

I scanned the swings—empty, the way I'd hoped—and made a beeline for the first one, not wanting to waste time. I lowered myself into the seat, gripped the chain with both hands, and pushed back with my feet. A moment later I was flying, pumping my legs to go higher. The adrenaline surge was awesome, as purifying as ever. I pictured myself as a child again, swinging alone, trying to work through problems too numerous and too deep to understand.

Suddenly, someone caught me on the back swing. I felt the jerk, and then strong hands gave me a push. I twisted around to see who my benefactor was. Vic, of course. Why was I surprised? His presence was so natural, it felt like air. For a time the problems between us evaporated, and we were just Marlene and Vic, swinging in the park.

He pushed me again, harder this time. I arched back, pointing my feet toward the sky. Higher and higher I flew, catching the wind through my hair. We didn't speak; words weren't needed.

After a bit, he caught me, stopping the swinging motion. My feet touched the ground, and I knew the time had come to talk. He led me to a picnic table and I followed, pulse fluttering like a drumbeat—whether from Vic and how much I loved him, or from pure guilt, I didn't know. He sat down and motioned for me to take the bench on the other side of the table. I swallowed, determined to tell the truth and put the deceitful years behind, no matter what the consequences. "How did you know I'd be here?"

"I was passing and saw you. The sight of you swinging took me back to old times. I remembered the park was your think tank."

"And the magic still works. Swinging relaxes me; helps put my thoughts in perspective."

"I didn't know it was a practice you continued."

I grinned. "I didn't. Wish I could, but I think my neighbors in Glen Ellyn would think I'm . . ." Not long ago I would have said *nuts*, but I'd decided I was going to start talking nicer to myself and about myself.

We sat silent for a minute before Vic spoke. "Ingrid all right?"

"Like always. She and Prue are still fighting over Eugene's foot. I can't imagine why either of them would want it, but they do." *Stop dallying, Marlene! Blurt it out! Let him blast you for the lies—the years of wasted trust!*

"Two stubborn women; might as well go along with their follies."

"Too stubborn for words." If only they would discuss the matter logically, their differences could be worked out . . .

Shut my mouth. Why did I think that way but refuse to practice my own remedies? The expectancy on Vic's face said he was thinking the exact same thing. The moment passed. Vic was too much of a gentleman to point out the comparison.

He shifted. "They'll work out the foot ownership, and if they don't, it gives them something to occupy their time. If not for our differences, what would life be?"

"You're right." Here it comes. Differences. Lies. Explosion. I opened my mouth to confess, but nothing came out. I couldn't bear to see the disgust on his face, the betrayal.

Silence.

I cleared my throat. "I'm working on a compromise acceptable to both Ingrid and Prue." I told him about my plan, and he agreed it could work.

"You're brave." He winked. "Don't be upset it they refuse to listen."

I picked up a dry twig from the tabletop and proceeded to break it into little pieces. "Joe was over and brought his latest invention."

"Ah, the Glass Robot? What'd you think?"

"Loud."

I piled the broken pieces of twig on the table, concentrating on what I was doing. Anything to keep from looking him in the eye.

I glanced up and his eyes were kind, but there was remoteness in his expression, one I'd never seen before. All was not well between us. Why didn't he confront me? Why didn't I tell him the truth? *Coward! You don't want the final break—the irreversible snap that can never be repaired.* I looked away. "Well, I'm finally coming to grips with my memories of Herman."

"That's good. You could never see your father the way the rest of us did."

I recognized the truth when I heard it. I'd wanted Herman to be like other people, not different. I'd been ashamed of the way he looked, the way he behaved, the comments sent our way.

"Not everyone liked Herman. You heard them at the meeting. Some of them were repulsed by him; others felt he was a nuisance." And they hadn't hesitated to say so, not caring that Ingrid and I were sitting in the same room, having to endure their remarks.

"You have to expect negative people," Vic said. "Not everyone has the maturity or ability to see beauty in someone like Herman. They tend to shrink away, afraid to touch or be touched."

"There but for the grace of God, go I."

"Most of us, when we look at another's misfortune, may sympathize. But a part of us will be thanking God it didn't happen to us."

I wasn't like that, was I? I thought back to some of the patients I'd worked with ... and cringed. Maybe I wasn't as far removed from that attitude as I liked to think.

"It's normal," Vic offered. "None of us want to be different. We all want to be accepted, to fit in. Herman never did and he knew it."

"Herman didn't choose his life." No one chose who they were born to or what genes they carried. Parents were a turkey shoot.

"God doesn't promise us the ride will be smooth, but he does promise to go with us every mile of the way."

For a moment I was caught up in silent thoughts. "It seems like he could prevent a lot of our problems, if he would."

"It doesn't work like that, Marly. God can do everything, that's true, but if nothing bad happened in our lives, we might get the idea that we didn't need him."

"So he lets bad things happen to show us we need him? I'm not sure I'm up to the test."

"You are. He lets life happen, and sometimes what we think is a burden is really a blessing. Herman touched a lot of people in this town, in ways he couldn't have done if he had been normal."

"I can accept that—I can even accept the differences in people and be glad of them, but it's been a long road getting here. It's been hard for me to see that each of us is a unique individual. I think if I were God, I'd have made everyone alike."

"Right." He grinned. "Could the world survive two Marlys?"

It couldn't.

He reached for my hand. "Think of how boring life would be if we were all carbon copies of one other."

"We could be perfect." I smiled when I said it, knowing that human nature being what it was, perfection wasn't possible.

"Perfect is highly overrated. God did a wonderful thing when he made us all different."

"I feel so guilty." I looked down at the table. "I didn't even try to accept Dad, not really. Something inside me cared more about what other people thought than about Herman's feelings, but I loved him, Vic. I'm just beginning to realize how much, and what I missed by not coming home more often."

"We can't undo the past; all we can do is ask for forgiveness and try to do better."

"It's surprising how each of us have different gifts. You have a gift with animals."

"And you have a gift with people. Nursing is a thankless job. At least my animals give me a friendly nudge every now and then."

Twenty-five years in the nursing field. Did I want to go back? Did I want the long shifts, the stress, eating poorly, and dealing with Sara's problems day after day . . . ? "Herman had simple gifts."

Vic agreed. "He was always happy, glad to see his friends, willing to help with anything they needed."

"And he loved animals. He was good with them too. It's fitting that he built the animal shelter. His gift to the town."

"He gave more than the shelter to the town. He gave the town his love. How many can say that?"

Sighing, my hands tightened on his. "He never seemed to mind that he was different, not openly. Maybe his difference didn't bother him the way it did me."

"What's the old saying? What you don't know can't hurt you."

"But in Herman's case it *did* hurt him, and by the very people who want to honor him now."

"Well, people change, grow older, experience life. They let us down, walk away from us."

There it was: the perfect opening for me to break down the wall, confess my sin and clear the air between us ... but I hesitated, and the moment passed. The old Marlene—the one who knew she'd lose him forever when the lie was voiced—shrank.

Sighing, Vic got up. "I have to go. Dad will wonder where I am."

I searched his face, looking for anger, but seeing only a remote sadness. "Yeah, Ingrid has probably called neighbors to look for me. She'll be sure something has happened to me."

The frown disappeared and he chuckled. "Your aunt is a piece of work—no disrespect intended."

"None taken." Ingrid was Ingrid; she never worried about how others would accept her behavior. She did whatever she liked, and if you didn't approve, you could get over it. If she and Millicent Spencer ever clashed, I wanted to be there to see it.

The chuckle turned to a friendly grin. "Good to see you, Marly. I'm glad Sara is doing better. I was concerned when I heard about the baby scare."

"Thank you. I was too."

He turned and walked away. Another opportunity, maybe my last, to make amends slipped away. Would I ever have enough nerve to talk to him about the truth? To make him understand why I would perpetrate this fraud on him — my best friend. I didn't know, but it was clear he didn't intend to make the first move.

"Vic!"

He turned around.

"Vic . . ." When I told him, it would be over. Forever. *God, grant me the strength to do this.*

"Yes, Marly?"

"I . . . have a good day."

Disappointment crossed his features. Had he expected a confession? I'd expected to offer one. *Father, I want to . . . I want to so badly! Inside I'm at war with evil and good. Please help me.*

"Yeah. You too." He walked on, and the moment passed — and I wondered if God would grant me another.

I looked at the swings, but the urge to use them had waned. I was right the first time: you can't go back. Swinging had been a nice interlude, but I wasn't a child anymore, and it would take more than youthful pastimes to help me with problems looming on the horizon like thunderheads.

Sighing, I got up and walked back to my car.

My faith in miracles was restored around one when the plumber arrived at Aunt Beth's house. By midafternoon, a new fifty-gallon hot water heater sat in the closet, and every sink in the house had either stopped dripping or had a new faucet.

Overhead, a new roof sheltered the old house; brown ceiling stains were spackled and painted. So impressed was I by the sudden whirlwind of repairs all coming together at the same time, that I phoned the realtor and then invited Ingrid over for supper. To my surprise, she accepted. It would be the first time Ingrid had stepped foot in her sister's house since she and Eugene parted, but it was time for celebration.

Tracey Haskins of Four Star Realty showed up as Ingrid and I were sitting down to eat.

"I'm sorry. I've caught you at a bad time."

"No, really, I'll show you the house. Let me check on Ingrid first." I returned to the kitchen and ran a quick glance over the table, making sure my aunt had everything she needed.

"If I'd wanted to eat alone, I could have stayed home," Ingrid stated.

I pushed her water glass closer. "This won't take long."

Tracey and I stepped outside and she took a few steps down the walk and looked back. Tracey sighed. "I've always loved this house. It would be beautiful painted a soft gray with white trim and charcoal accents."

I looked at the house, trying to catch her vision. Tall, two-story, with a wraparound porch, it had clean, elegant lines I'd never noticed before. It had always just been Aunt Beth's house, the place where I lived. For a moment, my heart ached at the thought of selling, and a deep longing swept over me.

I wanted to stay in Parnass. To live here, in this house.

The desire held me captive for one poignant moment before I regained my senses. I couldn't live here! I had a job, and Columbia was the closest hospital around. I'd been told by Beth's attorney that my inheritance would be sizable, but until properties were sold and the estate settled, I wouldn't know the full amount. It would be large, but how large? Large enough for me to retire, to quit my job? Or large enough to live comfortably but frugally? Enough to buy a yacht? Or enough to put the money in tax-free bonds for Sara's and the children's futures?

Besides, Sara would have something to say about where I lived. Or she would if she ever got over the sulks. My continuing absence would be driving her into a conniption fit. She still hadn't called, and I was starting to worry. I'd wanted to break her dependence on me, but it was altogether possible I'd broken more than I had intended.

I led the way into the house and Tracy stopped in her tracks, staring at the rocks in the living room. "Uh, those are rocks."

"They are indeed. Beth collected them."

Tracey shook her head. "Most people keep them outside."

"Beth wasn't like most people."

Tracy giggled. "Neither is Ingrid. How come *you're* so sensible?"

I didn't take offense. "Someone had to be. I got elected."

She bent over and picked up a fair-sized stone. "You could build a wall."

I stared at her. "Why would I do that?"

Color filled her cheeks. "Well, no, I don't suppose you'd want to do that, but if you did want to, you surely could."

I sighed. "I'll show you the rest of the house."

She whipped out her notebook. "Sorry, the rocks sort of threw me. They go with the house?"

"Absolutely, I'll even throw in additional ones if the buyer wants them." I figured the offer was safe. Who in their right mind wanted a house full of rocks?

She shot another look around the cluttered room. "Right. A whole lot of rocks. Well, I'll advertise the house as adventurous! Fun!" Her eyes focused on the rocks. "Perfect for the nature lover!"

We wandered through the house, with me pointing out the good points—high ceilings, which would be cool in the summer; oak woodwork; and a wide front porch. I pointed out the new roof, new faucets, and the repainted ceilings. Back in the living room, she raised her eyebrows again at the rocks.

"I'll get rid of those as soon as I can."

She nodded, apparently still at a loss for words.

We sat down in the living room, pushing sofa pillows aside, and took care of the necessary papers to list the house—a task I thought would be easy but proved to bring an unexpected surge of sentimentality. The house was part of my history, a past I would leave and never revisit. Closing doors to never be opened again was difficult—even for a rigid heart like mine.

Tracey filled out the listing form. "Old houses like these are easy to sell. Everyone wants to live in a piece of history." She jotted down a few notes. "Let's see, what was that asking price again?"

I gave her the amount Aunt Ingrid and I had agreed upon. She wrote it down. "Pity you can't move back here and live. This would be a beautiful home if it were fixed up."

That wasn't an option. I had responsibilities at home, Sara and my grandchildren. Besides, there was no place for me in Parnass anymore.

Tracey drove a For Sale sign in the front yard and then left, promising to stay in touch. Not that I expected too much. I didn't know the housing market, but surely there wasn't much demand for old rock-filled houses in this town.

I wandered back to the living room and sat down on the sofa. Rocks covered the floor, piled in the corners, reposed on the furniture. What was I going to do about them? I couldn't carry them all outside, and where would I put them if I could? No one would want to buy a house with a resident rock pile, whether the rocks were inside or out. Just one more problem on top of all the others. I leaned against the cushioned seat-back, staring at the ceiling. Painters, roofers, plumbers, Ingrid, Sara, Vic—all my troubles had names.

God, I'm going under here. Could you send a boat? Maybe an oil tanker?

If he did, with my sins, it would probably have a hole in it. Meanwhile, Ingrid was probably expiring from curiosity, and I hadn't had my dinner. I got to my feet and plodded back to the kitchen.

Ingrid steadily spooned carrots into her mouth. "Going to be odd to see strangers occupy this house."

"It's been vacant two years." I poured a glass of milk, then closed the refrigerator door with my hip. "I thought you might want to buy Aunt Beth's share of the property."

"Don't want anything that belonged to Beth. Good Lord knows we shared enough."

Bitterness. It never stopped.

I'd stacked the last dinner dish in the drainer when the phone rang. I lifted the receiver with soapy fingers. Tracey Haskins's excited voice came over the line. "We have a contract."

Blank, I stared at the mouthpiece.

"Isn't that wonderful!"

"An offer? Already?" *Great day in the morning!*

"No, ma'am, we have a signed contract with no addendums. Full offer. Once you sign, the house is sold. Will you be home for a few minutes?"

"Yes … I'll be here." I hung up. That had taken what? An hour? Property wasn't that scarce in Parnass, was it?

Marlene, your luck is beginning to turn. The Lord is shining on you. Don't question good fortune.

Idiot! You sold too cheap!

Still. An hour? It seemed sacrilegious to dissolve my past so quickly. What could I say? I'd asked for a boat and God had sent the Queen Mary.

Tracey showed up with contract in hand. I glanced down the page to the signature. *Vic Brewster*? Vic was buying Aunt Beth's house? I placed the contract flat on the table and fixed Tracey with a stern eye. "Why is Vic buying this house?"

She blinked. "He didn't say. Does it matter? He saw the sign when he turned into his drive and called me."

I thought about that. Did it matter? I wasn't sure, but I intended to find out. I hesitated to sign. Did I really want to do this? Then reason took over. I would inherit all of Aunt Beth's estate, but not until I sold this house. My bank balance hovered just short of empty, and I had the plumber and the roofer yet to pay.

A frown formed on Tracy's youthful features. "You *are* going to sign, aren't you?"

"Why?"

"Because I could use the commission. Business has been slow lately."

I could understand that. Without further hesitation, I picked up the pen and signed on the dotted line. The die had been cast. Beth's house was sold, and gone with it my only reason to remain in Parnass. Aside from Aunt Ingrid and the wretched battle over Herman's statue.

Tracey released a pent-up breath and got to her feet, gathering up her contracts. "We'll get this closed as soon as possible. Thanks, Marlene. I'll be in touch."

"Thank you, Tracey. I never expected to sell it this fast."

"Me, neither, but some things are meant to be, don't you think?"

"Yes, I do." Whether this was one of them, I wasn't sure.

After Tracey left, I took Aunt Ingrid home and then walked across the street to Joe's house. Usually he greeted me like a long lost friend, but tonight he wore a wary expression.

"Come into the kitchen. I'm working on this dratted robot. There's got to be a better way to control it."

Well, one could only hope. I sat down at the table and accepted the cup of filtered coffee he handed me from the only one of his inventions that really seemed to work. I had a feeling he knew what I wanted to discuss with him.

"Joe, why did Vic buy Beth's house?"

He concentrated on his robot. "You wanted to sell, didn't you?"

"Yes, but you never mentioned he was interested. Had I known, I could have sold it to him directly and bypassed a realtor's fee."

He examined the switch, giving it his full attention. "Vic and me, we're sort of particular about our neighbors. Figure he can rent the place out to good people if he wants. Make a nice little investment, and he kind of likes Tracey—wants to see that she does well in her business."

I nodded. That made sense, I guessed. Still, it left me with a disturbing feeling that something wasn't quite right, but I couldn't put my finger on it.

Joe screwed another piece of plastic onto his robot. "Vic could get married again. He's a fairly young man. Hard to tell what that boy's got in mind."

Vic was anything but a boy. My heart thumped erratically, reluctant to think of him married. The carnival came to mind, with Lana hanging on his arm. Perfect Lana. She'd be a good wife, but it broke my heart to think about it. Joe flipped the switch and the robot scooted across the table toward me. I flinched, and Joe caught the thing before it fell off the edge. He shut it off and blessed silence descended.

"You need to work on that noise. A woman wouldn't think of buying anything that noisy."

"I'm working on it—thinking I'll have to put in a smaller motor." He spoke absently, as if his mind was on something else. "You talked to Vic yet?"

I shook my head. "Not yet."

"What's stopping you? Longer you put it off, the harder it will be."

Exactly the comforting words I needed to hear. The situation was bad enough. "I haven't had a chance, with Ingrid and selling the house and all." A lame excuse, and I knew it, but all I had at the moment.

"What are you going to do about Beth's rock collection?"

"I'll put it out back, make a rock garden."

"You've got enough to build a good one."

"I'll start carrying them out tomorrow."

He shook his head. "You leave them alone. I'll hire a couple of high-school boys to do it. They're always looking for extra money."

"Good, I didn't know how I could manage it alone." What would I do without this man? Soon, too soon, I'd find out.

"What are you going to do about Ingrid?"

Yes, indeed. What was I going to do about Ingrid? I shrugged. "I don't know. I make plans, and then look at her and know she'd never go along with them. Ingrid has a mind of her own, set in concrete hard enough to discourage a jackhammer."

He laughed. "Always has been that way."

"Not shy about speaking it either. It's going to be a fight over that statue, isn't it?"

He nodded. "Afraid so. Ann Parish is just as protective as Ingrid in her own way."

"No one is as stubborn as Ingrid. They broke the mold when they made her."

Joe set the robot over onto the kitchen counter. "She's one of a kind, all right. Beth was too. Haven't heard you mention Sara much since you've been back. She doing okay?"

I was grateful for the note of concern in his voice. "All right, I guess. I haven't heard from her for a couple of days."

His brow lifted. "You two have a falling out?"

"Something like that." I didn't want to talk about Sara. The list of things I didn't want to talk about was getting longer all the time.

"They'll let you know if they need anything."

I hoped he was right. "I feel like I'm being pulled a dozen different directions. There's Ingrid and Sara, and the statue. I don't know what to address first."

Joe slapped a scratch pad down in front of me. "Make a list, putting top priorities first, and Marlene, don't leave God off. He'll help you if you give him a chance."

"Joe, I'm not a heathen." I'd drifted—snapped an anchor—but I still talked to God, still prayed, and I knew he'd been with me from the day Noel left. If anyone had stepped away or fallen aside, it was me. *Forgive me, Father ... don't give up on me. I'm slow, but surely learning I can't live without you.* I got up and set my cup down on the drain board. "I need to go. Talk to you later."

I left, still not sure why Vic had bought Aunt Beth's house, and wondering what Ingrid would have to say about it. I crossed the street, got my purse, and told Ingrid that Beth's house was sold to Vic, and then drove downtown. A light glowed in the vet clinic. Vic was working late tonight. He always put in long, hard hours; I hoped Lana would be tolerant of his schedule. The thought of Vic and Lana together, forever, stung like alcohol on an open wound.

This time I was determined to talk to him. My mind was made up, and I wanted to, but how could I face him and what could I say? A flick of anger brushed me. Vic *had* to know how hard this was for me. Why didn't he speak up? Irrational thoughts, I knew, but sometimes it was as if a demon invaded my mind, and until I kicked him, he refused to leave. I sat in the car for a long time, trying to get up enough nerve to go inside. *God help me ... God help me.*

Joe's voice sounded in my head: *"Longer you put it off, the harder it will be."*

I loved Vic. I knew that without a doubt, but could I face his anger, his disappointment in me? Would he forgive me? Could we begin anew, work toward a future together—Vic and Marly, the way it should have been.

I weighed the choices, good and bad. If I went inside, it could be the final curtain on our relationship. If I left now, I might still have a few days with him ... Just a few more days ...

Dropping my head, I breathed, "I'm hopeless, Lord." But was I? Or was I a woman trying to control my life, pushing God aside when his help wasn't invited. I had a sinking feeling the answer was the latter, and I think at that moment, I sank to a new low.

Twelve

Chad Hargrave in the meat department beamed at me on Thursday. "Marlene. I heard you were in town."

Like he could have missed that little tidbit. The CIA should study the way news circulated in small towns. Parnass Springs could have given them some real pointers.

"I'm here, Chad, but not for long. As soon as I get Ingrid settled, I'm headed back to Glen Ellyn."

He sobered. "Hear you're planning to put up a statue of Herman. Good idea. Man was a blessing to the town. We wouldn't have that dandy animal shelter if it hadn't been for him."

Mrs. Finney sidled up beside me. "Nonsense. You put up statues of important people. Herman never did anything important in his life."

Linda Scofford joined in. "What are you talking about? He loved this town and loved us. That should count for something."

Sadie Burton added her comments. "Granted, he loved the town, but do we need a statue? I mean, Herman wasn't the prettiest thing around. Seems to me we could find something nicer to look at."

The crowd gathered, and in a show of cowardice, I grabbed my package of ground beef and faded away. Joe was right—this town was divided worse than the North and the South in the Civil War. Brother against brother, and all that. I pushed my cart down the aisles, jerking things off the shelves and dumping them into my cart as if I were in a race for my life. I unloaded them onto the conveyor belt at the register. Sounds of upraised voices and unfriendly words drifted from the meat department.

Malinda Adams smiled. "Hear you're going to build a statue of Herman."

I rolled my eyes. "And you object?"

She popped her gum. "No, really don't care one way or another. Long as I'm not expected to pay for it, you can do anything you like."

"I believe the plan has private donors."

She shook her head. "Don't that beat all? People will pay for the strangest things. Ask them to pay for something sensible like new storm sewers, and they can't afford it. Something like this, and they have deep pockets."

Malinda gave me the total, and I paid my bill and departed. The squabble at the meat department was still going on, louder with every passing minute.

I drove by the post office to mail a card to Sara. I knew she would get over her snit, but in the meantime, she could learn independence.

Liddy Hunt was dropping her mail in the slot as I walked in. "Just the person I wanted to see."

"Liddy, if this is about that statue, I don't want to talk about it."

She frowned. "Well, no, that wasn't it at all."

"Oh, then how can I help you?"

She lifted an inquisitive brow. "Well, now isn't that peculiar? It's just gone right out my head. You ought not to have been so sharp with me, Marlene. Gave me a real start, it surely did."

I sighed. "I'm sorry, Liddy, but I've got a lot on my mind right now."

"Oh, of course. I understand, and I remember now. The Methodist church is having a rummage sale. Do you have anything to donate?"

I thought of the stacks of clothing, the boxes of junk crowding Beth's house. Rocks. "Yeah, I think I might. When will the truck come around?"

Her features scrunched as she gave it thought. "Next Monday."

"Monday would be great." We said our good-byes and I got in my car and left. I fueled the rental car, then drove past the clinic. Vic's truck was there, but I drove on. Ice cream—had to get home before it melted. Not that I was inclined to stop anyway.

The phone was ringing as I walked in. I dumped the plastic grocery bags onto the table and lifted the receiver. "Hello?"

"That you, Marlene?"

"It's me." I didn't recognize the caller.

"Prue Levitt Moss, calling from Maui."

"Oh, yes, Prue." I sank to the nearest chair. "How are you today?"

"Tolerable. Got a touch of gout in my knee. I moved here for a better climate for my arthritis and I get the gout. Way it goes."

I held the phone away from my ear, staring at the receiver. The *hussy* was calling me and being nice? What brought this about?

"You there?"

I put the phone back to my ear. "Oh, yes. How nice to hear from you." *Nice? Really, Marlene. You've been waiting on pins and needles for this call.*

"My lawyer has your proposition under consideration; we'll get back to you on it."

Good—this was good! "Thank you for calling. We'll look to hear from you soon."

"One other thing; if I come back to Parnass Springs, I'll pay my own way. I'll not be beholden to Ingrid."

"No, couldn't have that." I frowned. Was someone on the extension? I peered around the corner into the living room, but Aunt Ingrid was nowhere around.

Suddenly Prue laughed. "You're all right, Marlene. Not much like that sour-tempered aunt of yours. We'll get along nicely."

Good. "Get-along" was my middle name. Actually, I couldn't wait to see who brought the biggest, most outrageous floral offering to Eugene's grave.

Prue hung up and I started putting groceries away. Where was Ingrid? I hadn't heard a peep from her since I got home. She had a lot in common with Petey; anytime she got this quiet, I best check on her. She was asleep in her chair, no doubt.

I turned and started for the door as Ingrid walked in. I grabbed my chest, feeling my heart shift into overdrive. "You're walking!"

She stood straight and tall, both feet firmly planted, her ample form encased in an orange and yellow polyester dress. Circles of rouge the size of half dollars glaringly marked her cheeks.

She nodded. "Amazing, isn't it. I've been healed." She snapped her fingers. "Came over me just like that."

"That fast?"

"It doesn't take long when the Lord decides to move. I was just sitting in my bedroom when a voice seemed to say, 'Ingrid, stand up,' and I said, 'Who, me? Lord?' And then I got to my feet and I walked."

"Really?" I thought about the suspicious click on the phone line. Had she eavesdropped on my and Prue's conversation—of course! She figured she'd won and *voilà*, she was healed.

"I want you to take me to the church."

"Church?" I echoed, feeling like I had lost my final grip on reality. "Why do you want to go to the church? There's no one there."

She fixed me with an eagle eye. "Au contraire. God's there."

Au contraire? This from Ingrid? "Granted, but what will we do when we get there?"

"I'm going to light a candle."

I gawked. "You're what? They don't light candles in Mount Pleasant Church."

"I'll take my own. Quit arguing, Marlene. Let's get cracking."

"Yes, ma'am, whatever you say." I tossed a bag of chips on the table and reached for the car keys.

"No need for sarcasm, not when there's been a real-life miracle in our midst." She turned and walked out of the house with me trailing along behind. I'd ended up in cuckoo land. No doubt about it.

And I needed to find my way back to sanity.

Later I sat down with pen and paper. There were varying feelings in this town over Herman — some good, some bad — but everyone had something to say. Maybe someone should ask what I thought.

Maybe I should just tell them. I'd write an editorial and take it to the paper myself.

After staring into space for a few minutes, I started writing.

Dear Editor,

I find that disagreement is not only healthy, but encouraging. People of strongly differing views regarding a public statue of my father can have meaningful and frank discussions and still maintain friendships and respect for one another.

I reread what I'd written, frowned and scratched it out. These people wouldn't understand diplomacy. They needed hard facts.

Dear Editor,

Many think I was ashamed of my father, and often this was true. I didn't show him the respect he deserved because, like so many others, I didn't respect Herman's limitations; I resented them. As I've matured, I have realized that I was wrong. My dad wasn't the brightest bulb in the pack, but the light of human kindness, compassion, and love of fellow man shone most brightly when he was around . . .

My pen flew over the paper. This was my life, my heart I was hanging out for everyone to see. I should be more discreet, but then detachment had led me to nothing but trouble so far. It was time for a different tack.

It took awhile, but I finally got my thoughts down. My words were eloquent, full of passion, but dignified. I'd never considered myself a writer, but now I was rather proud of my accomplishment.

Bill Haskel, owner and editor of *Parnass Press*, looked surprised when I walked into the office around nine thirty. "Marlene. Good to see you."

"Hi, Bill. I've got an editorial. Will you publish it?"

He took the paper and read it. "Town's really heated up over this statue."

"I know. I'm hoping this will calm folks. I'd like them to hear a daughter's voice."

Bill read the editorial again. "You sure you want this in the paper?"

"Yes. That's what I want."

"All right, it's your choice."

Somehow I had a feeling *choice* wasn't the word he had in mind. *Funeral* hovered at the edge of my mind, but I dismissed it. The letter came from my heart. Pertinent phrases drifted through my mind.

"A simple child ... overlooked blessing to the world ... Devoted to Parnass Springs, heart full of love ... One of God's angels ..."

Nothing to inflame anyone. "You'll publish it?"

Bill nodded. "I'll send it to press, and then I'm going fishing."

I wished him luck and drove home, a warm, cozy feeling in my heart. Herman would have been proud. I was proud.

Joe popped over. He stuck his head through Ingrid's open back door. "Marlene! I'm taking Ingrid's Buick for a lube job. The key's in my truck if you need it."

I put the last load of wash in the machine and dumped in soap. "Thanks Joe!" Good ole Joe; he took care of Ingrid's car like he did his own. If she needed tires, he bought them; if she needed maintenance, he took care of it.

"If I need anything, I have the rental car."

"No you don't! It's got a flat—I'll fix it when I get back."

Another flat! The tire must have had a slow leak for me not to notice it sooner. I pushed the start button on the washing machine.

"Marlene?"

I glanced up, startled to find Joe now in the utility doorway. "I knocked but you couldn't hear me."

Resting my hand on my heart, I caught my breath. "You scared ten years off my life."

"I wanted to tell you that if you do take the truck anywhere and Ingrid goes with you, you'll have to help her up. She can't get in the cab on her own."

"Okay, but I won't be going anywhere this afternoon. Too much to do around here."

"Well, she's … er … quite a load."

"I know, don't worry. We're staying here all afternoon."

When I looked up again, he was gone.

I finished Ingrid's chores and was about to eat a bite of lunch when she came into the kitchen fussing under her breath. "Got to get it paid—never noticed the date."

"Did you say something?" I bent, rummaging in the refrigerator for leftover meat loaf.

"I've got to pay my electric bill."

"Do you need a stamp?"

"Stamp won't help. I have to pay it right now."

I closed the door. "Right now?"

"Right now. You'll have to drive me to the electric company."

"Can't you just mail it?"

"It's due today. If I don't pay it today, they'll tack a penalty on it, and I can't afford that."

I opened a sack of bread and took out a couple of slices, still under the false assumption that I'd be enjoying a meatloaf sandwich momentarily. "We'll have to wait until Joe gets back with your car."

"Can't we take your rental car?"

"No, it has a flat."

"Then we'll take his truck. He won't care—always leaves the keys in the ignition."

"I'm sorry, Aunt Ingrid, but Joe says you can't get in the cab without help, and I can't help you. I did something to my back trying to carry one of Beth's rocks outside."

The lower lip came out. "I can get in Joe's truck."

"He says you can't—not without help. He'll be back in a few minutes."

"I can't wait! The bill is due today, and if I don't get it paid, they'll penalize me."

"You *can't* get in Joe's truck on your own."

She crossed her arms. "I can so."

I smacked the bottom of the ketchup bottle, praying for restraint. A big blob shot out and spattered the front of my blouse. "You *can't.* Joe said you couldn't, and I can't help because I don't want to further agitate my back."

"I can get in that truck."

"You *can't*!" And I thought Sara was willful. Dealing with Ingrid was like eating a caramel and getting it stuck in your back teeth.

"You just watch me." Stomping to the back screen, she opened it, and was out the door in a flash.

Dropping the ketchup bottle, I bolted after her. By the time I ran across the street, she was at the truck. Jerking the door open, she shimmed up the high running board and into the front seat.

I arrived, breathless, and more than a little put out. Perched on Joe's truck seat, Ingrid stared straight ahead. "I'm ready any time you are."

Ready? No, I wasn't ready! I had a meat-loaf sandwich waiting for me, my blouse had a ketchup splotch, and I hadn't put on makeup today. But by now I was mad enough to bite nails.

"*All right.* I'll get my purse."

When I pulled up in front of the electric company, we hadn't said two words to each other. Ingrid sat in the passenger seat, purse clutched to her middle, looking neither to the right nor left. She reminded me of a female General Patton on a field mission.

"I'll wait in the truck." I killed the engine.

"I want you to meet Estelle."

"Estelle who?"

"Estelle Woods, my friend. She works here." *So. She did have a friend.*

Looking like Godzilla on a bad-hair day, I got out of the truck and followed her inside. After introductions, Aunt Ingrid lingered to chat with her friend. Twenty minutes later we came out of the utility company and walked to the truck. Ingrid paused on the passenger side.

"Get in," I called.

"I can't. You'll have to help me up."

I'd heard of people seeing red, but I'd never experienced it until now. I could not believe my ears. She *couldn't* get in?

"Get in, Ingrid. No kidding."

Her stance turned belligerent. "I can't. You'll have to help me."

I got out and slammed the cab door, then marched around the front of the truck imagining steam boiling from my ears. Facing Ingrid, I put my hands on my hips. "What do you mean, you can't? You got in by yourself before."

Her eyes narrowed. "I'm an old woman. I can't get in. You'll have to help me."

My mind raced. What was the penalty for cold-blooded murder? Manslaughter. Temporary insanity. Sure, I could plead insanity. Maybe get off with ten years—serve on good behavior, be out by the time I was ...

Whoa! Get a grip!

Marching back around the truck, I yanked open the door and searched for something—anything—to stand on. I spotted a block of wood on the floorboard.

The board landed at Ingrid's feet. She looked at it, then at me.

"Get in."

"I can't."

"You can!" I took her arm and nudged her onto the board. She balked, digging in her heels.

Finally I gave up and corralled her onto the running board, and then with my forehead bracing her generous backsides, I shoved. With an *oomph,* she settled, bringing her purse to her lap. She turned and met my furious look. "On the way home can we stop at the Dairy Dell for an ice cream? I'm in the mood for a Crusty Cow."

I'll give her a Crusty Cow . . .

My editorial was featured in Friday morning's paper. I read it over with a sense of prideful ownership. I had written this—every glowing word of it. I'd missed my calling. I should have been a writer instead of a nurse.

The phone was silent; no one called to compliment me on Herman's well-written and heartfelt accolade.

And Vic was still holding out.

Midmorning, Joe marched up Beth's walk, his bottom lip curled like a sausage link. What now? Everything was falling into place; one last town meeting regarding Herman and the statue, and I could go home.

The Parishes continued to garner town sympathy for their daughter while Herman's supporters wavered. Sometime during the night, I'd decided to withdraw my consent. Again. I knew my vacillating character would be perceived as true to form from the nutty Moss family, but events of the past day had made me realize that God wanted the fiasco over—finished. Or maybe I was the one who wanted it finished. I didn't know anymore. Vic had bought the house; Ingrid was walking again. Sara had cooled, so maybe the brief time I'd been away had accomplished what I'd hoped—a stronger, more independent daughter who knew Mom was nearby, but who was capable of running her own household. In essence, my job was over.

Joe reached the porch and rapped on the screen with a rolled-up newspaper. His heightened color indicated something big was brewing. When I opened the door, he sailed by me. "Town's gone nuts."

"Tell me something new." I lifted the coffeepot, motioning to an empty cup.

"No time for coffee this morning. Have you seen the paper?"

"Yes. Why?" I refilled my cup and set the chrome percolator on the counter. "I only had time to read my editorial."

"It's got the town in an uproar."

"My editorial? What's wrong with it?" I'd thought it was a nice tribute to my father. I took the paper and skimmed the column. My original letter, which had been written the day before, prominently led the discussion, but I had missed the long column of various letters either supporting me or taking me to task over my perspective.

"*What* are they talking about?"

"Your father. Seems the Parishes, and now your editorial, have set off a real stink bomb."

Stink bomb, indeed. My gaze followed a line of an opposing viewpoint:

Why the very idea of putting someone like Herman Moss on display for all to see . . .

Why couldn't people love? Why couldn't human beings see beyond the physical and reach to the heart of a man or woman. In today's world, perfection had replaced goodness. Their attitude hurt, but I'd done the best I could. If people were offended, that was their problem. I was through. I folded the paper and laid it aside. "Talk will die down when I leave."

"Leave?" Joe's brow jutted up. "You just got back."

"Vic bought the house. You know that, and you never did tell me what he plans to do with it." Putting Joe in the middle was unfair. I knew it but couldn't stop from serving my interests. "Will he live here?"

Joe turned the picture of ignorance. His face was a politically correct blank—a father's vacant look when being questioned about a son's business. "You know Vic. He makes investments. Never consults me. Just buys whenever the urge hits."

I studied my friend, my confidant, my surrogate father—and a terrible liar. Was he shielding me from more bad news? Reports of Vic and Lana. That was it! Vic purchased the house, and he and Lana's relationship was more serious than I'd thought—more than even Joe had thought. My brain raced with alarming possibilities.

How *dare* Vic buy Aunt Beth's house and move another woman in here!

"Marlene?" Joe's voice barely penetrated my sanctimonious fog. What a fool I'd been! I should never have signed the papers. I'd sold too quickly. I should have kept the house as investment property. Parnass Springs was small, and rental property hard to find. What had I been thinking? I could have purchased the house from the estate and increased my monthly income.

"Marlene!"

"What!"

"Sit down. You're white as a sheet." Joe pulled me down into a kitchen chair and drew a glass of tap water. "Drink this and calm down."

I couldn't breathe. *Air!* "I'm having a panic attack."

He grabbed for a plastic Wal-Mart sack lying on the counter. "Here, blow in this."

I batted the bag away. "I'm not hyperventilating—I'm having a panic attack. And you have to use a paper sack, Joe. Not plastic."

I picked up the glass and drained it in one long swallow. I'd thought I'd reached the peak of irrationality, but obviously not. Was it possible to cancel the contract? Let Tracey know I'd changed my mind and no longer wanted to sell?

"Talk'll die down." Joe obviously thought my distress originated from the editorial columns. Heated letters were nothing compared to the anguish coursing through my veins when I thought of Vic and Lana in Aunt Beth's house. Going about their lives, attending church on Sunday.

Dr. and Mrs. Vic Brewster.

It wasn't fair. I should be living here; I should be Mrs. Vic Brewster . . .

I caught my willful thoughts. I'd lost it. Somewhere between here and Glen Ellyn, I'd lost my last shred of common sense. I was freaking out over a man who at the moment had me at the top of his Judas list. A man I'd betrayed for years. I sprang up and refilled my glass with tap water and downed it. Joe watched, looking as though he might need to throw a net over me.

"It's the model upsetting you, isn't it?"

"Yes . . . no." I raised my eyes. "What model?"

"Of Herman. The one the shelter is unveiling at tomorrow night's town council meeting."

I continued to stare blankly at him.

"You know. The one the letters mentioned?"

I grabbed for the plastic Wal-Mart sack. "Missed that." *Air!* I needed air!

"Marlene." Joe cleared a spot on the cluttered table and unfolded the newspaper. Adjusting his glasses on the tip of his nose, he proceeded to read aloud.

" 'In deference to the growing controversy, the shelter has decided to order a replica of said statue. It is the committee's desire to allay fears of the monument's detrimental effect on Parnass Springs by showing the supreme craftsmanship and intent of proposed statue.' "

Yep. Missed that, and now Joe kindly pointed out my oversight. I slammed my hand on the table. "Heaven help us all!"

"I'm not so sure a replica isn't a good idea. Once folks see what's intended, the naysayers will back off."

"The Parishes will never back off, and I can't say that I blame them."

"What? I thought you'd decided to let the statue go up."

"I had, but after I met the Parishes ..." I bit my lower lip. "When I met them and saw the kind of people they were ... that they honestly wanted this whole painful thing to be over ... Oh Joe! I don't know what to do."

He shook his head. "On, off. On, off. You have to make up your mind, Marlene. Either you want your father recognized or you don't."

"Honestly? I don't know *what* I want." I told him about finding the cigar box and Herman's personal items. "It hit me hard that I'd never done anything to acknowledge my father. That's why I wrote the editorial, not because I wanted to persuade the opposition to let the statue go up."

"The editorial was quite touching. Herman would have been proud; I'm sure Ingrid appreciated the gesture."

My mind traveled back to the moment I'd shown Ingrid my editorial. I watched varying emotions play across her face, then tears swell to her faded eyes. She'd handed the paper back to me with a sanctimonious, "Well, Marlene. For once you did the right thing."

I'd felt my fingers curl in a death lock around the now rolled-up newspaper. If she'd been a fly, I'd have swatted her.

"You know Ingrid. Even if she did appreciate the effort, she'd die before she let me know it. She's funding the statue!"

Joe. Good old Joe leaned over and squeezed my shoulder. "You did a good thing, Marly. Don't let Ingrid rain on your parade."

"That's just it. This whole statue thing has turned into a parade, and I want it stopped. I'm going home, Joe. I'm going to the town meeting tomorrow night, and I'm withdrawing my support of the statue. After that, they can do what they want. Ingrid will be upset, but she'll get over it."

If she took to the wheelchair again, I'd have no choice but to take her to Glen Ellyn or put her in assisted living here. But I was through with Parnass Springs, through with Vic, and through with the whole mess.

Most of all, I was through with games.

And yes, if I intended to clean up my act, I had to admit to my foolish games. I was the one who lied. I needed to face Vic, and yet I'd taken the only way out I knew. The coward's way, shirking responsibility and leaving a path of devastation in my wake. No wonder the Lord remained vaguely detached from my frantic pleas for help.

Vic should have confronted me the moment my lie was exposed, declared his undying love and forgiven me in a gracious, Christlike way.

Well, isn't that what you expected, Marlene?

I should live in Aunt Beth's house.

I should be Mrs. Vic Brewster and live happily ever after.

I should know donkeys would line dance before any of the above happened. I'd sown my wild oats, and now I was stuck with nothing but runny oatmeal.

Joe might be mild-mannered, but he had mighty determination. Like father, like son. Vic had Joe's stubbornness, his resolve to face life head-on. Both shone brightly in Joe's face, and so did common sense. He never once led me wrong or gave me bad advice.

He sat me down, hands bracing my shoulders. Eyes so like Vic's pinned me to the seat. "Now you listen to me, Marlene. I haven't often been stern with you, but I am about to seriously hurt your feelings. This madness you've been carrying on year after year has to stop. You have seriously jeopardized any future you and Vic might have."

I shrugged his hands aside. "I don't need a lecture."

"You need a good time-out, young lady." Joe suddenly turned into a Joe I didn't know—he'd turned into Vic. Serious, no-nonsense Vic, and I didn't like the change. I wanted my old Joe—my kind, understanding let-Marly-alone Joe. This man was anything but sympathetic to my cause. Tired lines circled his eyes, and he seemed a bit more stooped than I remembered. Joe had seen and heard it all. How weary he must be of every excuse man had invented for self-interest and pitiless misery.

Right now he was looking at the world champion of both, and I wasn't proud of the title.

"You're right." I gathered my pride and replaced it with mock sarcasm. "I take it you have something you want to say to me."

"You take it correctly." He drew a chair closer and sat down. Crossing his hands, he studied his fingers. "Marlene. What I'm about say is unkind and I apologize, but you know you're the daughter I never had."

"I know . . . I love you, Joe."

"Very well and good, and I love you. But sweet talk won't get you out of what I'm about to say."

"Fire away."

"You are a spoiled, willful child in an adult body. Beth was too old to raise you, and Ingrid too wishy-washy. I watched you grow up in a world where everyone bent backwards to accommodate you because of Herman."

I didn't like Herman's and my situation spoken about with such open candor. Our situation was mostly addressed in whispered snatches. I squirmed, prickly beneath his penetrating gaze.

Joe's eyes softened, gentled. "Herman gave you life, but I like to think I helped shape that life, and you're not living the life we shaped together." He reached for my hands and his touch calmed me. Hands that had soothed childhood cuts and bruises, encouraged my dreams, and softened my letdowns. Disappointment warred with pride in his eyes.

"You're a lovely woman, and I'm going to tell you what others have only skirted around all your life. You got a rough deal; Herman had a worse one. I can't explain why God allows mental disability or senseless diseases—only he knows the answer. I do know that one day we'll have new bodies, and sickness, death, and pain will be no more. You were given the mental and physical abilities to overcome your family medical history; Herman is now free of his burden." His hold tightened. "Listen to me, daughter. You're still young. If God desires, you'll have many years ahead of you, years to realize your dreams, years to enjoy life, to love, to race with the wind. Go to Vic. Confess what he already knows, and make your apologies. I can't say with certainty what he'll do, but I know what the effect will be on you. You'll bloom into the woman God intended, a woman full of love and grace. All you have to do is allow the bitterness to drain away."

His words were like cleansing needles piercing ugly wounds. Not easy to hear, but healing. Lifting my eyes, I faced my accuser. "Do you think Vic will forgive me?" I clung to his hand, fearing that if I let loose of Joe, I'd let go of Vic too.

"Forgive you, yes. Will he forget, and will his love be strong enough to overcome the past? That's what you want, isn't it? To complete the dream that you and Vic began as children, to join as one, to grow old together?"

Pride fell away and I was so glad to rid myself of the burdensome garment. The missing weight left me buoyant, ready to do and face what I must. "I've dreamt of nothing less since the day I left Parnass Springs."

"Then for heaven's sake—and the sakes of everybody else who's been forced to stand by all these years and watch this drama play out—*go* to the man and tell him your feelings."

"Oh, Joe, he'll be so furious with me. All these years I've allowed him to think that Noel was still in my life."

"He's *already* furious with you! And the world! He's a good man, Marlene, but he has his limits." Joe sighed. "I pray daily you'll settle this lie, because it's strangling what could be a wonderful thing."

I reached for a napkin to blow my nose. "What if I go to him and he rejects my apology? His relationship with Julie was founded on trust." It'd be a cold day in August when he'd trust me again. "He loved her so deeply."

"He did." Joe's confirmation didn't do much to bolster my motivation. "But love comes in all forms, Marlene. You should know that. Your love for Herman was different than your love for Sara. Vic shared a deep and steadfast love with Julie, but Vic also remembers and grieves the love of his youth—the love of his life. And that's you, no matter how hard he tries to deny that fact, even to himself. Go to him, honey. Take advantage of what God has so richly put in your life. Not many find a love that spans year after year, trial after trial—and you and Vic *have* had your trials." He released another deep sigh. "Melba and I had that love. It's a rare gift, Marlene. Don't throw it away."

A priceless gift, love, and I'd had more than my share in life and failed to be grateful for it. Beth, though single and eccentric, and Ingrid, though staid and bitter at life, had nonetheless sacrificed to raise an infant.

Herman in his simple mind had allowed me angelic love; how many could claim that?

"I have so many apologies to make."

Joe shrugged. "Name me a person who doesn't? Isn't it fortunate we serve a forgiving God? Now go and be the Proverbs 31 woman."

He'd had me up till then. I was anything but a woman early-to-rise to serve my household with glee. But I could do better. And I knew exactly where I was going to start. I would confess my lie to Vic and face the consequences.

I hugged this man, without whom I could never have faced life. "Thank you."

He hugged me back. "Thank you for listening. Now go do what's right."

"I will." And this time I meant it.

That evening I showed Ingrid the cigar box. Her fingers stroked the worn lid. "Herman's treasures. The things he kept in here were important to him."

She opened the box and looked inside. I knew what she saw; things saved by the loved stepson who would never reach his full potential. She lifted the items, one by one. The pictures of me she placed to one side. "He was so proud of you."

"I know that now. I was too young back then to understand. Ingrid, do you think I was spoiled?"

"Back then, you mean?"

I nodded.

She sat in silence. "The past is gone; I'd say you grew to be as good as most. Maybe better." She picked up the cheap ring. "Herman's wedding band."

I stared at her, not sure I'd heard right. "His *what*? Herman was … *married*?"

"He thought he was. He and Lexy. Couldn't convince him any different. He wore that silly ring until it got too tight. I'd thought he'd lost it, but he put it in here."

Whoa! Hang on just a ding-dong minute here. Herman believed he was married to Lexy Parish. That was …

My eyes went wide. It was exhilarating!

My father thought he and my mother were married! Molestation had nothing to do with my conception, my birth. I was born out of commitment and love, not the adolescent hormones of two mentally challenged people. "Is that why I came into the world?"

She nodded. "He said they had the right. Seems he and Lexy loved children, maybe because they were both infants themselves. When the doctors told us about the pregnancy, it like to have killed us, but then we pulled up our socks and carried on."

That they had.

Herman's morals had been straight and honorable all along. He thought, in his simple way, he'd married the woman he loved. Suddenly I saw it as clear as day.

The heritage my father left me wasn't one of mental lack or scandal. Not hardly. My father's heritage was one thing. Love.

That realization firmed my resolve even more. It was time for me to act on my true birthright.

I left Ingrid's and drove by the vet clinic. The security light was off, and Vic's pickup was gone. The truck wasn't in Joe's drive when I left.

Where was he?

I called twice more before exhaustion drove me to bed. I slept fitfully. Confession weighed heavily on my mind. I tossed, getting up twice to peer out the window to the darkened cottage behind Joe's place. Vic's home remained dark.

Oh Vic, come home. Please come home.

Thirteen

I was up and dressed before dawn Saturday morning. I picked up the phone and dialed Joe. His sleepy voice came on the line. "'Lo?"

"Hi. I notice Vic's truck is gone."

"Yeah, you just missed him. He sat up all night with a sick animal—I heard him stop by a few minutes ago to shower and change, and then he was off again. Can I help you?"

"No, I need to talk to him. You have any idea when he'll be back?"

"He said something about vaccinating some cows. Good gravy, Marly. Do you know what time it is?"

"Very early. I apologize, Joe. Do you expect him back soon?"

"Should be back by early afternoon, I'd guess."

Joe wasn't thrilled that I'd roused him out of bed at this hour, but Joe was Joe, and for some inexplicable reason, he'd understood my need when I asked my next question.

"Joe, do you know where I can find my mother? I'm assuming that she is alive?"

I waited for his shock. Maybe even outrage. Instead, I heard him fumble for his glasses, then rustle some paper. What was he—?

"Woodland Health Care. It's an hour's drive from here. Here's the address and phone number."

He'd looked it up in the phone book. Good ole Joe.

"Thanks."

I moved so fast, I was probably halfway to Walgreens by the time Joe stumbled back to bed. I bought a small stuffed bear and candy kisses, and then, heart pounding, drove to the nursing facility. My resolve almost failed me when I arrived, and I sat in the car for thirty minutes trying to get enough courage to go inside.

Lord, please . . . help me. Am I doing the right thing? Don't let me make matters worse.

Sunlight filtered through budding oaks at the Woodland Health Care facility as dawn broke the eastern sky. My eyes swept the brick facade that had been my mother's home the majority of her life. Towering trees, an immaculate lawn, beds of colorful annuals already planted. The serene landscape lent a certain calmness and acceptance that immediately seized me.

And I knew. This *was* the right thing to do.

A warming breeze ruffled my arm, warning me that my light Windbreaker would be too heavy later. The weatherman on the radio was predicting "unusually high temperatures for this next-to-last day of April. And an 80 percent chance for thunderstorms by evening. Folks," he cautioned, "this is a big system, one we'll be watching closely."

Switching off the radio, I reached for the shopping bag I'd filled with the stuffed toy and Hershey's Kisses. Did my mother like chocolate?

She's a woman, isn't she?

Could I do this? Did I really *want* to do this?

The smell of breakfast lingered in the hallways when I walked into the facility. I sniffed—bacon and something sweet. Light streamed from a bank of floor-to-ceiling windows encircling the north end of the building. Carpeted seating areas were spotless from the work of morning cleaning crews. As health facilities went, this one was exceptional. The Parishes must pay a handsome amount to keep their daughter here year after year.

I located a bank of elevators, then the reception desk. Joe hadn't known much about Lexy Parish, other than he'd heard that she had been moved to Woodlands shortly after my birth. I handed the slip of paper with *Parish* written on it to the smiling, pink-smocked lady behind the desk.

"Lexy Parish? Yes." She typed in the name and a moment later wrote a room number on a pad. "Take the second elevator to the third floor and turn right."

Instead of a home, the facility suddenly felt like a hospital. Yet when the double doors opened and I stepped out into an atrium, I immediately relaxed. Birds flittered overhead. The soft but unmistakable trickle of a waterfall followed me down a warm, symmetrical-patterned tile walkway lit by soft landscape lighting. Benches nestled among exotic plants and palms that reached to the high-vaulted sky roof. My heart beat in my throat as I approached room 312—which, from what I could see through the slightly ajar door, wasn't a room but an apartment. I could hear the hum of a vacuum.

My nursing instinct kicked in, and I walked through the door before I realized I wasn't at work. Backing out quickly, I took a deep breath. No one had seen me. I'd stepped into a nicely appointed but empty sitting area.

I tapped on the door.

The vacuum hummed. I knew my timid knock wouldn't be heard above the noise. I stepped inside the room and rapped on the door facing. Still no response. Beyond the sitting room, I spotted a second room. Strip away the cold metal hospital bed in the middle of the floor, and the room would be a tastefully accentuated bedroom with three long floor-length windows on the east. Front row seats when Christ came again.

"May I help you?"

I jerked around and faced a housekeeper carrying a load of fresh linens.

"Ms. Parish? Is she accepting visitors?"

"Lexy? Sure, she's in here."

I trailed the young woman into the bedroom, my meticulously thought-out speech gone, my mind as empty as a pawnshop pistol.

My eyes focused on the woman sitting in a high-backed, damask floral-covered chair facing the window embankment. For a moment I thought Ann Parish was visiting and I panicked. What would I say to the elder Parish? How would I explain my impulsive visit?

How did I explain it to myself? I'd woken this morning with an insane urge to see my mother before I left. Not once in forty-three years had I experienced this drive, but suddenly it was imperative that I meet the woman who'd given birth to me. The woman Herman had loved and thought he'd married.

Now I was standing in the same room as my mother. The foreign sensation took my breath.

"Lexy? You have an early visitor today." The maid carried the linens to the bathroom as the woman in the chair turned to look at me—and I realized Ann Parish was right. My mother and I had the same warm, liquid eyes.

"Who are you?" Her voice was high-pitched, childish, the words slightly slurred.

Who was I? I didn't know if she knew that she even had a daughter. Summoning a smile, I stepped forward. "How are you today, Lexy?"

A smile lit the corners of her eyes. She was exquisite. Makeup impeccably applied even at this early hour. Thick, dark braided hair. She wore a simple band on her right hand. Even as I drew closer, I recognized the ring—the twin was wrapped in white tissue in the bottom of Herman's cigar box.

She reached out for my hand. I caught hers, and for a split second we embraced. "Lexy. My name is Lexy. What's your name?"

"Marlene." She didn't know me, and I didn't know her. I didn't feel any sudden rush of emotion—tears of a long-anticipated sentimentality. A basic twinge, maybe, curious definitely. This lovely woman looked nothing like I had expected. Maybe I'd expected a monster—some hideous-looking thing that drooled. As a health professional I should have known better. But for all of my training and experience, I hadn't ever been able to rid myself of those childhood fears. Those images that haunted me.

Now, as I looked at my mother, I saw how wrong those ideas were. Other than the surroundings, and a certain hint of something not quite right in her eyes, the woman sitting before me looked like any other woman her age.

"Marlene." She smiled. "I like that name. Wanna sit beside me?" She patted a seat beside her and I sat down, my gaze roaming the row of silver-plated picture frames on the table beside her. I recognized Grayson and Ann Parish. There was a picture of an older couple, perhaps my great-grandparents, standing beside a porch rail trailing red roses.

I nodded toward the mementos. "Is that your family?"

Her eyes switched to the frames. "Uh-huh. My momma ... and my papa. Grandma ... and grandpa." The words were slow, halting.

"Yes. Very nice." I returned her smile, and then fumbled for the shopping bag. "I have something for you."

"For me?" Childlike anticipation lit her eyes.

Why didn't I bring flowers? A simple bouquet of spring flowers instead of a stuffed toy. I almost didn't pull the bear out of the sack until she dipped her head to see around me. "Oh! A bear!"

I drew the toy out of the bag and gave it to her. You'd have thought I'd given her the Hope diamond. Her eyes misted. She tugged at the blue and green plaid shirt and jaunty hat, grinning. "For me? I *like* bears." She hugged it to her.

Herman liked bears too. He carried some kind of stuffed animal everywhere he went—including my prom.

"I hoped you might." I took out the chocolate kisses and again she was thrilled and offered me one. We sat in the tasteful bedroom and sucked on chocolate pieces. It was nice; a good daughter-mother thing we could share.

After a while, I noticed she seemed tired. When I attempted to take the bear, she drew the gift to her chest, holding tightly to the treasure. "My bear."

"Yes, he's yours. Would you like for me to help you back into bed?"

"Uh-huh. Can I keep my bear? No take-backs?"

"He's yours to keep." I slipped my arm around her waist and helped her into the bed. Out of habit, I straightened her pillow, put her call button close to her hand, and then tucked a blanket securely around the mattress. She clutched the bear to her chest.

"Will you come back and see me?"

"Of course I will. I had a lovely time. Thank you for sharing the chocolate."

She chuckled, a soft, whispery sound. "I like chocolate."

Yeah, Mom. A girl can never get enough chocolate.

I left the room a better person. Lexy Parish had no idea she'd just spent a few minutes with her daughter. I didn't know if she even understood that she *had* a daughter. The Parishes seemed to think that a statue of Herman in a town an hour away would be detrimental to their daughter's happiness, but I now knew that was propaganda—the protective parent kind. The statue would be detrimental to Grayson and Ann's happiness; Lexy wouldn't know or care.

But I did. I knew *and* I cared. The Parishes, by all appearances, were good people. The past should remain just that: the past.

I pushed the elevator button feeling better about myself and my past. I'd met my mother. Something I'd needed to do a long time ago. All my fear was for nothing. Sara was healthy—my mom wasn't the monster I'd pictured her to be. Dad was even turning out to be an okay guy.

The elevator doors opened, and I walked straight into Grayson and Ann Parish.

"Oh!" I stepped back quickly. "Oh!" I met my grandparents' startled faces. What did I say? How could I explain my appearance?

"Marlene?" Grayson was the first to recover. The door began to shut. He stuck out a hand and blocked the motion. Ann slipped out, and he followed. When the door closed, the three of us stared at each other. Then we all spoke at the same time.

"You must be wondering why—"

"Marlene?"

"How did you *know* where she was?"

"How? Joe told me. Joe Brewster."

Grayson took my arm and led me to one of the benches. A tearful Ann followed.

"I'm sorry. I know I have no right to be here, but I'm leaving town soon and I just thought since I'd never be back ... I just thought ..." The last thing I wanted was a scene. *I just thought*—that was my problem. If I wouldn't act on my impulsive thoughts, I'd be in better shape.

"No." Grayson's stern voice corrected me. "You have *every* right to be here."

"Grayson!"

"No, Ann. Enough is enough. Regardless of the circumstances, Marlene is Lexy's daughter. She has every right to meet her mother."

Ann sat down beside me, fumbling in her handbag for a tissue. I located one first and handed it over. "This is awkward. So terribly awkward."

She delicately blew her nose. "Grayson is right. Did you tell Lexy ...?"

"No! No. I didn't say a word." I searched my grandfather's eyes. "I didn't. She asked who I was, and when I changed the subject, she never mentioned it again."

The three of us sat in silence. Birds darted overhead. Everything *seemed* so normal yet our worlds had just collided.

Ann cleared her throat. "Why did you come?"

"I don't know. Until this business about Herman and the statue, I'd never thought much about her—Lexy. This morning I woke before dawn with this sudden need to see her. So

I got Joe out of bed, stopped by Walgreens and purchased a teddy bear and a bag of Hershey's Kisses, and made the hour's drive here." I paused and drew a heavy breath. "She's very pretty." I looked at Ann. "She looks like you."

Nodding, she wiped her nose. "And you look so much like her when she was your age. She named you, you know."

"No." I didn't know anything about my parents, not really. I leaned over and touched her arm. This had to be so hard on her. "I'm so sorry that Herman— "

"No." Grayson corrected me a second time. "Not Herman. Herman and Lexy. Both were responsible. We've skirted around the fact for years, and it's high time Lexy shared the responsibility."

"But— "

"Ann." Grayson quieted his wife. "Our daughter is not normal; she has many problems, but you and I both know the truth. What happened forty-three years ago resulted from an act carried out by two consenting parties."

My mind flew to the cigar box and the ring. "Are you aware that Herman and Lexy believed they were married?"

Ann looked up, her forehead creased.

"It's true." I told them about the cigar box, and the matching rings. Herman believed he had married his friend, Lexy.

"Lexy's worn that ring ever since." Ann's eyes met Grayson's. "She insisted they were married."

"And we never believed her."

"They couldn't have married. There was no ceremony."

"No formal ceremony." I took Ann's hand. "But one from the heart. Herman knew and believed in God. Ingrid made sure he understood. He knew, in his simple way, that there was a God."

Grayson sat down. "She'd never say where the ring came from. We thought she'd gotten it out of a cereal box."

"Herman probably did. He ate enough cold cereal in his lifetime to start a chain of trinket jewelry stores—a cereal-box jewelry chain, but a jewelry chain."

My offhand observation broke the tension. Grayson and Ann chuckled.

"My goodness," Ann whispered. "Those two thought they were actually married."

We sat talking—my grandparents and me, for the better part of the day and even had lunch together in the facility's cafeteria. I told them about my life—the honest truth. About Sara, and my fears when I carried her.

"It's odd, you know. When I took the pregnancy test, I was terrified it would be positive—then terrified it would be negative. I love children, and I would have had several if ..."

Grayson smiled. "If."

Ann bit her lip. "We have no idea why Lexy is the way she is. It's one of those unexplainable things. It just happened. We started noticing she wasn't developing properly around seven, and she got steadily worse. She's been institutionalized since she was fourteen. When she met Herman there a couple years later, she fell in love. It was impossible for us to make her understand that neither she nor Herman was normal—that they couldn't fall in love and marry like others."

"Lexy's an only child?"

"Oh, yes. The doctor said the chances of her condition being repeated with other children were slim, but like you, Grayson and I wouldn't consider having more, though we love Lexy dearly. We were afraid to risk it." She dabbed her nose. "But, oh! We've longed for grandchildren ..."

I smiled. "Well, you have a granddaughter. And a great-granddaughter and two great-great-grandchildren, one four years old, and one two. And one more on the way."

Ann gasped.

Cringing, I realized that I made her sound ancient since Sara was very young to have two children. "You're more than welcome to spoil them shamelessly—there's only one of me, and I'm doing a fair job, but I can always use help."

Then the emotion kicked in. Everything I should have experienced in Lexy's room but didn't. The love. The longing to be a family. The need to hug Pops and Grams and never let go.

Next thing I knew, I was weeping.

Grayson enfolded me, and then Ann. We stood in the quiet, curative foyer and hugged and cried.

"You don't know how much we wanted to claim you," Ann whispered. "We have relived our hateful words about considering you dead a million times—*praying* that we could someday retract and make up for what we said. We were so frightened. Can you understand? We felt we couldn't cope with two mentally challenged children—we didn't know what to do, so we lashed out at Ingrid and Beth. Thank God they insisted on keeping you in their family." Her hand tightened on mine. "We have scrapbook upon scrapbook of your pictures when you were growing up. Every week Grayson would drive by Beth's house and catch you in the front yard playing. Or he'd sit in the audience at school plays or music recitals and take pictures. He even caught you quite by accident the night of your prom. He was on his way to the drugstore and happened to see you and your date drive by. He wheeled around and snapped a picture as you walked into the gym."

Grayson smiled. "Today I would be arrested for stalking, or at least for suspicious behavior."

"How did Herman and Lexy meet? How ...?" I left the obvious question unspoken: how did they manage to be alone long enough to conceive a child?

"Herman came into the facility a few years after Lexy. They drew to one another instantly—they were seldom apart. They ate their meals together, did crafts together. We don't know how the pregnancy happened—the nursing facilities do the best they can, but sometimes—" Anne paused. "Later, Herman tried to be a man, tried to take responsibility for his actions, but of course, he was a child with a man's body."

She reached out and tentatively smoothed a stray hair from my forehead. Up close, I could see the years. She had to be near eighty. "I know you won't understand, but we thought it best Beth raise you, and for us to stay out of your life. We realized too late how foolish we'd been, but by then you were in your teens, and we couldn't bring ourselves to reopen the painful past. Then suddenly you were gone, married. We knew we would never see you again, and our hearts ached."

I embraced her. There'd been a lot of mistakes in the past. Mine as well as theirs. But this was one family legacy that would stop. Here and now.

We returned to my mother's room and spent the day with her. We played games and sang songs. She seemed content—happy with her new friend.

Until that day my past hadn't been important to me, but this afternoon had changed everything. I carried the thought with me as I left the building and checked the time. Four thirty. I'd promised Ingrid to be home in plenty of time for the town council meeting at seven. I'd have to hurry.

But now, facing tonight's chaos didn't seem so insurmountable.

I'd state my position, once and for all, and it would be over. I'd go home, to Glen Ellyn where I belonged.

A new beginning. Grayson and Ann could come and visit Sara and the children. Life would be different. I'd have family now, close family, except for one notable exception. The past between Vic and me was still unresolved.

I had to find him and talk to him. Now.

Thunder shook the ground as I got into the car. A hot wind buffeted the car; thick storm clouds built in the west. I took a second to change my cell so Vic's ring tone was "Amazing Grace." I wanted to be sure that if Vic *did* call to talk, the credit went to the proper source.

Fourteen

Hail bombarded the car as I turned out of Woodlands. Pea-sized, and then nugget-sized chunks pelted the hood. An ugly gray-green cloud hung overhead as I swerved off the outer road and onto the highway. More rain? Spring was indeed fickle. Two ducks flew by, moving with the wind. Concerned about the worsening weather, I flipped on the radio and tuned in to a local station as the tornado sirens went off.

A chunk of hail the size of a baseball hit the windshield, shattering the safety glass. I yelped and jerked the wheel, careening toward the shoulder. The hail suddenly stopped and a dead calm settled over the area.

Stunned by the onslaught and terrified to drive any farther, I sat parked by the side of the road, the motor idling. The entire sky to the left, southward, was a pleasant, warm blue with golden sunlight. Everything to the north was a roiling, pitch-black cloud. I rolled down the window and craned my neck, staring at the cloud. I could make out a distinct clockwise rotation taking shape.

Tornado. My breath caught in my throat.

Warning sirens wailed. Motorists flashed by me, some screeching to a stop under a nearby underpass. I glanced to my right and left. No ditches in which to take cover. A gust of wind rocked the car. I slid the transmission into gear, deciding to make a run for cover.

Wheeling back onto the highway, I floored the gas pedal. The car fishtailed before rubber gained traction. The overhead underpass quickly filled with panicked drivers. I spotted an empty space that I could wedge into and mashed harder on the gas, fear rushing my throat. Then I heard it. A grinding sound, like a huge cement truck backing toward the highway. Huge, sucking, coming right at me.

I'd been in one other tornado in my life. Aunt Beth had pulled me from bed one August night, wrapped me in a blanket, and carried me to Aunt Ingrid's root cellar. The storm had destroyed half of Parnass Springs and claimed three lives.

Violent wind rocked the car; I kept one eye on the underpass and another on the ominous-looking cloud that was quickly closing in. Suddenly I knew I was about to face death.

Please God, please God. Let me make it to the underpass.

I was almost there, but the funnel was moving unbelievably fast. The apocalyptic black curtain cut off the sky, whipping round and round, snapping trees in half. My ears started popping. Wind rocked the car, dust blinded me. A bush, broken off at the roots, rocketed past, and I involuntarily ducked. Then it happened.

The car lifted—I felt it leave the pavement. Everything tilted, turned upside down. Wind shrieked past the windows. I gripped the steering wheel, holding tight. Only the seatbelt held me in place.

The compact tumbled over and over, like a child's toy. My eardrums ached, threatening to burst from pressure.

A piece of tin—maybe a highway sign—slammed the passenger side. Debris poured through the shattered windshield. I quit trying to hold on to the steering wheel. Grit and bits of rubble stung my exposed flesh. My hands flew to my face, a shielding defense. A female's frantic screams rang in my ears. Mine?

Something large and heavy hit the hood of my car. My hands dropped, and I saw a commercial trash bin sail off into the churning blackness.

God, help me! I was in a funnel cloud. A whirling sheet of tin roofing flew past, missing the car by centimeters.

A fragment of a verse in Hebrews flashed through my mind: *"Just as man is destined to die once, and after that to face judgment . . ."*

This was my appointed hour. Something slammed through the windshield and exited the back window. Screaming, I slid down as far as the seat belt would allow. Not far enough.

Joe's earlier warning flashed through my brain: *Make your amends today, Marlene. Tomorrow isn't promised to us.*

Falling, falling. *Vic!* The car plunged end-over-end before slamming down, hard. It bounced twice, landed on its side, and slid infinite feet before stopping.

Pain shot through my right shoulder. Streaks of light blinded me. I slumped against the wheel, hurting as if someone had used me for a punching bag.

A second later a mangled motorcycle hit the ground beside the car. No sign of the rider. I struggled to sit upright, took one look at the carnage around me, and passed out.

I opened my eyes again when a couple of farmers began to pull me out of the wreckage. Rain came down intermittently, cold and pitiless. An elderly man towered above me. He had to stop and catch his breath every few moments, but he was doing his best.

"Hold on little lady, we've about got you clear."

I could barely hear above the whine, some sort of a saw, and I realized there must be firemen and EMTs present.

"Am I alive?" I was still groggy, having trouble focusing.

"You're one lucky lady." Strong arms lifted me from twisted metal. Rain sluiced down in buckets, wind gusting. An immediate chill wracked me. Someone wrapped a blanket around my shoulders and led me to a waiting car. Pain shot up my left leg when I tried to put my weight down. White-hot needles stabbed my ankle. My rescuer had an arm around my waist, supporting my weight to the car. The moment I was seated, I took inventory. I couldn't feel my right arm, my front teeth seemed to be intact, my left ankle felt swollen to twice its size, and when I licked my lips, I tasted salty blood.

"How many injured?" I asked.

A medic shook his head. "It's bad." Outside power lines were spitting sparks in the dark.

Vic. Joe. Ingrid ... I struggled to sit up, but firm hands held me down. An IV went into a vein. "Woodland Health Care facility?"

"No damage assessment yet—"

Darkness claimed me before I heard the rest of the answer.

Hours later, I walked out of Boone County Hospital's emergency room doors, wondering what to do next. The hospital staff released me on my assurance that I'd go straight home and see my doctor; I was in no shape to leave, but bed space was limited to the severely injured. With a broken right arm, sprained left ankle, numerous cuts and lacerations, I was one of the luckier ones. I was nicked and bruised, particularly across my stomach and chest where the seatbelt had cut into me. I would be a colorful character tomorrow, but I was alive.

I'm not complaining, Lord, just grateful.

A quick inventory confirmed I was missing my purse and cell phone.

According to news reports, the tornado had cut a wide swath. Phone lines were down for fifty miles. So far, twelve had died in the storm, and damages were estimated to be in the millions.

Cabs were nonexistent. My rental car was a twisted heap lying in a farmer's field, but one thought filled my mind. I had to find Vic.

Dear God, don't let it be too late.

I struck off, hobbling toward the busy highway with enough Vicodin in me to fight bulls.

I limped along the roadside, blubbering as the realization of how close I'd come to checking out sank in. How easily I could be lying in the car wreckage, leaving behind so many unsaid thoughts, so many messes I should have cleaned up.

Thank you, God. I don't deserve what you've done for me, but I'm grateful. You know that.

Hitchhiking was foreign to me, but that was the good thing about tragedy: the sap of human kindness oozes out of mankind when there is a real need. I'd barely thrown my hand in the air when a brightly lit semi braked and the driver asked if I needed help. Sporting a head bandage, a cast on one arm, numerous facial stitches, and a crutch (that I insisted I didn't need but the hospital said I did) I conceded that yes, I could use a little help. "I need a ride to Parnass Springs."

"Climb aboard!"

I focused on the high step. No way could I climb that. Seconds later the driver bounded out of the cab, and with a gentleness that surprised me, lifted me onto the seat, then handed me the crutch.

We edged down the road, dodging downed trees and power lines. Carnage was everywhere. Flattened farms, houses, and barns. Businesses destroyed, building roofs blown off, animal carcasses, pieces of clothing, shoes, lawn chairs. Pink house insulation draped downed fences and severed lines. My hands were shaking so hard that I stuffed my uninjured one into my Windbreaker pocket. I'd never witnessed anything like this. It looked like a bomb had gone off.

My trucker was a burly young man with dark hair pulled back in a ponytail and a tattoo of an eagle clutching an American flag on his right forearm. He grinned over at me. "Name's Chuck."

"Marlene."

"So what happened to you?"

There wasn't an inch of flesh on me that didn't feel battered and bruised. The seatbelt on the compact had almost cut me in two. "I got caught in a funnel cloud. Lifted my car off the highway and whirled it around in the air like cotton candy." I shuddered, realizing what a narrow escape I'd had. My poor rental car. The second one I'd demolished. Avis would blacklist me forever.

Chuck whistled. "That right? You're lucky to be alive."

"Lucky? I suppose so, but I believe God gets the credit." I shivered, recalling the last harrowing half hour.

He shrugged. "God, huh? If he exists, it doesn't seem like he's doing much good, considering the mess the world is in." Chuck shot me a skeptical glance. "You one of those Bible-thumpin' women?"

"Can't remember the last Bible I thumped." It was hard to carry on a coherent conversation with my head pounding like a jackhammer. Where was my migraine medicine? In my purse. Where was my purse?

Chuck waved a beefy hand at the devastation lining both sides of the road. "You telling me a fair God would let something like this happen?"

I closed my eyes. "Look, I don't pretend to have answers—even *an* answer. I'm not a theologian. I'm just an ordinary woman who believes in God."

"Rose-colored glasses."

"Faith."

He fell silent, then changed the subject. "Parnass Springs your home?"

"For the time being. My aunt lives there and I'm here to settle an estate. My home's in Glen Ellyn, Illinois."

"Near Chicago, huh? You're a long way from home."

"So where are you from?"

"Oklahoma City. Drive a rig out of there, hauling canned goods and produce for Clemons Wholesale Grocery. You ever hear of them?"

Who hadn't heard of Clemons? They were one of our biggest grocery chains. At my nod, he continued. "They've got a big warehouse in Oklahoma City. I come this way twice a month."

"Well, I'm certainly glad you came this way tonight."

He braked to avoid a couple of cows crossing the road. They eyed us placidly before stepping off the blacktop. Chuck eased past them and they scampered away.

He shifted gears. "Got any kids?"

"One, a daughter. Two grandkids and another on the way."

"Nice. I've got two girls and a boy. They're something else." He grinned and pride dripped from his expression.

I laughed. "They always are when they're ours."

He shook his head. "Amazing, isn't it? I was kind of wild, you know, and then I met Kelly and we got married and started having kids. Now I look back and see how little I used to have and how much I've got now." His cell phone rang, and from his end of the conversation, I realized it was his wife.

He ended the call and grinned. "That was Kelly. She works in a convenience store—some customer came in and told her about the tornadoes. She was worried."

The destruction hadn't gotten any lighter the closer we got to Parnass. I had people I loved out here. Were they all right?

The hour drive took twice as long as normal. I stared out the truck window watching for something familiar, but the tornado had changed the area into an alien landscape. "How could one storm do so much damage? It's destroyed everything."

"Forecaster said there was a line of them. Seventeen funnels have touched down, worst outbreak in years."

"Seventeen!"

"We're almost to Parnass. Maybe it won't be so bad in your neighborhood." I clenched my teeth to keep from crying. The devastation was so complete, I couldn't see how anything could survive. I clasped my hands tightly in my lap, praying to see something still standing. A heap of rubble marked the place where a truck stop used to be. A couple of big rigs were lying on their side, tossed like toys in a child's fury. Fence posts were ripped from the ground and left in a splintered heap. A sheet of tin roofing wrapped around the lone tree left standing.

Large round hay bales littered the road. Chuck slowed, weaving his truck through them. We should have been in Parnass before now. Part of me didn't want to arrive; afraid of what I would find, but another part of me was frustrated about how long it was taking. Aunt Ingrid. Vic and Joe.

Oh, Lord, let them be all right.

When the big truck pulled into town, my heart dropped. Not much was left standing. The café had half its roof blown off. A dozen or so houses, the gas station—all were destroyed. Homes left standing had extensive damage. Chuck stopped the truck and turned a worried countenance in my direction.

"You okay?"

"I don't know." I was numb, incapable of thought.

"I'd take you to your house, but I don't think I can get this rig through the mess." He released the air brakes and climbed out of the cab. Moments later he lifted me down and handed me the crutch. We stood for a moment, watching dazed residents sift through debris.

"You sure you'll be all right?"

"I'll be fine, Chuck. I'd offer you something for gas, but I haven't seen my purse in hours."

Chuck grinned. "I wouldn't take it anyway." He sobered. "I hope your family made it through all right."

I nodded, biting back tears. Joe and Ingrid would be in the cellar. You didn't live in these parts and not take a storm seriously. But what about Vic? Where was he when the storm hit? In a farmer's field, delivering a calf? Doctoring a sick horse? Where was he at this moment? Lying hurt and alone in a pile of rubble ... I couldn't bear the thought.

I reached out with my one good hand and Chuck grasped it. "I hope you meet God one of these days."

He grinned. "You never know."

No, you never knew when God would show up.

He climbed back into his rig. There wasn't a lot of room to turn around, but he kept maneuvering until he finally got back on the road. He lifted a hand in farewell. I waved back.

I took off hobbling down the street toward Ingrid's house, terrified of what I'd find when I got there. It must be after midnight—or early Sunday morning. I'd lost all track of time.

A large tree lay across the road, ripped out by the roots. I worked my way around it, trying to protect my injured ankle. This was an endurance test and I was losing. Downed power lines littered the ground; I trod warily, knowing I was in dangerous territory, one wrong step and instant electrocution.

When I approached our street, I saw that the front porch and part of the roof had been torn off Aunt Beth's house. Aunt Ingrid's house looked to have fared better. The old oak was uprooted near the cellar door. She'd complained about that tree earlier, that the roots were penetrating the cellar. I'd promised to have it removed. Another thing I'd not gotten around to. It looked like nature had taken care of it for me. Half the shingles were gone off her roof, but the structure looked intact.

A pile of broken boards and rubble blocked my way. I inched around it, taking me off the road and through the Brewsters' front yard. I paused in front of Joe's house. The back cottage was gone; the garage was sitting in the lane at the back of the lot. Half of Joe's house remained. The kitchen was mostly rubble. I spotted the coffeemaker, the odd looking contrivance with all the hoses running from it, sitting on the kitchen counter untouched.

Neither Joe nor Vic were anywhere around.

I picked my way to Ingrid's ground cellar and pounded on the door, yelling her name.

Her voice came back. "Here! In here!"

"Are you all right?"

Please, God, let her be. She sounded scared. With good reason, considering what she'd been through. I should have been here with her, instead of at Woodlands with Lexy. My heart lurched. Lexy! The mother I'd only just met. Had she survived the storm?

"We're fine. Are you all right?"

"I'm okay." Except for a few bruised and broken areas that were giving me a lot more trouble than I appreciated. I felt like I'd been beaten with a clu—

Wait! She said *we. We're fine.* Of course! Joe and Vic would have taken shelter with her. "Is Vic in there with you?"

"No. Joe is—and Mrs. Potts."

"Where's Vic?" I held my breath. *Please, God, let the news be good.*

Joe's voice came through the heavy door. "He went to immunize Pete Chaffee's herd around one o'clock. I haven't heard from him since."

"Marlene?" Ingrid again.

"Yes?"

"You've got to get us out of here. There's something across the door, and we're trapped."

The old oak was blocking the door. It was practically sitting in the middle of it. "It's going to take awhile before I can get someone to cut the tree away from the cellar door."

"Why's that?"

"The town is destroyed. I don't know where to find help, but I'll try."

"You've got to get us out! These walls are closing in on me. I'm likely to get the paralysis again."

"No, you *won't*! *Don't* you pull that on me, Ingrid. I've been picked up by a tornado and dropped, been in the hospital, and hitched a ride home with a trucker who had more tattoos than a circus act. I'll get you out of there; I don't know how, but I will, but you pull that paralysis thing on me again and I'll leave you in there. I mean it!"

I shut up. Leaning close to the cellar door, I listened. Real quiet. I realized I'd been screaming earlier. Not a sound came from the cellar. Had I shocked Ingrid into cardiac arrest?

A meek voice filtered through the wooden door. "Whatever you say, honey. Just do the best you can and we'll be satisfied."

My shoulder slumped as I stared at the door. I must have sounded deranged. I took a deep breath and held my aching side. "I'm leaving now to get help, but I'll be back. I promise."

The same meek little voice replied, "You do that honey, but don't rush; we'll be here when you get back."

I could not believe it. I'd finally gotten her to back off. Favoring my bad ankle, I clumped down the street looking for a Good Samaritan with a chainsaw. Eons later, the sound of saws drew me. A group of men was trying to remove a tangle of tree limbs and broken lumber.

I snagged one of them. "I need help."

He glanced at my bandages. "Looks like you do. Do you need a ride to the hospital?"

I pointed back the way I had come. "My elderly aunt and two neighbors are trapped in a cellar. A tree has fallen across the door."

He shook his head. "Can't help, we're trying to clear the road."

Tears rolled down my cheeks, as if someone had opened the floodgates. He frowned. "Here! Don't do that! Let me talk to Frank."

Apparently Frank was the broad-shouldered redhead wielding a saw like a weapon. The man was flat-out clearing brush. After a few minutes the first man returned.

"Okay. Where's that cellar?"

I pointed back the way I'd come. "Over that direction."

"Can we drive there?"

"Most of the way." I was so tired and battered, I wasn't sure of anything anymore. We got in a pickup, and he drove in the direction I indicated. After a few minutes he said, "This looks like Joe Brewster's neighborhood."

"It is. He's in the cellar with my aunt."

He turned and squinted at me. "You're Ingrid Moss's niece?"

"Yes. Marlene."

His features softened, as if by not introducing himself he'd committed a breach of conduct. "Dave Anderson. Joe's my pastor, or he was. He's retired now."

"I know. I was at his retirement party."

"That's right, you were. You look different."

"My car was picked up by a funnel and ... oh, never mind." I was too exhausted to repeat the scenario.

We braked in front of the house and he opened the pickup door and got out. "Where's the cellar?"

Now that help had arrived, Ingrid wanted out! She screeched and pounded on the door. I assured her I was doing all I could, but my mind was on Vic. He was hurt, I was sure of it. I couldn't say why, but I was. I knew he was lying somewhere injured and alone, and I had to find him. But where did I start?

"Aunt Ingrid?"

"Yes—are they working?"

"They're working. They should have the tree cleared in another half hour. I'm going to look for Vic. Where is the Chaffee farm?"

"Oh, three, four miles out."

"Ingrid, I need *exact* directions."

Joe shouted. "Go to the highway and turn left. Then go about two, two and a half miles and you'll come to a row of mailboxes. There's a big feed sign opposite the mailboxes."

"Turn there?"

"No, go on past the mailboxes another mile or so and you'll see a big mulberry tree. That's where you turn. Go on down the road another mile or so and you'll ford a creek, then at the top of the hill, the road forks off. Take the left fork; it'll take you straight to the Chaffee place." His tone sobered. "Call me the minute you hear anything from him, will you?"

"I will, Joe." For all the good it would do. I seriously doubted phones of any kind were working yet.

Transportation. I couldn't get a car through the streets. Too much debris. I hobbled back across the street to the Faradays'. Their house looked to be intact but battered. Discarding the crutch, I pulled myself up the porch railing using my one good arm and the handrail and hit the doorbell. Minutes passed and no one answered.

Sitting down on the concrete porch, I lowered myself step by step until I touched ground, then stood and hobbled to the back of the house. I had to shove the garage door aside, not an easy task, but I found what I was after. Fred Farraday's motor scooter. The key was in the ignition.

By the grace of God, I managed to mount the scooter and with one hand, turn the machine, pointing the wheels toward the street. I switched on the key and the engine puttered to life.

Getting a solid grip on the handle, I eased my sprained ankle to the footrest, then gave the machine a little gas, lifted my good foot, and roared out of the garage.

If it wasn't my time to go, I was sure pushing it.

Fifteen

Fallen trees and metal made for a harrowing ride through town. Crews were clearing the streets and highway, but it was still a tortuous maze. I couldn't gain any speed because of debris cluttering the road. I scooted around a pile of lumber that looked like it had once been someone's shed. A downed tree blocked half the road, but by concentrating, I eased past. Power lines snaked and sparked on the highway. One swerve, one mistake, and it would be my last.

God, give me safe passage and let me find Vic.

Thunder rolled in the distance; a light drizzle dampened my jacket. Parnass Springs would never be the same. The town would rebuild—people here were tough—but it would not be the same.

I slowed to let a horse cross the road. Where did he belong? It would take weeks to sort personal property.

The scooter tooled down the highway. I was surprised at how easily I'd adapted to the cycle. At first I was scared to death and in agony, but now my former riding skills came back, and I was comfortable behind the handlebars. When Vic and Fred taught me to ride in my youth, neither would have envisioned a time when I would be racing down the road on a rescue mission. I moved as one with the machine, grateful for the wheels beneath me. My mind thumped an erratic mantra: *Let me be in time, please God. Let me get there in time to help Vic.*

For all I knew, Vic had sat out the storm safe in the Chaffees' cellar or basement; every rural household had one or the other. But I couldn't rest until I knew for certain that he was safe. That this worry gnawing at me was unfounded.

I located the mailboxes, and a mile farther, the mulberry tree came into sight. High winds had taken out the trunk and branches, but it was a big tree and it was beside the junction of a new road, so I assumed it was the right landmark.

Without letting up on the gas, I made the turn, slid, then righted and gunned the machine down the gravel road. My ankle throbbed and my broken arm reminded me of the insanity of the ride, but I had to find him—needed to feel his calm assurance. Maybe he would never forgive me for the deception I'd perpetrated. Maybe he didn't feel the undying love Joe had spoken about. But I had to find him, no matter what. Never had my love for Vic Brewster been more passionate, more urgent, than now, when I didn't know if he was alive or dead.

The scooter flew down the road throwing mud and gravel. The creek came into view, swollen by heavy rain. I plowed through churning water without letting up on the gas. Water showered, blinding me, but the cycle emerged on the other side and I gave the engine full throttle. The road was clearer here, not as much debris littering the way. I had to watch out for the occasional tree, but I was making excellent time.

Rain clouds roiled overhead. Another mile and what was once a farmhouse and barn appeared. Both were flattened, as were the outbuildings. The Chaffee farm had taken a direct hit from the tornado. Could anything have survived?

I pulled up in front of a pile of rubble and let the machine idle. A man, woman, and three kids ranging from around ten to teenager looked up when I braked. I stared at the small cluster of the Chaffee family, searching for Vic. He wasn't among the dazed survivors.

Mr. Chaffee approached. "Do you need help?"

"Vic Brewster. His father said he was out here."

The man nodded, brow furrowed. "He was. We were working cattle in the pen back of the barn when we saw the storm brewing. Barely had time to drive the herd out to pasture and get my family into the shelter before it hit."

"Vic? Did he go into the shelter with you?"

He shook his head. "I tried to get him to, but he was worried about his dad. Said he had to get back to town and make sure he was okay."

"He left?" I couldn't believe what I heard. *Left.* He forfeited a storm shelter to drive into the teeth of the storm because he was worried about Joe. Only Vic would have done that. "How long ago was that?"

"I'd say ten minutes before the storm hit. He was driving fast, maybe he made it back to town okay."

I shook my head. "He never made it." The words dropped like ten-pound bricks in my heart. *Where are you, Vic?* I hadn't seen a sign of his truck on the ride out.

Mr. Chaffee frowned. "Could have taken cover somewhere along the road. I wouldn't worry; Vic Brewster grew up in tornado alley. He knows all about storms. He wouldn't let himself be caught out in one."

I wanted to believe, wanted to so desperately, but I knew Vic. He hadn't made it back to town.

Mrs. Chaffee had been sorting through the rubble that once had been her home. Now she held something out to me.

A picture frame with cracked glass revealed a smiling bride and groom. The Chaffees, older now, but there was still a glow in her eyes when she looked at him. Would Vic ever look at me like that again?

Frank Chaffee's eyes followed his children. "We're all alive, unharmed. That's the important thing. God was good to us—you'll let us know about Vic? We've been worried sick."

"I will—thank you."

Anxious to be on my way to find Vic, I asked the Chaffees if they needed anything. When they said they didn't, I turned the cycle, preparing to leave. The farmer's truck had been slammed into a tree. The car's hood was sprung, knocked upright and blocking the windshield. His tractor lay tossed aside, upside down.

I left, going slower this time, searching the ground for tire tracks. Vic had to be somewhere.

I was begging now, all pride thrown to the wind. I had to find him, had to tell him that I loved him and was sorry for deceiving him. Had to know he was all right. If necessary, I'd drive this road until I ran out of gas; I had to find him.

Oh God, please. I'll do anything—I'll never miss another Sunday service; I'll do my Bible reading religiously—not religiously, faithfully. I'll never tell another lie; I'll spend every vacation working at a homeless mission ...

On and on I promised, trying to bargain with God, though I knew better. Bartering wasn't the way to get God's attention. Finally I stopped the cycle in the middle of the road and bent my head, letting the tears course down my cheeks.

God, he's yours, I know that, but please, allow me one more chance to make amends, to tell him I love him and how deeply sorry I am for betraying him all these years. I'm undeserving of your grace, but Vic isn't. I'm the culprit, not him.

Calm settled over me. Now I cruised more slowly, searching both sides of the road. Halfway back to Parnass Springs I found the tracks where a large vehicle had gone off the road. The ruts veered down an embankment toward the creek. With my heart in my throat, I climbed off the scooter and peered over the embankment. I spotted Vic's truck, lying on its side.

I half climbed, half slid down the bank, praying with every breath. The passenger's door had been ripped off. The truck's interior was a shambles. I spotted a bag of jelly beans, split open, the contents spilling on the inside floor. I caught back a sob. Vic and his jelly beans. Jelly beans, for him, were other men's cigarettes and coffee. His lunch box lay on the creek bank, mashed into a distorted tangle.

"Vic!" I held my breath, listening. Nothing. I shouted again and again, walking up the gravel bar, searching. Finally I shuffled back to the truck. He *had* to be somewhere in the vicinity.

I called until I was hoarse.

Nearly defeated, I walked around the truck, powerless to leave until he was accounted for. I gave one last, desperate call, terrified there wouldn't be an answer. *"Vic!"*

The sound was so faint I almost missed it.

"Marly?"

I stopped dead in my tracks. "Is that you?"

"I knew you would come."

I went lightheaded. He *knew* I'd come? He had that kind of faith in me? Tears blinded me. "Where are you!"

"Under the truck. There's some sort of depression here; I'm pinned down. I can't move."

"Don't worry, I'll get you out." I limped around the truck and still couldn't see him. I had no flashlight; I hadn't thought to bring one. And it was dark, so very dark.

"I don't think you can get to me. You'll need help."

"I'll ride back to town and get someone. I won't be long. Hold on." *Oh God, let me find someone to get him out before it's too late.*

"Marlene, wait! Dad?"

"He's okay. He and Ingrid were in her storm cellar when I left town. Is the pain bad?"

He didn't answer.

"I'm going for help! Hold on!"

My eyes were so blurred with tears, it was a miracle I could see to climb the steep embankment. Vic was alive. Now I had to get him out of there and see how badly he was hurt. He'd sounded weaker with each word.

Pain seared my ankle. I bit back tears as the medication began to wane. Every bone in my body burned with white-hot torture, but none of that mattered now. The scooter roared as I raced off.

The trip back to town seemed interminable. The situation there hadn't changed much. The whine of chainsaws filled the air. It took half an hour to locate a truck with a winch to lift the pickup off Vic. At first Tate McNeal refused to come with me, but when I told him Vic needed help, he dropped his protests and agreed to go. Tate and Vic had been friends since high school. I knew I could count on him. I struggled into the cab and gave him directions to the Chaffee place.

"He's gone off the road and down the creek bank. A little farther and he'd have been in the water." The thought scared me so, I had trouble breathing. I had come that close to losing him. If the truck had landed on him in the water, he'd be dead by now.

Tate braked when I pointed out the jagged tire tracks. We piled out and started down the rocky embankment. When Tate shined the flashlight, the wreckage looked even worse. How could anyone be alive under that mangled truck? It would take a miracle to save Vic, but God was in the miracle business. I hoped he was ready to send another my way.

Tate eyed the truck's grotesque angle. "You say Vic's under there?"

"Yes, I talked to him." But he wasn't talking now. Was he still alive? I knelt by the front bumper, trying to see in the darkness. "Vic? Can you hear me?"

Nothing. Tate rounded the front of the truck. "Here. Let me see."

He knelt, shining the light underneath the pickup. After a moment he got to his feet. "He's there, all right. But he's not moving. We've got to get him out."

"How?"

He flashed the light up the creek bank. "I've got to find a way to get the truck down here so I can hook onto Vic's pickup. That bank's too steep for me to navigate. I'm going to walk down the creek a ways and see if I can find a place to pull in."

I watched him walk away, taking the light with him. Thunder rumbled in the distance. Lighting flashed. The storm had moved on, but light showers persisted. Unable to do anything, I half-crouched beside the pickup and prayed as I'd never prayed before, prayed that Tate could find a way to get his truck down here, and finally I prayed for myself. That God would give me the courage to accept whatever happened.

The rumble of Tate's truck broke the silence. I watched as he drove slowly down the creek bank toward me. He stopped at a wide space and turned the truck around. For a heart-stopping moment I was afraid he would get stuck, but he managed to gain traction and ease the rig around until it was pointed back in the direction he had come.

He gave a sharp whistle. "Over here! Take the flashlight and shine it on Vic's truck, so I can see where to back up. Tell me when I get close enough."

My teeth chattered in the night air as Tate climbed into the cab and slowly backed toward the wreckage while I held the light steady. Inch by inch he eased back. I held my breath. This had to work; it was our only hope.

"Stop!" I screamed the warning, afraid he couldn't hear me over the sound of the diesel engine. Red taillights spilled over the creek bed.

Tate got out and walked to the back. "I'm going to hook onto the front bumper and winch it up. When I get it off of him, you pull him out."

"We don't know how badly he's hurt. I'm afraid to move him."

"Look, Marlene. The way that thing is lying, and as close as it is to him, I'm afraid to leave him there. One slip and that pickup could do him in. You read me?"

I read him, all right. "Okay, you lift the truck off him. I'll get him out of there." Tate was right; we didn't have time for proper protocol. We'd worry about the consequences later.

The motor growled to life, and the chain tightened with a jerk. "Keep going! It's moving. It's in the air!"

Slowly, the front end of the pickup rose until I could crawl under and get a grip on Vic's shoulders. I pushed backward, dragging him with my one good hand. Pain shot through my body—agony nearly blinded me—but I pulled with every ounce of remaining strength. Eternity passed before we were clear of the pickup. I collapsed next to Vic for a moment, trying to catch my breath.

Tate sprang out of the truck and crunched across the gravel toward me. "What's the story?"

I knew what he meant: Is he alive? I reached over and checked Vic's vitals. He roused enough to open his eyes and attempt to speak, but he was confused, barely aware of who I was. His breathing was heavy and uneven. "We've got to get him to the clinic."

"Negative. Not sure Doc Johnson's place is still standing. He could be hurt himself."

"We'll find an ambulance, then, to take him to Boone County Hospital."

He shook his head. "None available. They're all out. No other way to do it, we've got to take him ourselves."

I glanced at Vic, unconscious now. "We can't move him without the proper equipment. I need blankets, saline solution, a stabilizing board for his leg, I need—"

Tate's voice held a world of patience. "I know that, Marlene, but we have to make the best of what's available. Vic needs help and he needs it now. We've got to get him to Columbia."

He was right. I was confused—disgracefully confused for a nurse. We would have to move Vic. We'd be as gentle as feasible, and pray we didn't inflict further injury. Tate searched the riverbank and came up with a thick branch. By working together, we managed to stabilize Vic's neck. It wasn't much, but it would help.

Tate scooped Vic up into his arms, and like a small baby, carried him around the truck to the passenger side. We struggled to load his unresponsive body into the cab. His left leg was broken; a bone poked through his torn jeans. I had Tate rip a piece of my blouse tail and made a compress to stop the bleeding.

"Hold on darling ... I'm here." Crying didn't help but I couldn't seem to stop. I wanted to tell him everything ... the lie, the years of deception ... everything, but he couldn't hear. Confession would have to wait a few hours longer.

Tate stepped back, breathing hard. "Get in. Let's get this show on the road."

I clumsily climbed into the cab and cradled Vic's lifeless form against me. He moaned and I caressed his cheek. "It's all right. Marly's here."

"Marlene?"

My heart stopped when I heard him murmur my name. "Yes, darling. I'm here."

"Marly." He sighed and fell silent.

I groped for his pulse, weak and thready. Shock? I hugged him closer for warmth. He wouldn't have survived a night on the creek bank, wet and cold. Nights were still chilly and the air was unseasonably cool after the storm. It could have been several days before anyone found him, given the wide destruction.

Tate climbed behind the steering wheel and winched Vic's truck down. In a few minutes he had it unhooked, the cable back in place, and was back inside, slamming the door behind him. I held my breath as he slowly drove up the creek, looking for a place to get back on the road. The tires spun a couple of times before he kicked it into four-wheel drive. We shot up onto the road and I breathed normally again.

Vic stirred, and I patted his cheek, knowing little else to do. I wanted him to remain unconscious until we reached the hospital and he could be given something for the pain. His injuries made my own barely mentionable.

Sirens sounded, and Tate pulled off the road to let an ambulance race past. I was mentally wringing my hands by the time we rolled into Columbia's city limits. Damage here wasn't as widespread. Evidently they'd been on the edge of the storm. The outlying areas had taken the brunt of the violence.

Tate pulled up to the emergency entrance of Boone County Hospital. The dash clock said 7:10 a.m. "You stay put, Marlene. I'll get help."

I nodded, too drained to argue. Security lights fully revealed Vic's condition, and panic seized me. His face was bruised and bloody. A jagged cut marred his forehead. His clothing was stiff with mud. I jerked around as someone opened the passenger door. A hospital employee motioned for me to get out. Together, the orderly and Tate got Vic out of the truck and onto a stretcher, then wheeled him inside. I limped after them. In all of the excitement, I'd forgotten my injuries. I was numb to my soul.

For the second time that day, I entered the hospital emergency room, only this time behind a gurney instead of lying on one. How was I going to let Joe know that I'd found Vic? I didn't know his cell phone number. The hospital would have a phone directory, but landlines were most likely out of order. Joe had to be worried sick.

Tate led me to the waiting room, and then said he had to go. I understood. "Listen Tate, go by and tell Joe where Vic is. He'll be likely to set out on foot looking for him."

"Will do. Do you need anything?"

"Nothing. I couldn't be in a better place, for Vic or myself."

He grinned. "I'll be getting back then. They need help in Parnass."

"Thanks, I don't know what I'd have done if you hadn't been there."

"I think a lot of Vic. Always liked you too, Marlene. About time you came home."

He left, but his words remained in the empty waiting room. Home? Parnass Springs was home? Somehow that sounded right. A moment later I realized I should have asked Tate for money for a cup of vending-machine coffee. I was chilled to the bone, teeth chattering. I'd lost my Windbreaker somewhere, and I didn't have a clue what had happened to my cell phone, purse, or credit cards.

I sank down in a waiting room chair, resting my throbbing head on the cool metal back, and tried to make out the time through my shattered watch crystal. No luck. I glanced at the wall clock: nine fifteen. The day that wouldn't end.

I couldn't sit still. Finally, giving into temptation, I got up and limped to the pay phone, sticking my fingers in the return change cup and wiggling them. I silently squealed when two quarters dropped down. *Yes! Thank you Lord!*

Seizing the prize, I bought a cup of hot coffee.

Sixteen

Over an hour later, the double doors opened and a young female doctor wearing blue scrubs approached me. "Are you a member of the Brewster family?"

Don't I wish? "No, I'm a family friend. Vic's father is in Parnass Springs. I brought Vic to the hospital."

She nodded. "His leg's broken in three places, and he's got a couple of cracked ribs. Otherwise I'd say he survived the accident in good shape." Her eyes skimmed my arm sling, muddy ankle bandage, face stitches, and abrasions. "Weren't you in here earlier?"

I nodded. "You wouldn't believe my night."

Vic's injuries required a hospital stay. When he came out of the anesthesia, he slowly opened his eyes, adjusting to the light. His cloudy gaze focused on me. "Marly?"

"Hi. It's about time you woke up, sleepyhead."

He reached for my hand, and I was relieved to feel his strength. He was going to make it. *Thank you, God.* He'd given me my umpteenth chance. This time I wouldn't waste it.

"Where am I?" Vic half-raised off the bed, and I gently pushed him back to the pillow.

"You're in the hospital. There's been a storm—a tornado, actually."

"Storm ... yes, I remember ... I couldn't get to shelter ... how bad are the injuries?"

"You have a broken leg and some cracked ribs, but everything considered, you've fared well."

Suddenly his eyes cleared and he became more alert. "Dad? Dad doesn't know if I'm dead or alive." Worry was clear in his eyes. "He'll be beside himself, Marly. Go home and let him know I'm okay."

"Tate will tell him. He promised, and I saw a CB in the truck cab. He'll get the message through."

Vic frowned. "Tate? What does he have to do with anything?"

"Tate winched the truck off you, and we brought you here."

"How did you find me? I remember talking to you, didn't I? I'm a little foggy."

I laughed. "It's a long story. First I broke into Fred Faraday's garage and borrowed his scooter."

He gave me a dubious look. "You didn't. He's nuts about that thing, won't even let his own kid ride it. You didn't put any scratches on it?"

Quickly I explained my adventure, but my injuries were the least of my concerns.

His eyes skimmed my bandaged arm and cuts and bruises. "You're hurt! How ..."

I covered his mouth with my hand. "You need rest. We'll talk later when you're thinking more clearly."

"Good idea." He lay back on the pillow and closed his eyes. "Go home ... get some rest, honey. I'll be fine ..."

Honey? Had he just called me *honey*? Or had he asked for money? Maybe he needed something. My head whirled. "I don't have a ride home, and besides, I don't want to leave you."

I lay my head on his bruised hand. *I don't want to leave you.* It'd been light years since I'd been free to express my feelings, and regardless of my aching ankle and arm, I couldn't leave.

His hand closed around mine. "We've got all the time in the world. Now go. You need to be in bed yourself."

True, but if I ever lay down, I feared I wouldn't be able to get up again. Ever. My body was coming apart at the seams. Besides, I had something to say that couldn't wait. "Vic."

"Yeah?"

"I'm sorry I lied to you about Noel."

He took the confession more easily than I'd expected—almost in stride, or more like he'd been waiting a long time to hear it—too long. "Why did you do that, Marly?" Instead of anger, I heard deep regret.

"Pride." My hand stroked his bruised arm. "I hated lying to you. Every time we talked and you asked about Noel, I hated what I did, but you were so happy, so settled with Julie. I'd made such a mess of my life, running away from you, from Parnass Springs. I couldn't bear to admit my mistakes because there were so many. I knew I'd probably never come back here so the lie seemed safe enough. Then Julie died, and suddenly you were single again. I was caught in this horrible web, one of my own making, and I didn't have enough nerve to break free."

His hand tightened around mine. "Why did you run away from *me*?"

"Because I knew if I stayed, I would marry you. I loved you too much not to marry you, and then you would want children—"

"I never insisted on having children. I knew your fears about your mother and father, and as far as I knew, they were legitimate."

"But I would have *wanted* to give you children and knew I didn't dare."

We sat in silence, holding each other's hands, he gently stroking my muddy hair. "Want to hear something not so funny?"

"Sure. I could use a sad tale about now." After all, hadn't the night been one hilarious episode after another?

He gently eased me upright until our eyes met. "I can't father children."

"W-what?"

"I can't have children. Julie and I tried for a couple of years and then decided something was wrong. Turned out I couldn't father a child."

"Oh, Vic." I lay my head on the side of the bed. *Oh, Vic.* That's all I could think to say. All those years of regret, of hopelessness, and if I'd just trusted God ... just followed his plan for my life.

Forgive me, Father. Forgive me for being such a fool.

Images of my life flowed through my mind. Pictures of my childhood, my marriage, of the nurse handing a tiny bundle to me, saying I had a daughter. I saw Sara as she held her first child, felt my grandbaby curl those tiny fingers around my thumb ...

"You're not laughing."

"I have so many regrets, Vic. And yet ..."

"And yet?"

"For all that I wish things had been different, I wouldn't give up Sara and the grandchildren. And I don't think you want to give up knowing and loving Julie." I stroked his hand. "Even when we rebel, when we go our own foolish way, God is there. And he still cares for us, doesn't he?"

"Yes, he does."

"He even brings us joy in the midst of our mistakes."

Free choice. Isn't that what I'd promised Chuck, the truck driver? God gave us free choice, but he didn't leave us alone in our choices. He was there. All along. It'd taken me forty-three long years to learn this; I prayed my daughter got it a lot sooner.

"Vic Brewster."

"Yeah, Marley Queens?" His eyes locked with mine, and I could quite happily have drowned in the love I saw there. Love. Forgiveness. Dedication. Expressions I'd waited a lifetime to see in his eyes.

"I'm going to kiss you, Vic. I'm going to kiss you because I love you—no, I adore you. I always have and always will."

"Really?"

"Yes. Really." I'd already made up my mind. Game time's over.

One dark brow lifted.

"I'm going to kiss you, and it's going to be with all the pent-up emotion and love that I've carried for you since I was five years old."

One side of his mouth lifted. "*Really.* You'd take advantage of a man in my weakened condition?"

"Yes, I would. In a nanosecond."

I kissed him, and then I kissed him again, then again with as much care as I could manage for a man lying in a hospital bed with a broken leg and cracked ribs.

And when his arms tightened around me possessively? That's when I really let him have it.

On Monday morning, the hospital staff arranged for a car to take me to back to Parnass. April had gone out like a lion, and May sauntered in like a lamb.

Joe and Ingrid were helping neighbors dig through rubble when I got out of the car. Joe threw his shovel aside and ran to meet me.

"Vic's fine." I struggled out of the back seat. "I couldn't call. I lost my cell phone and my purse, plus phone lines are down everywhere."

"Tate told us. Thank God you're both okay!"

Ingrid came to my side, and between Joe and her, they got me into the house. Ingrid had some rain damage inside, and the furniture sported a sheen of dust, but all in all, her house fared better than most. She clucked like a hen over my injuries. Joe immediately sat me down, bowed his head, and holding my hand, he thanked God for my and Vic's safety. When he'd finished, I echoed his prayer with a grateful and heartfelt amen.

While Ingrid made me a cup of tea, I told them about the night's events. "Vic's truck is demolished. It went off an embankment, almost landed in the creek."

"Doesn't matter, trucks can be replaced." Joe's fingers gripped mine. "Thank the good Lord for taking care of him.

We couldn't hold services yesterday—first Sunday in forty years I haven't been in church."

Minutes later, Joe left for the hospital in a neighbor's car, and Ingrid heated a bowl of soup to accompany our tea. I hadn't eaten much since Saturday at noon in the cafeteria with the Parishes. Ingrid and I chatted as I ate and downed another pain pill.

"Most of the town's buildings are gone." My aunt sat down, misty-eyed. The storm had taken the fight out of her. "We'll rebuild. Parnass Springs will be even better. The old bridge wasn't touched, they say, and that's a blessing." Her eyes darkened. "The new shelter is gone, Marlene. I walked over there earlier. It's rubble."

"I'm so sorry, Aunt Ingrid." All the fuss of the past few weeks gone in a matter of minutes. Shouldn't that be a lesson to me? Only the eternal things mattered.

She stared off into the distance. "Just brick and wood. I'm glad we didn't have a chance to build Herman's statue—it'd be gone, too, and I wouldn't have wanted to lose him twice."

"We could have rebuilt the statue."

She glanced at me. "You'd do that?"

I reached over and took her hand; aware the medication was starting to do its thing—sweet, sweet lessening of pain. "I'd have done it then, and we'll do it together now. For Dad."

A smile chased away the earlier worn lines circling her eyes. "You've come a long way, Marlene."

Almost too late. Vic and I still had over twenty-five years of baggage to sort through, but I had hopes now that the lies were out of the way. Surely our lives would be better. How could they not be if we were together? The *three* of us: Vic, me, and God.

I studied my aunt. "Do you know where I was when the storm hit?'

"No, you hadn't said where you were going Saturday morning. I was worried—I didn't know where to begin to look for you."

"I'd gone to Woodlands."

Her lower lip tightened. "Isn't that where—"

"Lexy Parish is. Yes. I went to visit my mother."

Ingrid stared at the tablecloth, and then picked up a spoon. "And?"

"And ... she's lovely. Have you met her?"

"Once, when she was carrying you. You favor her, did you know that? Same color of eyes."

"I know that what Herman and Lexy did all those years ago wounded you deeply." I thought of the cigar box in my bedroom, the simple ring. "But it hurt the Parishes too. Remember how Grandpa Parnass used to say, 'let bygones be bygones.' Both families have to do that, Ingrid. Let bygones be bygones."

Her features hardened. "I don't want anything to do with those people. They objected to Herman's statue—they're heartless."

"They were hurt by the scandal. And mystified. Just like you."

"Their girl ruined Herman's life. Folks thought worse of him after ... Before, they knew he was simple and didn't understand like most folks. They accepted him. Later they blamed him, whispered ugly things behind his back."

"They were both involved. Willingly. They loved each other, Aunt Ingrid. And that love resulted in me."

"And I'm glad it did."

I looked at her. "Really?"

She dismissed me with a wave of her hand. "Of course. Might not say it much, but you know I love you. Why else would I leave you my entire estate when I'm gone."

It was a good thing I was already sitting down. I don't know what I'd thought Aunt Ingrid would do with her money—truth be told, I hadn't really thought about it.

"Eugene left Herman a large trust."

"Eugene?" I frowned. "Did he make that much as a salesman?"

"Don't be ridiculous. His family had old money. Eugene didn't have to work a day in his life, but he loved adventure. Always said he couldn't sit still." She lifted her tea for a sip. "That's why Herman chose to stay with me when Eugene left. He might have been simpleminded, but he knew he'd never have a real home with his father. After Herman died, and I followed his wishes to have the animal shelter built and give a large grant to the public library, I set up a trust where the remainder of your father's estate, as well as mine, would go to you upon my demise."

"I don't know what to say."

Another wave of the hand. "No need to say a thing. We're family. That says it all."

So it did.

I eased back in my chair, my mind returning to a day thirty years ago—the day Herman found God.

The sunny June morning stood out in my mind as clearly as if it happened yesterday. Ingrid, Beth, and I had left the church and headed for the car when we heard Herman burst from the side entrance, yelling at the top of his lungs.

"Good news! Good news!"

"Marlene, go get him and tell him to hush!" Ingrid snapped.

I bounded out of the car and headed for him. He spotted me, his face lit with an angelic glow. "Marly! Good neeeeews! Good neeeeews!"

He raced across the lawn, shouting, stumbling over his two big, too-awkward feet. His usual mismatched pants and shirt looked even more out of place this morning. Heads turned. Smiles turned to scowls.

"Stop *shouting*, Herman! Ingrid says for you to get in the car!"

He reached me, eyes bright, his grin spreading from ear to ear. "Good news, Marly! Jesus *loves* me!"

Jesus loved Herman. Even now, the sheer euphoria on his face brought joy to my soul. *Good news! Good news! Jesus loves me!*

That day, Herman got what some geniuses failed to get their whole life. So who was truly mentally challenged?

I smiled at my aunt. "Herman understood what was important. He understood that he was special because God loved him. We'll rebuild the shelter; we'll make it even larger so when we look at it, we'll be reminded of the size of my dad's heart."

Ingrid reached to wipe tears. "I didn't give birth to him, but I loved him like my own—maybe loved him more than my own. When Eugene left and Herman chose to remain with me—why, he was all I had. I had to protect him, to shelter him from the world."

"Oh, Aunt Ingrid. Haven't you realized it yet? Herman was an *angel.* You didn't need to shelter him. He was sent to deliver a message of a deeper meaning to life, to enable us to sort through what counts and what doesn't. That was Herman's mission, and he performed it well."

It might have taken all these years for his lessons to sink in, but I finally got it. Ingrid was about to. I leaned over and squeezed her hand. "Good news! Good news! Aunt Ingrid, Jesus loves you."

Late that afternoon I borrowed a neighbor's cell phone and called Lana. I knew that she worked at the local bank, which the storm most likely had damaged, but she might be around to help with the cleanup. The bank had one of the few landlines in operation. When I told her about Vic and the accident, she immediately volunteered to drive me to Columbia, where she dropped me off at the emergency entrance.

"Tell Vic I hope he's better real soon."

Surprised, I turned to look at her. "Aren't you coming inside?"

"No." She offered a look that only two women in love with the same man could understand. "We both know Vic Brewster wouldn't know I was in the room if you were there."

"Oh, Lana." She knew. She knew that an irrevocable bond held Vic and me—and she'd just given her blessing.

The moment I walked into Vic's hospital room, Joe discreetly excused himself, saying he was going to the cafeteria for a bite to eat.

Vic motioned me closer. When I reached for a chair, he patted the space beside him and smiled. A weak one, nevertheless, a living, breathing smile.

"You look considerably better than the last time I saw you." I moved IV tubing and sat down. His color, though pasty, had improved. They had just given him pain medication and he had the look of giddy oblivion.

"Little Marly."

"Big ole Vic."

His grin turned into a forgiving smile, which I offered back. At least he was speaking to me.

I'd left him, knowing we'd crossed a bridge onto common ground, but still I'd worried that once the crisis passed, the old tension between us would resurface. He didn't appear intent on a grudge, but right now he wasn't feeling anything but good. Real good.

"Guess I owe you one."

Shaking my head, I fiddled with the tubing. "We both owe the Lord one. I couldn't have found you without his help."

He shook his head. "I can't believe how fast the storm moved in. It was foolish to try to outrun it, but I was worried about Dad."

"Well, God's still in the miracle business." I checked the thick, heavy cast covering his leg suspended in the air. "Three breaks, huh?"

"That's what they say."

"What about your practice?" Between therapy and healing, he'd be off for months.

"Dad talked to a fellow vet in Columbia. He's going to cover for me until I can get around."

My heart twisted. "That will be awhile."

"Yeah, awhile." He laced his fingers through mine. "I'm counting on you to help with the therapy."

The old, teasing Vic was back. *Hallelujah!* But were his good spirits and the teasing glint in his eye the result of medication or amnesty? What I'd done was a serious infraction, one that a few halted confessions couldn't heal.

"Vic—"

He stopped me. "With time we're going to get past this." His hold tightened around my hand. His voice began to rise. "Right now I'm working through the anger. You've got to know I was furious when I found out that Noel was dead—had been dead *all those* years! How did you think that made me feel, Marly?"

"Betrayed."

"Exactly!"

"Don't yell at me."

"Didn't you trust me to understand?"

"It wasn't just you. I'd deceived everyone; Ingrid, Beth, Joe—and there's something else you need to know. Noel walked out on me when Sara was two."

"What?"

"He left me and married this—this woman—this psychiatrist, when Sara was two."

"Noel's not only been *dead* all these years, he wasn't even your husband?"

I nodded, miserable. What had possessed me to think that I could keep this part of my life a secret?

Vic shook his head. "I can't believe this."

"I know—and I'm sorry, Vic. I'm *so* sorry. I know how lame that sounds for what I've done, but I deeply regret my actions from all these long years."

"Did you perpetrate this lie to keep me away?"

"Keep you away? You were *married.*"

"I know I was married, and I loved my wife, but when Julie died? What about then, Marly? Nothing prevented you from telling me the truth, yet you still continued the farce. For *years*, Marlene. Were you afraid I would pressure you into coming back here?"

"No, of course not."

"Pressure you into seeing me again?"

"No, I wanted that more than life itself. Every time we talked, I died a little more on the inside. You have to know that. It's just that . . ."

"What? Please tell me. Help me understand."

"I was ashamed. It was my pride, foolish pride, that kept me away, and the lie held me in bondage. My life stank, and you'd made lemonade of yours."

"I can't believe that you didn't tell Dad."

"I couldn't face him with the truth, couldn't face his disappointment in me."

"What about *my* disappointment?"

"That, most of all." I eased closer until there was a hair's breadth between my lips and his. "Don't you think I've paid dearly for my mistake? When I heard Julie died, I wanted to run to you, to comfort you—to confess my lie, to beg your forgiveness and in time hope that we could begin a new life together. But you were shattered. Then, when you began to move past the tragedy, I'd retreated, believing that what we had was in the past. I was so sure that after letting the lie go on for so long, even if I confessed, I'd never regain your trust. When I came back, I had every intention of disposing of my past—to put you and Parnass Springs behind me once and for all."

"But God had other plans."

I sighed. "He always does."

"Don't you think he's trying to get your attention?"

"Yes." I bent and lightly kissed him, testing the waters, tracing the corners of his oh-so-familiar mouth with the tip of my finger. "While I'm confessing, I might as well tell you this. I didn't faint the night I knocked that display of Cokes over."

"You faked *that*, too?"

"I'm not proud of my choices."

"I hope you've learned from them—please tell me you've learned from them."

"I have. I promise." I eased closer. "You said you were working through your anger; do you have reason to believe the issue can be successfully resolved?"

His answer? A long, oh-so-thorough kiss.

Later I nudged him. "There's one other thing I need to know while you're working through things."

Grasping my shoulders, he gently moved me back. "What's that?"

"That you love me."

His gaze gentled. "Isn't that obvious?"

"Well ... no. You've never said you did—"

"Hold on a minute. How many times have I told you I love you?"

"Now? When we're adults?" I asked.

"All the years leading up to adulthood."

"Oh. Well." I grinned. "Quite a few." Too numerous to count.

"Nothing's changed on my part. How about you?"

"Nothing's changed here, either. You have my solemn promise, Vic. I will never lie again, to you or to anyone else. I've learned my lesson. Sin does not pay."

Gathering me close, he rested his chin on the top of my head. "I love you, Marly Moss. I have from the moment I laid eyes on you, and that has never changed."

I closed my eyes, savoring his declaration. Only one more obstacle to overcome. What I was about to say might intimidate some men. I wasn't sure how the man I love and planned to spend the rest of my life with would feel. "Ingrid told me this morning that I'll inherit her estate. And that Eugene left Herman quite a sum, which was then left to me in a trust. And then there's the matter of Aunt Beth's estate . . ." I sighed. "You know Ingrid and Beth lived like paupers, fought like men, and did anything possible to spite the other at times. Would you ever have guessed those two women were sinfully wealthy?"

He stopped me with a long kiss. Afterwards, he said, "What you're trying to say is that I'm in love with a wealthy woman?"

"Very wealthy—"

He frowned. "You don't have a rock fetish, do you?"

I giggled and hugged him tight, delighted to have my old Vic back. "No."

"Then we don't have an issue."

I whirled when I heard children's and adult's voices coming down the hallway. I quickly removed myself from Vic's side into a chair as Joe entered the room, trailed by Aunt Ingrid.

The pastor grinned. "Feeling up to more company?"

"Aunt Ingrid—" I struggled to my feet.

"In the flesh. Here. Someone dropped these by the house as we were leaving." She handed me my lost purse and cell phone. I seized the items; I'd been completely lost without them.

Ingrid grinned. "I also brought company."

Sara and Pete appeared in the doorway. "Mom!" My daughter flew into my arms, babbling like a frightened four-year-old. "We've been so worried! When I couldn't reach you after the storm, we got in the car and drove all the way to Parnass." She paused, inspecting me. "Look at you! You look *wretched.* Black eyes, cuts—stitches! Is your arm *broken*?"

I stuck out my bandaged foot. "Sprained ankle too." I wasn't getting much sympathy these days; might as well milk this for all its worth.

Petey dove into my lap. "Me-maw!"

Emma Grace bucked in her father's arms, clearly wanting some attention. I clasped Petey to my hipbone and reached for Emma with my one good arm. Liquid happiness rolled down my cheeks as I engulfed my family in a wide hug.

"You drove all the way from Glen Ellyn, with the children?"

"Well, we tried, but we had to stop around three this morning. Pete had worked a twelve-hour shift and the kids kept waking up in the car. We stopped at a Holiday Inn Express and slept a few hours, then we were back on the road before dawn." Sara burst into tears. "Oh, Mom. I was *sick* with worry. Are you okay?"

"I'm fine, honey. Terrific. And Ingrid and Joe weren't hurt. We have much to be thankful for."

Pete introduced himself and shook hands with Joe. Vic lay in bed, his eyes on the spectacle. Suddenly I realized he'd never met my child and grandchildren.

"Sara." I pulled my daughter closer to the bed railing. "This is Vic Brewster, town vet and acting mayor of Parnass Springs."

Sara flashed a grin. "Hey Vic. Looks like you didn't fare so well during the storm."

Vic focused on Sara; he was clearly drinking in the sight of my daughter. In a way, she was a part of his past—a part he'd never met.

"Yeah, had a little tangle with a tornado."

Pete stepped to the bed, and the two men engaged in conversation. Docs. They were seldom at a loss for words.

The room took on a carnival-like atmosphere; conversations flowed on every side of the bed. I stepped back to catch my breath, suddenly so full of love I was about to burst. I'd made mistake after mistake, but God was still on his throne, still in the blessing business.

My dad's words, shouted on that Sunday so very long ago, penetrated my mind, and I heard Herman's joyful cry above all others in the crowded hospital room.

Good news! Good news, Marly! Jesus loves you!

Seventeen

And so, it is with great pride, that I dedicate the Herman Moss Animal Sanctuary to the town of Parnass Springs, Missouri. Because my father, Herman Moss, loved animals, all animals, this shelter is a no-kill, nonprofit sanctuary dedicated to helping any needy animal, regardless of species or breed."

A year had passed since that stormy night; one unbelievable but exhilarating year. I grinned as applause filled the common area. A blue May sky formed a canopy over the enthusiastic crowd.

With one snip, the scarlet ribbon fell away, and the gleaming rebuilt glass and polished-wood structure officially reopened. When clapping died away, I nodded to Petey and Emma.

"Now Me-maw?"

"Now."

My precious little rug rats skipped to the canvas-covered statues, and when I gave the signal, they pulled on one set of ropes and canvas fell away to reveal a bronze Butchie.

Giving a second nod, the children raced from canvas to canvas, jerking coverings away. Nine Butchies in all, each one an original. Herman's Butchies hadn't been cut from the same mold, and most called them mutts, but he loved each one. The compromise had thrilled the town. Applause swelled.

Stepping down from the podium, I went straight into Vic's arms and we embraced.

"Nice job, Mrs. Brewster."

"Thank you, Mr. Brewster. I'm envious that I didn't think of the idea first."

Everywhere one looked, they were reminded of Butchie and how each dog had enhanced a simple but smarter-in-ways-that-count life. I was grateful that for every time I'd failed my dad, a Butchie had been there to soften the rejection. But most of all, I was thankful for the one man whose elemental goodness and innocence had changed my life.

"Mom! What a great idea! Dogs!" Sara approached and wrapped her arms around my waist.

"Not just dogs—Butchies." I grinned. We hugged, our eyes on Petey and Emma playing on the statues, romping, laughing with other children. What a glorious day. What a glorious life!

"Mom, you're serious about staying here, aren't you?"

My alarm bell went off. The past year had been a taste of heaven, starting with Vic and our wedding nine months ago. Sara had been accepting of my "newfound love," even when I'd told her that love had been around a lot longer than she had. Even the fact that we had decided to live in Aunt Beth's house while Vic had it remodeled hadn't upset her. The old home was lovely beyond words, with a new sunroom, three-car garage, and the interior restored to the day Beth first purchased it. Vic's former cottage in back of Joe's house had been replaced. Parnass Springs had rebuilt, and all that remained of the storm were memories shared at the local café over mugs of strong black coffee.

Ingrid approached, walking right sprightly for a woman her age. The Parishes trailed her. The three had formed a tenuous friendship over the past year; Ingrid even visited Woodlands on occasion. Lexy was overjoyed with her new friend. I visited my mother fairly often, never revealing to her who I was. Lexy loved me, the way she would love a friend who faithfully came to visit. She knew me only as Marly. As far as I could tell, she never remembered having a baby and, with the exception of the ring and a tattered crayon picture of a clown with Herman's name scrawled across the bottom, I could find no evidence that she remembered my father. When asked who drew the picture, she'd only smile and say, "my best friend."

My thoughts returned to Sara's question. "Yes, honey, I know you're disappointed I'm selling the Glen Ellyn house, but baby, I'll fly home every three weeks and stay a week." My groom suggested the compromise, and like anything Vic Brewster said, I thought the plan was brilliant. After all, he *was* brilliant, and the good Lord knew money wasn't a problem.

"That's not good enough, mom." My daughter's tone took on an edge that I knew meant trouble. "Petey, Emma, and baby Ellie are growing up without you, and I don't like it."

"I don't like it either." Separation from them was the one fly in the ointment, as Ingrid liked to remind me. Now that we were a family—a real family—Sara, Pete, and the children were the only missing pieces.

My daughter flashed a grin. "Well, who knows? One of these days, Pete may decide to move his practice." Her eyes skimmed the area. "And Parnass might need a new doctor. Someday."

For a split second I wasn't sure I'd heard correctly. My eyes flew to Vic, who was now deep in conversation with Pete. The two men had taken to one another like sidewalk chewing gum to shoe soles. Vic had baby Ellie in his arms, like any doting grandfather. I giggled. Vic a grandpa. The handsome, virile man I'd married was *anything* but grandfatherly.

I swung back. "What?"

"Mom. Did you hear a word I said?"

"I think you said … no. I must have heard incorrectly."

"I said Parnass isn't *so* wretched. Golly, who knows? Maybe Pete and I and the kids will move here someday so we can be closer to you." When I just gawked at her, she silently mouthed. "Parnass Springs. Build a home here. In Parnass? Someday. Maybe."

"Here—*this* Parnass—the jumping off place of the earth?"

"Yeah … maybe. No promises, Mom, but—"

Who squealed? Me! I lunged for her, catching her close. "If you're teasing me, young lady, I'll ground you for months."

"Ha! I'd like to see ya try it." Her cheeky grin was as cheerful and unexpected as her bombshell.

Vic and Pete sauntered over, Pete grinning like a shelter cat. "What are you two giggling about?"

I clamped my lips shut. "Pete … I …" Emotion overcame me and I stepped into my son-in-law's waiting arms and bawled. Someday, God willing, Sara and Pete and my grandchildren would be with me. *This is too much, God. You're too good!*

Ingrid and the Parishes stopped, and I blurted out Sara's thoughts.

Ingrid beamed. "My goodness, we'd be family, a real family." Her eyes misted over. "Shame Beth couldn't be here to see this."

A cell phone tinkled. Seven of us fumbled in pockets and purses, but Ingrid calmly reached and unhooked a snap on a belt clip and pushed the talk button. "Ingrid Moss speaking."

I gaped at her, then at Vic. Ingrid with a cell phone? What was the world coming to?

My aunt's features turned brittle. "I thought we'd settled this."

Someone said something on the other line.

"Fine."

Someone said something else.

"Fine."

Someone must have clipped a threat.

"Have at it."

Someone hung up.

Ingrid calmly replaced her phone on the belt clip. When all eyes were on her, she shrugged. "The hussy won't give up."

"Prue?"

I thought the matter over Eugene's foot had been settled a year ago; I'd even mailed a round-trip ticket to Maui two months ago. What happened? "She *still* wants Eugene's foot?"

"No, she wants to be buried on the other side of Eugene. It's *my* lot. Bought and paid for with my money. Now *she* wants to be buried there." My aunt threw back her head and guffawed. Immediately sobering, she said, "When pigs fly."

That's when I mentally threw up my hands. *All* life's problems couldn't be neatly wrapped in a tidy bundle.

"Pops! Hey Pops!" Petey bounded for Vic, Emma close on his heels. Vic passed Ellie to me and then scooped the two imps into his arms, nuzzling their necks.

Closing my eyes, I breathed deeply of clean air and friendly fragrances. A person couldn't pick a better place to live than Parnass Springs. Just ask me.

I'm an expert on happy endings.

Read a sample chapter from Lori Copeland's *Monday Morning Faith*

I manhandled my carry-on luggage and an oversized umbrella down the long jet bridge, aware of the *thump thump thump* of my rubber-sole shoes against the carpeted floor. I sounded like a butter knife caught in the disposal.

As I entered the plane, my heart rate accelerated. *This was it.*

No turning back now.

The point of no return. The real thing.

I squeezed past the smiling flight attendant, passed the stairway on the plane to the upper lounge, and made my way through first class into the cabin section. I paused, overwhelmed by the sheer size of the 747 Boeing aircraft. My eyes traveled row upon row of cabins. How would they ever get this thing off the ground? They would—I knew from prior experience—but right now my fact meter had blown a fuse.

Moving along, I passed the galleys, glancing at my ticket and excusing myself when I stepped on toes or bumped into a fellow passenger blocking the aisle. I eased through business class, past even more galleys, the lavatories, and the coach/tourist/economy section. I studied my ticket. My seat was in the back of the plane. So were the majority of bathrooms.

At long last, I spotted my row. With my purse on the end of an armrest and my oversized umbrella tucked underneath my arm, I swung around—almost knocking a man unconscious with the clumsy rain gear. When I heard the solid *thwack!* I spun, horrified. The wounded passenger clutched the side of his head. For a heartbeat my voice failed me, but I managed to sputter out a weak, "I'm *so* sorry!"

I turned back to store the umbrella in the overhead bin, but the burdensome wood handle nailed a woman seated next to the aisle and flipped her spectacles two rows up. She grabbed for the flying missile and missed. Squinting, she glared up at me.

By now all I wanted to do was crawl in a hole and pull the dirt in behind me. Everything I did drew more attention to my clumsy entrance. Glasses were passed back, and the hostess appeared with an ice pack for the passenger's smarting injury. I tried to stuff my carry-on in the overhead bin; the hostess took the umbrella and assured me she'd give it back when we landed.

I sank into my seat and wanted to die.

And I figured I would. This monstrosity—this jumbo jet—would never get off the ground, let alone fly thirteen hours over land and sea. Had I done that once before? Me. Johanna ... Johanna ...

What *was* my last name?

I brushed at crumbs on the front of my suit jacket. I had yet to walk through O'Hare and pass a hot dog stand without indulging. Chicago Dogs.

Starbucks.

See's Candies.

My nerves and I hit them all; I was eating my way to the hereafter. I pushed my glasses up on my nose. Contacts would be impractical where I was going. The climate was far too hot. I'd left them at home with my wool coat.

I glanced out the window a final time. Saginaw, Michigan—and Mom, Pop, and Nelda—was eons away. My entire existence had been marching toward this moment in time. Would I measure up?

Of course, since this man-made contraption would never get off the ground, I wasn't sure it mattered whether I did or not.

Sniffing the faint scent of wieners in the air, I settled back to await my death.